Who Greatest: Elvis or The Beatles?

First Revised Edition

Mike Shellans
Arizona State University

and

Bill Slater
Capella University

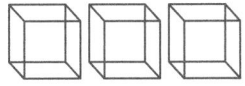

Dorset Group

www.dorset-group.com
Orders: customercare@dorset-group.com

Cover Concept Design: Bill Slater

Cover/Interior Design: Carlisle Publishing Services

Composition/Illustration: Carlisle Publishing Services

Photo credits: Credits for photos reproduced with permission in this book appear on the appropriate pages within the text.

Printer/Binder: Victor Graphics/Baltimore, MD

ISBN-10:   0-9768021-4-7
ISBN-13:   978-0-9768021-4-3

Copyright © 2011 by Dorset Group, LLC. All rights reserved. This publication is protected by Copyright and permission should be obtained from the publisher prior to any reproduction, storage in a retrieval system, or transmission in any form or by any means, electronic, mechanical, photocopying, recording, or likewise. For information regarding, permission, please write to: Rights@dorset-group.com

10 9 8 7 6 5 4 3 2

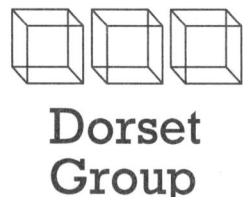

Dorset Group

www.dorset-group.com

Acknowledgements

Mike Shellans

I would like to thank Dorset Group and Carrie Cantor for their enthusiasm, wisdom, positive reinforcement and unyielding dedication to quality in the creation of this book. Special thanks also to Wayne Bailey, Karen Bryan and Gerry Magallan for their innovative vision and unending support of online Popular Music education. And lastly, love and appreciation to Nan van der Steur whose unwaivering encouragement, love and sense of humor continue to sustain me.

Bill Slater

I would like to thank Carrie Cantor and everyone at Dorset Group for their help on this book. Thanks also to my lovely wife Deborah, and my children Justin and Alicia, who put up with my long hours working on the text. And a very special thank you to Prem Rawat, who has taught me what is truly worthwhile.

Contents

Preface   vii
Prelude   ix

1 The Extraordinary Lives of Elvis and the Beatles   2

2 Musical Influences and Performance Styles   26

3 Management and Production   56

4 Elvis and the Beatles in Film and Television   92

5 Drugs and Alternative Lifestyles   122

6 The Business of Being a Pop Star   136

7 The Manias That Wouldn't Die   162

8 Charts and Sales by the Numbers   174

Appendix A: Elvis's Musicians   191
Appendix B: The Beatles' Use of Outside Instruments   201
Conclusions from the Authors—Who Is the Greatest?   205
Bibliography   207
Index   215

PREFACE

It is said that behind every legend, there is reality and a large grain of truth. Unfortunately, this truth becomes obscured in the telling and retelling of stories, until the living person becomes a myth. As it has happened to so many historical figures, so it has also happened to Elvis Presley and the Beatles—John, Paul, George and Ringo. They have all reached such mythic status to the average person that the truths of their lives are no longer as important as the tale. The tales grow in the telling, spawning more half-truths and hopeful lies, and eventually leading to the inevitable angry discussion volatile question "Who is the greatest, Elvis or the Beatles?" There are so many levels and varieties of categories that are involved in this simple question; there is probably no definitive answer, as each individual can venture his or her own opinion with total commitment and validity.

But what can be determined are the facts, about which there have been hundreds of books and endless pages written in mind-numbing detail. This book acts as a sieve to these details and half-truths, sorting out one from the other and presenting them in a logical progression. The authors hope this book will function in several capacities, from settling bar bets over statistics and sheer numbers to presenting anecdotal and factual information about these great artists perhaps unknown or forgotten by the reader. Ultimately, the authors wish to challenge the reader's opinion as to whom he or she believes really was No. 1, Elvis or the Beatles. Perhaps through comparisons of their personalities, lifestyles and music, this book will shed light on one of the most burning questions in Rock 'n' Roll history.

Finally, this book was written as an homage to ". . . two of the greatest acts in *Rock and Roll.*" It is intended to be as inclusive as possible, but of necessity distills that history to a manageable size. Therefore, it should be seen in that light and not as an instrument to end all arguments about Elvis or the Beatles. Those who spend their lives collecting trivia about either Elvis or the Beatles and those who have only the briefest exposure should find something of interest in these pages.

PRELUDE

"Before Elvis, there was nothing."
—John Lennon

"Remember, there's four of them and only one of me."
—Elvis about the Beatles

"What kind of person are you, an Elvis fan or a Beatles fan?"
—Uma Thurman in Pulp Fiction

One of the milestone facts about Elvis and the Beatles is that they actually met—all five of them—on one very special occasion. There have been scores of pages written about this first and only time that Elvis met with all four of the Beatles, so sifting out the truth of the matter takes some doing. But one thing we know for sure is that they met on August 27, 1965.

Journalist Chris Hutchins, who wrote for the music magazine *New Musical Express,* claims to have engineered the famous encounter and also was lucky enough to witness it. Hutchins was personally known to the Beatles, who had invited him to join them on the American leg of their tour. As a result, Hutchins was privy to the backstage antics of the Beatles and their entourage, which explains how he could have such close insider information. He detailed the meeting between Elvis and the Beatles in his book *Elvis Meets the Beatles: The Untold Story of Their Entangled Lives,* which he coauthored with Peter Thompson.

Initially, Elvis was reluctant to meet with the lads from Liverpool. Some stories hold that he was adamant about not having them at his California house, but he was dissuaded from this attitude by Colonel Parker, who set up the meeting particulars through Hutchins with Brian Epstein.

When *The Beatles Anthology* was published in 1995, the story gelled into a cohesive whole through actual quotes from many interviews both past and present. Though Hutchins's report and the *Anthology* description do not always match, the combination nevertheless provides a glimpse into the events of that famous encounter when, in Hutchins's words, a "billion dollars worth of talent" played music together for just one night in the late summer of 1965.

Elvis Meets the Beatles

The Beatles met Elvis Presley in Los Angeles on August 27, 1965, at the tail end of their 1965 tour of America—the one that began with their concert at New York's Shea Stadium and peaked with their performance at the Hollywood Bowl in Los Angeles. At the time, Elvis was making movies in Hollywood (which he came to despairingly call "my travelogues") and living in a mansion at 565 Perugia Way in Bel Air.

The Beatles, their manager Brian Epstein and their roadies Mal Evans and Neil Aspinall were all driven up into the Hollywood Hills to Elvis's abode. There are no photos or audio recordings of the subsequent meeting, although there is a fan photo taken from a distance of the aftermath. (According to Hutchins, Elvis's manager, Colonel Parker, insisted that no photographs or recordings be made of the encounter. One has to wonder if Parker would have chosen otherwise had he realized how priceless such documentation would have been.)

However, Elvis tried to make them feel at home. According to Hutchins, Elvis sat on the couch, while Paul and John were to one side of him (on his right) and Ringo was on the other. George sat cross-legged on the floor. A huge color television was on in the middle of the room with the sound off, while a record player was playing the latest tunes. Several minutes ticked by and no one said a word. Elvis finally broke the silence that had fallen over the room by tossing his remote control on the table in front of him.

Hutchins recalls Elvis started the conversation. "Look, guys," he said, "if you're just going to sit there and stare at me, I'm going to bed. I didn't mean for this to be like the subjects calling on the King." He smiled, and everyone laughed. "Let's talk a bit, huh? . . . And then maybe play and sing a bit?" John then said that that was just what they all wanted to do. One of Elvis's staff brought drinks for the guests, but while the Beatles all drank scotch-and-coke or bourbon-and-7UP, Elvis had only 7UP, and he didn't touch any of the cigarettes that were offered, unlike the Fab Four. After a bit, Elvis said, "Somebody bring in the guitars." One of his men jumped up, and within moments three electric guitars had been plugged into the amplifiers in the room.

Elvis took a bass guitar, and John took a rhythm guitar. Paul sat down at a nearby piano. Elvis obviously wasn't that familiar with his instrument, so Paul gave him some instructions. "Here's how I play the bass," Elvis said, strumming a few chords. "It's not too good, but I'm practicing." Paul then remarked, "Elvis, lad, you're coming along quite well. Keep up the rehearsals and me and Mr. Epstein will make you a star."

George was busy looking over his instrument, and it was a few minutes before he joined in. They had at last found a way of communicating, through music. Only Ringo looked a bit down, as he could only watch the others and drum on the side of his chair. "Sorry there's no drum kit for you," Elvis told Ringo. "We left that back in Memphis." "That's okay," Ringo replied. "I'd rather play pool." Eventually he moved over to the pool table and shot pool with Mal.

While all this was going on, Brian Epstein and the Colonel sat chatting at the back of the room. Then, they went out into the game room to play some roulette. John remembers, "I think Brian won a bit, and the Colonel lost a little."

"What's it gonna be?" asked Elvis. "Let's do one by the other Cilla [not Priscilla Presley], Cilla Black," said Paul, leading into "You're My World." "This beats talking, doesn't it," said John. Elvis was getting into it. "This is what you guys gave me for my thirtieth birthday," he said, referring to the song he was about to play. "It made me sick." (It made him "sick" presumably because it was so good, and so successful, and Elvis was in competition with the Beatles.) He laughed and played the bass riff from "I Feel Fine."

"Why have you dropped the old stuff? The rock?" asked John. "I loved the old Sun records." "Listen just because I'm stuck with some movie soundtracks doesn't mean I can't do rock 'n' roll no more," Elvis replied, testily. "I might just get around to cuttin' a few sides and knockin' you off the top."

Hutchins further relates that "Playing the instruments certainly helped [them] feel at ease with Elvis. After about an hour [they] stopped and began to talk about the thing [they] all knew best—entertaining. In particular, the experiences [they] all had on tour." "Some funny things happen to you on the road, don't they?" Elvis smiled. "I remember once in Vancouver we'd only done a number or two when some of the fans rushed the stage. It was lucky the guys and I got off in time. They tipped the whole damn rostrum over!"

Paul immediately followed up Elvis's words. "Yes, we've had some crazy experiences, too. I remember one fellow rushed on stage when were performing and pulled the leads out of the amplifiers. Then he turned to me and said, 'One move and you're dead.' " Elvis replied, "Yeah, it can be pretty scaring at times." John said, "When the fans went for you, you were up there all alone. With us, it's four against everybody and we can draw support from each other."

It was 2 a.m. when things wrapped up. As they were about to leave, Paul said, "Elvis, we'd like you and the other guys to come up to the place where we are staying tomorrow night." "Well, I'll see," Elvis replied. "I don't know whether I can make it or not. But thanks all the same." He smiled and they all shook hands. John recalls, "We never saw him again. It was Elvis's sense of humor that stuck in my mind. He liked to laugh and make others laugh, too. Which was why I put on a Peter Sellers voice again as we walked out of the door and said, "Tanks for ze music, Elvis—and long live ze King!"

"It was one of the great meetings of my life," said Paul in an interview in 1995. "I think he liked us. I think at that time, he may have felt a little bit threatened, but he didn't say anything. We certainly didn't feel any antagonism. These were great times, so even if you didn't enjoy all of the events that much, you could still go home to Liverpool and say, "Well, you know who I met?" I mean, to meet Elvis, or anybody like that, or to say you've been to Sunset Strip—it was very impressive.

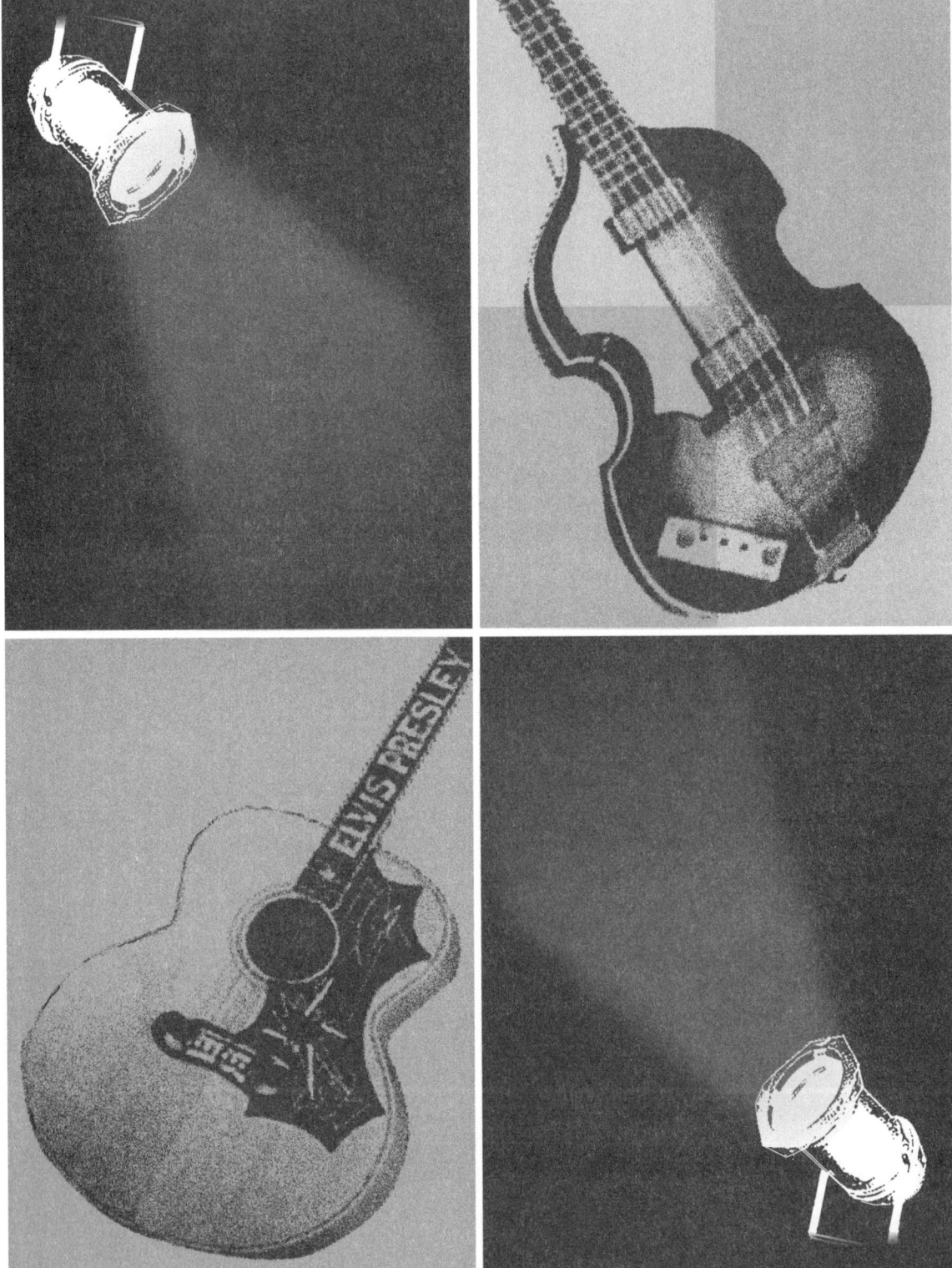

Chapter 1

The Extraordinary Lives of Elvis and the Beatles

Elvis

On January 8, 1935, Gladys Presley gave birth to twin boys in a small house in East Tupelo, Mississippi. Jesse Garon, the elder sibling was stillborn. The other twin was named Elvis Aaron Presley. Gladys doted on Elvis and always told him he had the power of both twins.

Elvis and Gladys were close throughout their lives together; she rarely let him out of her sight and acted as his confidante, guide, and most trusted friend. Gladys worked as a seamstress and homemaker, and she and Elvis enjoyed a relationship stronger than any he would ever forge with his lackluster father, Vernon, or his inner circle later referred to as the "Memphis Mafia." (So dubbed by the media, the Memphis Mafia referred to Elvis's entourage of family, boyhood friends, and early business associates who handled his security, touring, and public appearances.) They often wore suits, ties and dark glasses, and looked the part of "Mafioso." When Vernon was sentenced in 1938 to Parchman Penitentiary for

> **COLD HARD FACT**
>
> **Was Elvis's middle name spelled Aron or Aaron?**
>
> Elvis was named after his father, Vernon Elvis Presley, and a family friend in Tupelo, Aaron Kennedy. Aron was the spelling that Gladys chose, apparently to make it similar to the middle name of Elvis's stillborn identical twin, Jesse Garon Presley.
>
> Later in life, Elvis began looking into changing the spelling of his middle name to the traditional "Aaron." In the process, he learned that official state records had inexplicably listed it as "Aaron," and not "Aron," as it was written on his original birth records. Knowing Elvis's plans for his middle name, Vernon chose the "Aaron" spelling for Elvis's tombstone. "Aaron" is the spelling Elvis's estate has designated as the official one when the middle name is used today.

forging a check to $8 (serving eight months of an eight year sentence), Elvis grew even closer to his mother. Gladys took Elvis everywhere with her, and when Elvis began attending school, she would walk him there and home again.

When he was in the fifth grade, Elvis's teacher invited him to enter a talent contest on Children's Day at the Mississippi-Alabama Fair and Dairy Show. At the age of ten, dressed in a cowboy suit and standing on a chair to reach the microphone, Elvis sang his rendition of Red Foley's "Old Shep" and won second place, a five-dollar prize, and a free ticket to all the rides. On his birthday the following January, his parents gave him a guitar that they had purchased from the Tupelo Hardware Store for $12.95. Over the next year, Elvis's uncle (Vernon's brother, Johnny Smith) and Assembly of God pastor Frank Smith (no relation) gave Elvis basic guitar lessons.

In 1948, after Vernon lost another job, the Presleys moved to Memphis. Gladys's brothers got Vernon a job at the Precision Tool Company, and the Presleys moved into a small apartment at 370 Washington Street where the rent was eleven dollars a week. Elvis enrolled at L.C. Humes High School. Starting in his sophomore year, he worked in the school library and, after school, at Loew's State Theatre. In 1951, he received his first driver's license, joined the ROTC unit at Humes High, tried out for the football team

> **COLD HARD FACT**
>
> During his first appearance on *The Milton Berle Show* on June 5, 1956, Elvis's hip-swiveling leg-shaking performance ignited the first real controversy of his career. Though the audience fans squealed with delight, television critics across the nation called the performance "vulgar" and "animalistic" and observed an "appalling lack of musicality." In July of that year, Elvis appeared on *The Steve Allen Show*, and Allen, not an Elvis or a Rock 'n' Roll fan, insisted that the "new and improved" Elvis wear formal white tie and tails while singing this song to a basset hound. The good-natured Elvis obliged and later laughed all the way to the bank.

(he was cut by the coach when he refused to trim his sideburns and ducktail), and in his spare time hung around the black section of town, especially on Beale Street.

Elvis grew up hearing basically three styles of music: church music; Country & Western (C&W), which he heard on the radio; and black Gospel styles, which he heard from the traveling tent shows that sometimes set up camp across the railroad tracks from the Presley home. When he and his family moved to Memphis in 1948, Elvis was exposed to Traditional Blues and Rhythm & Blues (R&B) music and was immediately drawn to the sound and style of artists such as B.B. King, Howlin' Wolf, and Sonny Boy Williamson.

In the summer of 1953, Elvis dropped in at the Memphis Recording Service (Sun Studios) and recorded "My Happiness" and "That's When Your Heartaches Begin" as a birthday present for Gladys for a cost of four dollars. Thanks to smart-thinking secretary Marion Keisker, Sun Studios owner Sam Phillips heard the recordings and in 1954 called Elvis to team him up with local musicians Scotty Moore, on guitar, and Bill Black, on bass. On July 5, they recorded Arthur "Big Boy" Crudup's "That's All Right (Mama)." This song, backed with "Blue Moon of Kentucky," became the first of five singles Elvis released on the Sun label. When Memphis radio station WHBQ began airing it two days later, the record became a local hit and Elvis began touring the South and appearing at the Grand Ole Opry, where he was not initially well-received, as he was a bit "wild" for the Country and Western crowd. The Opry stage manager actually told Elvis to quit music and go back to driving a truck.

Elvis performing in the studio, January, 1956. © *Bettmann/CORBIS*

Elvis poses for the camera during his military service at a U.S. base in Germany, October, 1958.
© *Vittoriano Rastelli/Corbis*

In August 1955, Elvis was signed by Hank Snow Attractions, a management company jointly owned by country singer Hank Snow and a man named Colonel Tom Parker. A few months later, Parker took full control and arranged for Elvis to move over to RCA Records and do his recording in Nashville and New York City. In January 1956, his first RCA single "Heartbreak Hotel" became a huge hit, launching him onto the national music scene. Elvis's star power expanded swiftly, interrupted only by his two-year stint in the army from early 1958 to early 1960.

Meanwhile, as Elvis's career soared, his mother's health declined. She became nervous and easily agitated, began drinking too much, and gained a lot of weight. When Elvis was inducted into the army and sent to Germany, she became even worse, until, in August 1958, Vernon had her taken to the hospital. She appeared jaundiced,

Elvis kisses his mother, Gladys, on the eve of his induction into the Army. At left is his father, Vernon.
© *Bettmann/CORBIS*

with a yellowish cast to her skin, and, as Vernon said, was "suffering for breath," but her doctors could not come up with a diagnosis.

Elvis was able to get emergency leave home to visit her in the hospital. She rallied when he came but then later passed away in her sleep. Elvis, twenty-three, was devastated by this loss. Many times throughout the rest of his life, he commented that he had never fully recovered from her death. Many believe that Elvis had lost the only person in his life that could keep him on the straight and narrow.

Following his return from military service, the quality of Elvis's recordings dropped, and Elvis himself became dissatisfied with the direction his career took over the next seven years. To satisfy his multiple film contracts, he took on an overly demanding schedule that precluded creative recording and public performances. Beginning with *Love Me Tender* (opened on November 15, 1956), Elvis starred in thirty-one motion pictures—mostly musicals—as his public persona transformed from one of rebellious Rock 'n' Roller to wholesome family entertainer. *Jailhouse Rock* (1957), *King Creole* (1958), and *Flaming Star* (1960) were considered his best films, though *Blue Hawaii* (1961) and *Viva Las Vegas* (1964) were also highly praised.

In the musical arena, however, Elvis's star began to fade. In 1960, his album *Elvis Is Back* came out to mixed reviews. The social upheaval of the 1960s and the so-called "British Invasion" of Rock 'n' Roll acts from the other side of the Atlantic, spearheaded by the Beatles in 1964, pushed Elvis somewhat into the background, no longer on the cutting edge of the times.

On May 1, 1967, Elvis married Priscilla Beaulieu, (whom he had met in Germany in 1958 when she was only 14!) and nine months later, on February 1, 1968, their daughter Lisa Marie was born. The marriage didn't last long. Elvis had affairs with other women that he did not take great pains to hide, most notably with singer Nancy Sinatra (daughter of Frank) and the actress Ann-Margret. Elvis and Priscilla separated in 1972 and divorced in 1973.

At the end of 1968, Elvis made a very successful comeback by returning to his Rock 'n' Roll roots. His superb performance in the televised special "Elvis," sponsored by Singer Co. (more commonly known as the *'68 Comeback Special),* which aired on NBC on December 3, 1968, was well received. And in 1969, he returned to live performing, starting in Las Vegas and then moving across the country. His shows sold out and set new attendance records. The King was back.

After seven years off the top of the charts, Presley's song "Suspicious Minds" hit No. 1 on the Billboard music charts on November 1, 1969. It was to be the last time any song of his hit No. 1 on the U.S. Pop charts while he was still alive (although "Burning Love" got as high as No. 2 in September 1972). He continued, however, to reach No. 1 on charts around the world.

Elvis loved the Hawaiian islands and, in January 1973, performed in Honolulu in the first live concert to be broadcast worldwide via satellite. This event enabled him to reach his biggest audience ever. His subsequent *Aloha From Hawaii* album became another No. 1 record.

During the mid-1970s Elvis became increasingly isolated, battling an addiction to prescription drugs that took a toll on his appearance, health, and ability to perform (see chapter 5). Elvis's

> **COLD HARD FACT**
>
> Elvis was strongly influenced in his dress, hairstyle, and mannerisms by watching Tony Curtis. As an usher at Loews Theatre, he had every opportunity to see the films starring his hero again and again, and the sultry looks and popularity of Curtis with the teen girls wasn't lost on the young Elvis.
>
> Early photos of Elvis with his D.A. (short for Duck's Ass or Ducktail, a combed-back hairstyle popular during the 1950s, which made the back of the head look like a duck's rear end), look remarkably like Curtis, including the trademark lip curl! Throughout his career, Elvis was a master at acquiring other's styles and making them his own, while infusing what he copied with his signature manner.

final live concert appearance took place in Indianapolis at the Market Square Arena on June 26, 1977.

During his last few years, Elvis recorded a number of country hits. His album ironically titled *Way Down* was moving quickly up the country charts shortly before his death on August 16, 1977, and hit No. 1 that week, topping the U.K. Pop charts as well.

THE BEATLES

Young John Lennon

John Lennon was born to the sound of Hitler's *blitzkrieg* bombs in Liverpool on the night of October 9, 1940. His mother, Julia, gave him the middle name Winston in tribute to Prime Minister Winston Churchill. His father, Alfred, a ship's steward, was at sea at the time of the birth and was to spend most of the war years away, either at sea or AWOL. This meant that Julia had no income, so she continued to live at home with her father, Pop Stanley, and her sister Anne (Nanny).

Alfred returned home from the war in 1944, but, by 1946, John's parents' marriage was over. Alfred returned to sea and John did not see him again until John was famous. Julia met and moved in with John "Bobby" Dykins. It was a small apartment, and Mimi (Julia's older sister) did not approve of Bobby and Julia's living there with young John. One day, Mimi turned up at Julia and Bobby's apartment with a social worker and John's grandfather. Initially, the social worker felt John should stay with his mother, but when Mimi pointed out that the apartment had only one bedroom, the social worker handed John over to his grandfather, who immediately put him in Mimi's care. While growing up, John saw his mother only occasionally. Mimi always told John that his mother lived far away, even though she was just three miles from Mimi's house.

Growing up with his Aunt Mimi and Uncle George Smith at "Mendips" on Menlove Avenue, in a working-class section of Liverpool, John had, by all accounts, a happy childhood. Contrary to the myth, it was a comfortable existence. His four aunts and his cousins surrounded him. When his Aunt Elizabeth (Mater) moved to Edinburgh, John would spend his childhood summers with her in Durness, in a remote area of Scotland, a place he adored.

John's love of reading, writing stories and poems, and drawing emerged early. But he was naughty and often up to mischief, so much so that he was expelled from kindergarten before going to Dovedale Road Primary School. He entered Quarry Bank High School in September 1952. John was bright and clever, but he took no interest in conventional education and consequently left Quarry Bank with no formal qualifications. Yet, with the help of his headmaster and a portfolio of his work, he was accepted at the Liverpool College of Art, which allowed him to indulge in the Teddy boy dress and behavior of the time, much to his Aunt Mimi's disapproval.

John's mother, Julia, was more easygoing about how he looked and behaved. She also encouraged his early interest in music. John's frequent visits to see Julia and his half sisters, Julia and Jackie, typically turned into musical sessions at which Julia would sing and play her banjo. She taught John to play the banjo, which led him to want a guitar of his own.

John pestered his Aunt Mimi for a guitar, and it wasn't long before she purchased him one. From then on, he would sit on his bed making up tunes and singing to them. The noise often got on Mimi's nerves, and she'd banish him to the front porch with the

> ## COLD HARD FACT
>
> In Britain in the 1950s and early 1960s, a teenage fad known as the "Teddy boy" was all the rage. The name derived from the Edwardian style of period clothing that the teens affected. The clothing that the Teddy boys wore was designed to shock their parents' generation. It consisted of an outrageously "camp" Edwardian-style drape jacket, suede Gibson shoes with thick crepe soles, narrow "drainpipe" trousers (known as drainies), a smart shirt, and a loud tie. The Teddy girls adopted American fashions, such as toreador pants and circle skirts, although they tended to wear low-cut tops to make themselves look less proper. Girls wore ponytails, and the boys tried a number of hairstyles. The boys' favorite hairstyle was the overblown quiff with a DA at the back, originated by movie star Tony Curtis, and emulated by Elvis! The Teds' chosen music was American Rock 'n' Roll and the British bands that adopted the same style. They formed gangs, which sometimes wore a common uniform, such as a particular color of jacket or socks.

words that have since become immortal: "The guitar's all very well, John, but you'll never make a *living* out of it."

In early 1957, John and his best friend, Pete Shotton, formed a Skiffle band called the Quarry Men. (The name was related to the name of their high school). Skiffle was a distinctly British musical style combining regional folk music with quicker tempos and instruments, such as the washtub bass and the washboard for percussion, considered to be a distant cousin of American Folk Rock and forerunner of British Rock 'n' Roll. The Quarry Men began performing at parties and Skiffle contests around town.

In July 1958 (coincidentally, only a month before Gladys Presley died), John's mother, Julia, was tragically killed. She had been to visit Mimi and was on her way to the bus stop when a car driven by an inebriated off-duty policeman ran her over. Mimi said that after John got the news, he "just went to his room into a shell." Some years later, John recalled the incident as the worst night of his life. "I lost my mother twice. Once as a child of five and then again at seventeen. It made me very, very bitter inside. I had just begun to reestablish a relationship with her when she was killed."

John Lennon live on stage at the Cavern Club on Matthew Street, Liverpool, England, December, 1961. *(Photo by Evening Standard/Getty Images)*

> **COLD HARD FACT**
>
> John's mother was killed just one year after John and Paul first met. The fact that both John and Paul lost their mothers during their teen years was the basis of an unspoken bond between the two young men.

Young Paul McCartney

James Paul McCartney was born June 18, 1942, in Liverpool, England, five months after the Nazi bombings had ceased. His parents were Jim and Mary McCartney, a working-class couple.

Young Paul saw tragedy at a very early age. When he was just fourteen, his mother succumbed to breast cancer.

After his mother passed away, Paul asked his father to buy him a guitar. His father, who was a musician (front man of the silent-cinema accompaniment and traditional jazz band group the Jim Mac Jazz Band), was thrilled that his son, who always excelled academically, was also interested in music. Despite his meager salary as a cotton salesman, he bought his son a trumpet. However, Paul quickly discovered that it was more impressive to his friends if he played guitar, so with his father's permission, he exchanged the trumpet for an acoustic Zenith guitar.

Young George Harrison

George Harrison was born on February 24, 1943, to Louise and Harold Harrison. He had two brothers, Harold Jr. and Peter, and a sister, Louise. His father was a bus driver, and his mother a housewife. George's interest in music began at the same time the Skiffle craze hit Liverpool. He played in a Skiffle band with his brother, Peter, but because he was so young, he and his brother had to sneak out of the house to practice.

George met Paul McCartney in 1955, when both boys were regularly taking the bus to the Liverpool Institute. (George's Dad was the bus driver.) The two shared a love for the guitar and for American Rock 'n' Roll, and soon began to get together in the evenings to practice their distinctive versions of "Don't You Rock

Me Daddy-O" (recorded by Bill Sherrell for Tyme Records in 1957) and "Besame Mucho" (first recorded by the Jimmy Dorsey Orchestra in the mid 1940s). Paul brought George into the Quarry Men shortly after he himself joined the band at the behest of John.

Young Richard Starkey

Richard Starkey was born in a small two-story terraced house in the poor Dingle area of Liverpool on July 7, 1940, making him the oldest member of the Beatles. His father, whose name was also Richard, was originally a Liverpool dockworker and later worked in a bakery where he met Ringo's mother, Elsie. His parents broke up in 1943, and Elsie later married Harry Graves.

Young Richard managed to remain cheerful throughout his childhood, even though he often lived it in the hospital. At age six, he suffered appendicitis and went into a coma for two months. At thirteen, he caught a cold that developed into pleurisy, causing him to miss much school. By age fifteen, he could just barely read and write.

Like the other Beatles, young Ritchie also eventually became caught up in Liverpool's Skiffle craze. In 1957, he started his own group with Eddie Miles called the Eddie Clayton Skiffle Group, then joined the Raving Texans, a quartet that featured Rory Storm as lead singer, in 1959. At around this time, he got the nickname Ringo, because of the rings he wore, and because it sounded "cowboyish." He took on the last name Starr.

Come Together

On July 6, 1957, John was introduced to Paul by a mutual friend, Ivan Vaughn, after John's group, the Quarry Men, gave an afternoon performance at the St. Peter's Parish Church Garden Fete in Woolton, Liverpool. John was immediately impressed by Paul's knowledge of Rock 'n' Roll songs and his ability to properly tune a guitar! (John had learned slightly different ukulele tunings from his mother). Fearing that Paul might form his own competing group that summer, John asked him to join the Quarry Men, and Paul said yes the next day. Paul debuted with the group at the New Clubmoor Hall Conservative Club in Liverpool on October 18.

Paul then invited George to join the group. George was only fifteen but able and determined, and George's mother kindly

> **COLD HARD FACT**
>
> Alan Freed was the disc jockey credited with giving Rock 'n' Roll its name. His "Moondog" show broadcast live R&B performances. His show often promoted black artists for the first time to white audiences, including the young Beatles, via high-wattage radio stations out of Philadelphia and New York.

allowed them to rehearse at their home. In late August, the group (John, Paul, and George on guitars, and John Lowe on piano) recorded several songs, including Buddy Holly's "That'll Be the Day." Later that same month, the band performed at the Casbah Club (run by Mona Best, the mother of future Beatles drummer Pete Best). In November, they changed their name to Johnny and the Moondogs, reflecting their interest in Alan Freed's "Moondog" Rock 'n' Roll radio shows, which they heard via off-shore radio broadcasts.

By early 1960, a friend of John's from art school, Stu Sutcliffe, joined the band as the bass player. At Stu's suggestion, they became the Silver Beetles and then the Beatals (because the style of music they played was often called "Beat" music), touring Scotland under both of those names. In August, Pete Best joined the group on drums (replacing the very capable Tommy Moore, who went off to work in the steel mills), and the group made its first trip to Germany. While in Hamburg, singer Tony Sheridan convinced the Beatles (changed to this permanent spelling by John), to serve as the backing band on some of his recordings for the German Polydor Records label, produced by bandleader Bert Kaempfert. At the first session, in June 1961, Kaempfert signed the Beatles to their own Polydor contract.

Later that year, the Beatles were back in Liverpool, performing regularly around town, when a young record-store manager in Liverpool named Brian Epstein found he was having trouble fulfilling his customers' requests for a single the Beatles had recorded in Germany with Sheridan. When he couldn't locate copies from usual sources, Epstein ventured to ask the band themselves, and attended a lunchtime Beatles show. He was struck by both the musical talent and the charm of the four young men, while the Beatles quickly appreciated the value of Epstein's business acumen and experience. In January 1962, Epstein signed a five-year contract to manage the band. In June, after having been rejected by almost every other record company in the U.K., he brought the Beatles to EMI's Abbey Road Studios in London. George Martin, the principal producer with EMI's Parlophone label, decided to grant them a contract. At this time, Pete Best was fired and replaced by Ringo Starr, who was considered a better drummer, and much better liked by the others.

The Beatles' first recording sessions produced a minor U.K. hit, "Love Me Do," which charted, followed by a second single "Please Please Me." Three months later they recorded their first album (also titled *Please Please Me*), a mix of original songs by John and Paul along with some covers. While the Beatles were popular on the U.K. charts starting in early 1963, Beatlemania did not break out in the United States until December of that year, when "I Want to Hold Your Hand" was first played on New York radio. The song was No. 1 on the charts for three weeks before the Beatles' first appearance on *The Ed Sullivan Show* on February 9, 1964. (They appeared on the next two episodes of the show as well.) In the summer of 1964, they set out on their first world tour, but their touring days ended just two years later when they played their final concert in San Francisco on August 29, 1966. Fed up with the fan hysteria, they chose to channel their collective talents into studio recording.

Epstein died of a drug overdose in 1967. His loss turned out to be devastating to the band.

In January 1968, the Beatles formed a company called Apple Corp., Ltd., which included its chief division, Apple Records, housed in a building on Savile Row in London. Nevertheless, Epstein's absence, combined with Paul's unofficial and largely unwelcome takeover of the managerial role, took a heavy toll on the

COLD HARD FACT

The Beatles met Ringo Starr (who was drumming with Rory Storm and the Hurricanes on their German tour) on October 15, 1960, when he sat in for the busy Pete at an impromptu recording session featuring the Beatles and Storm's guitarist, Wally Eymond. Two years later, John, Paul, and George, feeling that Pete was not working out personally or musically, asked their manager, Brian Epstein, to fire Pete and hire Ringo. And, as they say, the rest is history.

band members, and the Beatles as an entity began to disintegrate. In January 1969, they performed their final concert on the Apple building's rooftop, which was filmed for their *Let It Be* movie. They released their last recorded album *Abbey Road,* in the summer of 1969, before officially breaking up in April 1970 as the *Let It Be* album was released. Each of the Beatles then went on to have a successful solo career.

During their time as a band, the Beatles released thirteen albums and five films in seven years, and were one of the most famous and successful bands in popular music history.

Paul, George, and Ringo famously reunited in 1994 to release the first of the Beatles' *Anthology* albums, consisting of outtakes and live recordings of Beatles songs. Two other volumes were released the next year. They also created two new Beatles songs by layering new music on unfinished tracks John had made before his death. DVD releases of the Anthology followed in 2003, with a new set of both mono and stereo remastered CDs released in 2009 to huge sales. The Beatles: Rock Band interactive music video game hit the shelves in 2009, with fans swarming to purchase the vocal and instrumental play-a-long song collection for their homes. Also in 2009, the release of an apple-shaped USB drive containing all fourteen remastered Beatles albums with art work, photos, and new and expanded descriptive rides the wave of the latest technology.

The Adult Life of John Lennon

In 1962, just as the Beatles were becoming popular in the U.K., John married Cynthia Powell, who was pregnant with their son, Julian. But in 1968, he met a Japanese-born artist named Yoko Ono, at London's Indica art gallery where she was showing her work, and the two began having a very public affair. Cynthia filed for divorce later that year. John married Yoko in March of 1969. Her constant presence, even at Beatles' recording sessions, was one source of tension among the Beatles (though certainly not the only one), and for this reason, many observers blamed Yoko for breaking up the Beatles.

While he was still a Beatle, John and Yoko recorded three albums of experimental electronic music. John's first "solo" album of popular music was *Live Peace in Toronto 1969,* recorded in 1969 (prior to the breakup) at the Rock 'n' Roll Festival in Toronto with the Plastic Ono Band. He also recorded three singles in his

John and five-year-old Julian Lennon and Yoko Ono watch to the rehearsal of the *Rolling Stones Rock 'n' Roll Circus Show,* December 10, 1968. © *Bettmann/CORBIS*

> **COLD HARD FACT**
>
> After both John and Yoko were injured in the summer of 1969 in a car accident in Scotland, John arranged for Yoko to be constantly with him in the studio (including having a full-sized bed rolled in) as he worked on the Beatles' final album, *Abbey Road*.

initial solo phase, "Give Peace a Chance," "Cold Turkey" (about his struggles with heroin addiction), and "Instant Karma!"

After the Beatles' breakup in 1970, John released the *John Lennon/Plastic Ono Band* album, followed by *Imagine* in 1971 and *Mind Games* in 1973. John's personal life then went into turmoil when Yoko kicked him out of their home. He lived for a time in Los Angeles with a friend of Yoko's, May Pang. In 1974, he released *Walls and Bridges,* before reuniting with Yoko in early 1975. That same year, he released the *Rock 'n' Roll* album, which featured his covers of old Rock 'n' Roll songs.

When Yoko gave birth to their son Sean in 1975, John retired to spend time with his family and try to be a better father to Sean than he had been to his first son, Julian, whom he had neglected. The retirement lasted until 1980, the year he released his last complete album, *Double Fantasy,* a collaboration with Yoko that focused on their relationship. He then began work on a new album to be called *Milk and Honey.*

Tragically, on the night December 8, 1980, John was murdered in front of his apartment building on the Upper West Side of New York by a deranged man named Mark David Chapman right before Yoko's eyes. He died of shock within a couple of hours. He was forty years old.

The Adult Life of Paul McCartney

Paul married the American photographer Linda Eastman in 1969, and they remained married until her death in 1998. He adopted Linda's daughter from a previous marriage, and together they had three children of their own, two daughters and a son.

Paul launched his solo career in 1970 with the album *McCartney,* which contained the hit song "Maybe I'm Amazed." *Ram,* released in 1971, was credited to both Paul and his wife, Linda.

> ## COLD HARD FACT
>
> In the late 1990s, Paul feuded with Yoko over the writing credits on a number of Beatles songs. He wanted to change the credits from "Lennon-McCartney" to "Paul McCartney and John Lennon" on songs that had been primarily composed by Paul. Yoko felt this would be a betrayal of the agreement John and Paul had made many years earlier. George and Ringo backed Yoko, and Paul gave up his effort.

In 1971, Paul formed the band Wings, in which Linda played a prominent role, despite much criticism from observers about her lack of musical talent. Wings went on to become one of the most popular bands of the 1970s, releasing ten albums over ten years, including the acclaimed *Band on the Run* in 1973. Wings also recorded the hit theme song to the James Bond film *Live and Let Die*.

In 1980, Wings broke up, but Paul continued to enjoy success as a soloist in the early part of the decade. His song "Coming Up" hit No. 1 in the U.S., and his duets with two other major Pop stars—"Ebony and Ivory" with Stevie Wonder and "The Girl Is Mine" with Michael Jackson—were both very popular as well. In the late 1980s, he formed a songwriting partnership with Elvis Costello, out of which came, among other things, the 1989 hit "Veronica" (on Costello's *Spike* album). In 1989 to 1990, Paul went on a very successful world tour that featured him performing many Beatles songs for the first time since the breakup. He did a similar tour in 1993.

On March 11, 1997, Paul was knighted by Queen Elizabeth II. In 1998, his beloved wife and musical partner, Linda, died after a long struggle against breast cancer, the same illness that had taken his mother when Paul was only fourteen. Paul continued to release Pop albums throughout the 1990s and into the first decade of the new century. In June 2002, he married Heather Mills, an anti-landmine activist and former model, and continued to give live concerts throughout the world. Paul's song "When I'm Sixty-four" came true on June 18th of 2006 when he turned 64. After a new release and a series of secret and surprise gigs in small New York, Los Angeles, London and Paris clubs in 2007, May of 2008 saw a messy divorce between Paul and Heather, resulting in a huge payout to a woman some describe as a "gold-digger." Paul continued

> **COLD HARD FACT**
>
> In December 1999, George was attacked in his home by a crazed fan and stabbed multiple times, resulting in a punctured lung. He and his wife were able to detain the thirty-five-year-old attacker until the police arrived, but the man was later acquitted of any crime on grounds of insanity.

touring through 2008 and 2009, appearing on TV and releasing a live CD of his very successful New York concert.

The Adult Life of George Harrison

George married British model and photographer Pattie Boyd in 1966, who famously left him in 1971 to marry his best friend, rocker Eric Clapton. George remarried in 1978, to Olivia Trinidad Arias, with whom he had one child, their son Dhani, born that same year.

George wrote a few very popular Beatles songs, such as "Taxman" "Something" and "While My Guitar Gently Weeps," but his talent as a songwriter was largely stifled and overshadowed by John and Paul. While still a Beatle, George became interested in Hinduism and Indian music. He studied with East Indian Classical Musician Ravi Shankar, whom he helped to popularize in the West, and introduced Indian musical instruments such as the sitar into a number of Beatles songs. For the rest of his life, this Indian influence played a huge role in both his worldview and in his music.

George had a mostly successful solo career after the Beatles broke up and came into his own as a songwriter. His major hits included "My Sweet Lord" (1970), "Give Me Love (Give Me Peace on Earth)" (1973), "All Those Years Ago" (1981), and "Got My Mind Set on You" (1987). He organized the first large-scale charity concert, the Concert for Bangladesh, which took place on August 1, 1971. He released a total of twelve albums—not including compilations, box sets, and soundtracks—as a solo artist.

In the late 1980s, George helped form the Traveling Wilburys with Roy Orbison, Jeff Lynne, Bob Dylan, and Tom Petty. The all-star band released two albums and five singles between 1988 and 1991.

George died on November 29, 2001, at the age of fifty-eight, succumbing to lung cancer that had metastasized to his brain.

Harrison's final album, *Brainwashed,* was completed by his son Dhani and Jeff Lynne and released in 2002.

The Adult Life of Ringo Starr

Ringo married Maureen Cox in 1965, and they had three children. The couple divorced in 1975, and Ringo married actress Barbara Bach in 1981.

Of all of the Beatles, Ringo did the least singing and songwriting but nevertheless managed to have a moderately successful solo career, particularly with his 1973 *Ringo* album. Altogether he released fourteen studio albums, six live albums, three compilation albums, and a handful of singles, including "Photograph" and "You're Sixteen," which were No. 1 on the U.S. charts in 1973 and 1974, respectively. Ringo also had some success as an actor appearing in such films as *Candy* (1968), *The Magic Christian* (1969), *Son of Dracula* (1974), and *Caveman* (1980). He starred as Larry the Dwarf in Frank Zappa's *200 Motels* (1971). His voice is featured in Harry Nilsson's animated film *The Point!* (1971). He was especially well-received in the British film *That'll Be the Day* (1973) where he co-starred as a Teddy boy. He also played "The Pope" in Ken Russell's *Lisztomania* (1975).

Beginning in 1989, following a stint in detox for alcoholism, he organized a series of concert tours under the name Ringo Starr and His All-Starr Band, featuring other well-known musicians. The eighth such tour took place in 2003. In 2007, Ringo released his nostalgic *Liverpool 8* CD, with tours and TV appearances through 2008. Ringo and Paul reunited on stage briefly in April of 2009 for a well-received benefit concert.

"The King" and His Most Inspired Follower: Elvis and John

"Before Elvis, there was nothing."
"Nothing really affected me until I heard Elvis. If there hadn't been Elvis, there would not have been The Beatles."
—*John Lennon*

Elvis Presley and John Lennon each created some of the greatest music on their continents during their short lives. Besides their great musical accomplishments, there were many parallels in their personal lives. Neither John nor Elvis were particularly good students, though both were quite intelligent. John always displayed a sharp verbal wit, much to the dismay of his teachers, and he used it to keep unwanted attention at bay. Elvis was a quiet loner who had a nearly photographic memory but did not fit in physically or personally with the traditional Southern school system. Elvis would forgo the standard cowboy shirts and jeans in favor of colorful shirts and dress pants more akin to the styles of the black youth of the day. John adopted the rebellious "Teddy boy" look, which included black leather jackets, tight jeans, and dark t-shirts, derived from American films featuring Marlon Brando and James Dean. Both Elvis and John were outsiders in school who did not make friends easily and turned to music as an outlet for self-expression and a means of alleviating frustrations.

Both men needed partners throughout their lives. For young Elvis it was his high school friend, Red West, who saved him from a gang of toughs who wanted to cut Elvis's hair in the school lavatory. West stayed by Elvis's side throughout his career, as his driver and member of his inner circle (the so-called Memphis Mafia). For John, that partner was, at first, Paul, an easygoing natural musician who balanced his own acerbic edge and became a songwriting partner as well as a friend. Then later it was Yoko Ono, his second wife.

Throughout their lives, neither Elvis nor John ever lost touch with his roots, and each considered himself the product of his socioeconomic position in society. Elvis always retained his "poor country boy" demeanor, and John even sang of himself as a "working-class hero." And though both men became hugely famous and wealthy beyond their dreams, each craved privacy and peace and disdained the privileges heaped upon royalty and members of the upper class.

Both John and Elvis had quick tempers, sometimes acting out violently toward their spouses or those around them. John's sharp tongue was often his weapon of choice, whereas Elvis was quick to use his fists or even pick up a gun when frustrated. Both also used hard drugs, the effects of which directly impacted their personal and public behavior and revealed their need to escape from reality and the pressure of their highly public lives.

John and Elvis both sought spiritual enlightenment through various means during their relatively short lives. Elvis, who attended church as a child, embraced Gospel music early on, and later in life explored mystical texts describing New Age philosophies and the search for God. John looked for "truth" through mind-expanding substances, such as LSD and transcendental meditation. Both Elvis and John seemed fascinated with death, and each man was still exploring these spiritual areas in their lives when they passed on to the great beyond and finally received their answers.

Comparison

Elvis's childhood was characterized by a number of things that also marked the early years of the four members of the Beatles: working-class roots, self-taught musical origins, love for African-American music, and a desire to break free from humble surroundings and become famous. All five grew up with strong mother figures, with a lesser influence from their fathers (except for Paul's musical dad), and saw music as the ticket to self-realization and personal fulfillment. But rather than follow the musical trends of their time, they all rebelled, choosing to synthesize prior styles and create new musical territory—Rock 'n' Roll and "British Invasion" music.

All five artists had to struggle to break into show business. They paid their dues in small clubs and on grueling tours for years before making it big and never forgot their roots along the way. They loved their families, and all were dedicated fathers (though it took John a while to become one). They strove to express their true selves through their music, which made them vulnerable but also attractive, powerful, and seemingly magical in their deceptively easy way of performing.

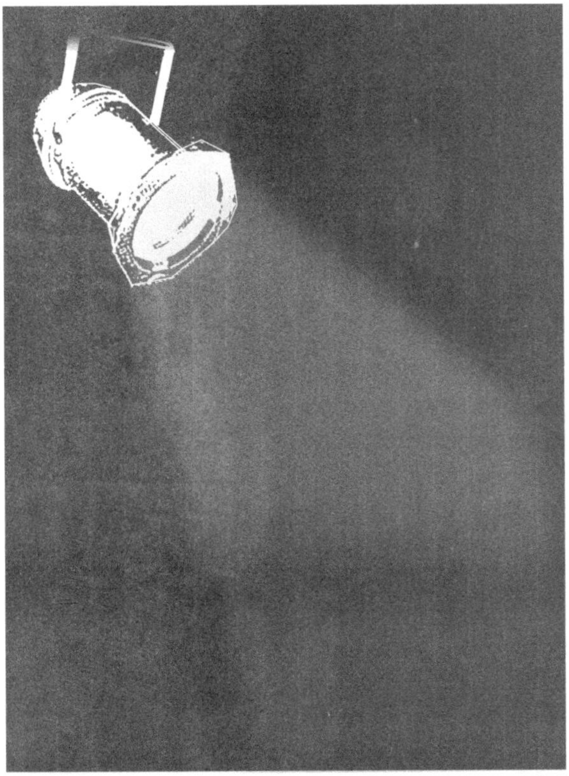

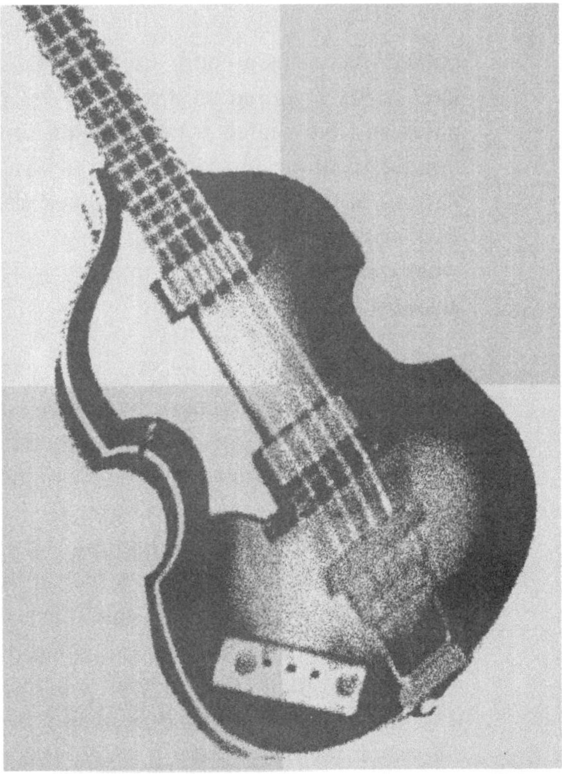

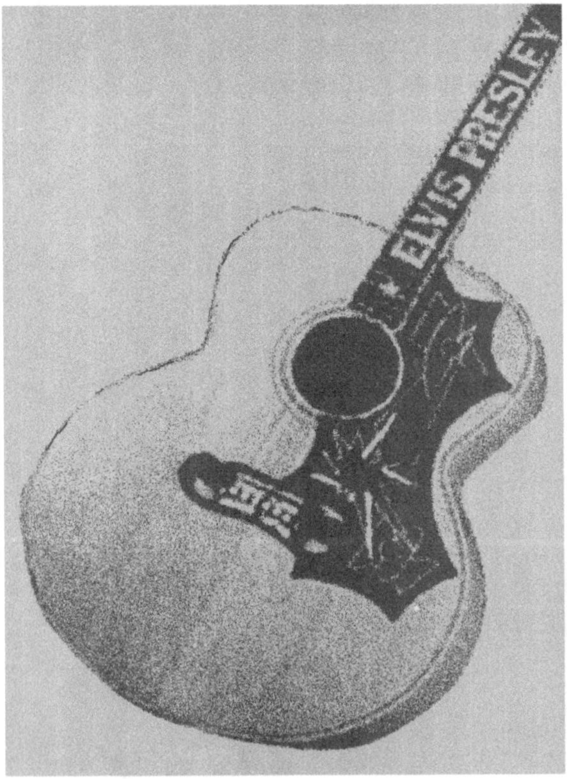
ELVIS PRESLEY

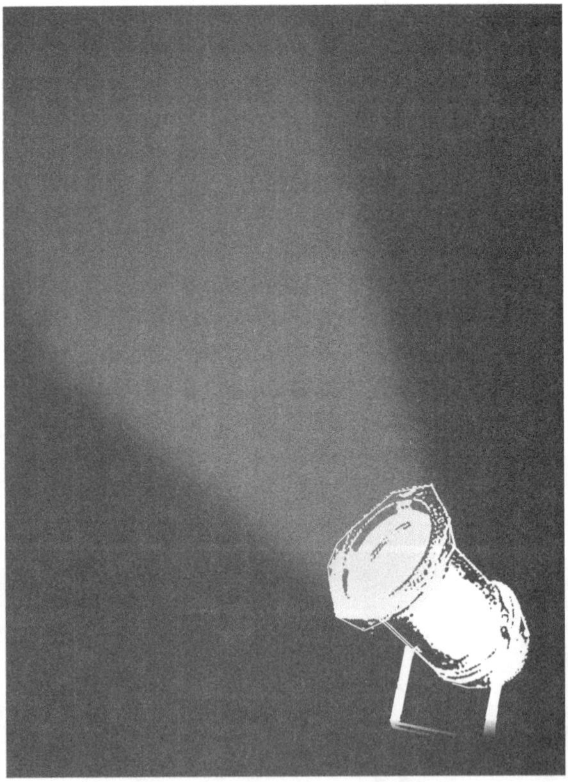

CHAPTER 2

Musical Influences and Performance Styles

Elvis

Musical Influences

Elvis entered the American music scene in January of 1956 with the release of "Heartbreak Hotel" and the first of several appearances on the Jackie Gleason-produced Dorsey Brothers' television show. The new freedom teenagers were finding in African-American music, called Rhythm and Blues (or R&B), in the mid-fifties was spearheaded by disk jockeys such as Alan Freed, who played black music (called "race records" until 1949, then "R&B") to national audiences over the airwaves. White American teens (and some adult listeners as well) were searching for fresh musical sounds after the Swing and Big Band music of the 1940s, and R&B offered them a new musical palate. The syncopations of the "rhythm" aspect of R&B, the blues scales and melodies derived from African tonality, and the humorous, double-meaning lyrics became the foundation of Rock 'n' Roll (R&R) and of Elvis's music later in the decade.

Elvis Presley performing his infamous hip swivel, in Hollywood, California, June, 1956.
© *Bettmann/CORBIS*

A musical sponge, Elvis was perhaps the first truly biracial musician. He did not simply cover or redo black R&B songs: He synthesized them and the style traits through his own musical personality based in cowboy songs and the church music he grew up hearing. This combination of musical influences helped create Rockabilly, the unique sound of young white southerners (and some mid-westerners) covering, or redoing, R&B songs with a Country and Western (C&W) base. It can be heard in the early music of Jerry Lee Lewis, Carl Perkins, and Buddy Holly, but Elvis also symbolized the new emerging musical form we call Rock 'n' Roll.

It was daring for Elvis to cross the musical color lines, singing R&B songs with a C&W backup band, as Benny Goodman and a few others had only briefly touched upon integration in Popular music in the Swing era. Bill Haley had preceded Elvis with this concept, but he could not physically personify the emerging R&R sound to young audiences. (Haley, already in his thirties, appeared

> **COLD HARD FACT**
>
> The story of Elvis in Las Vegas is a record-breaker. In 1968, Elvis signed a performance contract with the International Hotel (eventually purchased by Hilton Hotels) for him to perform for five years, four weeks per year, two shows per night for $500,000 per year. The showroom at the International held two thousand people, so a little bit of math reveals that Elvis averaged an astounding half a million paying audience members under this contract.

rather stiff, was moderately heavy-set, balding with a spit curl in the middle of his forehead, and had one glass eye!) In contrast, Elvis looked the part of a young Rock 'n' Roller and embodied the sexuality of the new style. Elvis was only copying the upfront sexuality of black performers, who utilized stage antics such as strutting and suggestive hip, arm, and leg movements as part of their musical interpretation. But Elvis created his own unique hip swiveling and sneering appeal to capture the attention of the teen audience and their buying market.

One of Elvis's unique gifts was his almost photographic musical memory, which allowed him to quickly learn and reproduce songs from a wide variety of styles throughout his career. Elvis loved ballads—slow, romantic songs—and culled these from Pop artists, both black and white. The music in his films, for example, covers a wide range of styles, including Blues, Country, Latin, Native American, Hawaiian settings, Funk, and Hard Rock. His post-army music may have started out as little more than snarling, shouted Rock 'n' Roll to more Pop-oriented singles, but Elvis also recorded light Classical pieces ("O Sole Mio," for example, made into "It's Now or Never"), many Pop ballads, Soul-style songs ("In the Ghetto"), and Grammy-winning Gospel songs such as "How Great Thou Art." His successful televised *'68 Comeback Special* was a tour-de-force of these different styles, and his televised 1973 *Aloha From Hawaii* included the epic "American Trilogy," a patriotic anthem combing three traditional American Folk songs. During his touring and Las Vegas years of the 1970s, Elvis covered a variety of songs by his contemporaries, including pieces by Creedence Clearwater Revival, Bob Dylan, Roberta Flack, James Taylor, and, yes, the Beatles.

Elvis tended to focus on singles as his preferred means of musical transmission, although he did do a few albums, such as his Gospel and Christmas releases and soundtrack recordings. But the 45 single was Elvis's main domain, and he ruled the charts in this aspect. A majority of his albums were compilations of his greatest hits or live recordings, according to the fashion and preferred marketing strategy of the record industry in the 1950s. The basic concept for packaging and marketing albums prior to the Beatles' innovations was simply to compile and package an artist's biggest song, and release the record with a staged photo on the cover and a songlist on the back, perhaps with a short bio. Elvis knew nothing of marketing or packaging albums, but concentrated on songs and singles, always looking for a new hit tune. He cared little about how his albums were constructed and released.

Elvis was always a solo artist, even when surrounded by guitar players, bassists, drummers, vocalists, and a forty-piece orchestra, as he was during the 1970s. Elvis's strength was his individuality, uniqueness, and self-sufficiency as a performer, with all other musical participants simply playing supporting roles during his career. As grandiose as he and his stage productions became, Elvis was always the main attraction and remained simply a solo artist backed by an enormous conglomeration of voices, guitars, strings, and horns. The fans came to see Elvis Presley; the other performers were icing on the cake.

Instrumentation and Orchestration

Elvis began his musical journey with just his voice and his guitar, an effective combination that proved to be the essence of Elvis's unique sound throughout his career, even when surrounded by dozens of other musicians. In 1953, Elvis first recorded "My Happiness" and "That's When Your Heartaches Begin" with just his voice and a guitar at Sam Phillips's Memphis Recording Service. Within a year, Sam had teamed Elvis with Scotty Moore on lead guitar and Bill Black on acoustic bass. Both of these musicians came from a C&W background and only moved toward R&B under the influence of Elvis and his musical tastes. The "Blue Moon Boys" (so named after their recordings of this song and "Blue Moon of Kentucky" became popular) soon added drummer D.J. Fontana, whom Elvis had worked with on the Louisiana Hayride performance circuit during 1954 and 1955. The Jordanaires, an outstanding Gospel-oriented male vocal quartet out of Nashville, joined Elvis in 1956, and this ensemble combination performed support harmonies behind Elvis during his glory years of the mid and late 1950s. Soon Elvis added pianists such as Floyd Cramer and Dudley Brooks for recording sessions. But Elvis was always the focal point, the lead singer, front man, entertainer, and box-office draw.

After his service in the army, Elvis added vocalist-guitarist Charlie Hodge to his entourage, but performed rarely during his moviemaking years (1961–1969). The exception to this was his outstanding televised 1968 *Singer Special* (also known as *The '68 Comeback Special),* in which Elvis performed live in an informal setting with Hodge, Scotty Moore, and D.J. Fontana and with a studio orchestra for the first time. Elvis knew this was the sound he had been looking for to accompany his style, a larger-than-life, grandiose wave of full orchestral music that matched his transition from young Rock 'n' Roller to mature Pop star. The Rock 'n' Roll Elvis spearheaded as a youth thrived on the relatively stripped down sound of guitars, bass, and drums, but this new, thicker orchestral texture reflected Elvis's emerging style as an adult Pop performer.

As Elvis evolved as a musician and performer, several of his old-guard performers, such as Scotty, Bill, and D.J., left his group and were replaced by younger musicians with a fresher, more modern approach. Bill and Scotty, particularly, were still C&W musicians at heart, thrust into Rock 'n' Roll via Elvis's initial tidal wave of popularity, and were never really comfortable in their role as "Rock stars."

Elvis realized the need to keep up with the times musically, especially once the "British Invasion" hit American shores in the mid 1960s, so his band roster changed accordingly. He used such innovative guitarists as Tommy Cogbill, Tiny Timbrell, Hank Garland, and Reggie Young. When Elvis returned to Las Vegas in 1969, his new band included guitarist James Burton and Glen Hardin, pianist and former member of the Crickets. By the 1970s, Elvis toured with a cohesive rhythm section, hiring local orchestras to augment his huge musical entourage.

Elvis himself played many instruments in his career, including acoustic guitar, electric guitar, electric bass, ukulele, and acoustic piano. (See Appendix A for a list of which musicians played which instruments on Elvis's recordings.)

As Elvis toured and played Vegas regularly, the Jordanaires preferred to remain in Nashville, so Elvis would enlist vocalists that included the Imperials (a male vocal quintet), the Sweet

Inspirations (an African-American female trio), and Millie Kirkham or Kathy Westmoreland on high female vocals. J.D. Sumner and his group, the Stamps, joined Elvis in the early 1970s, and other vocal groups, such as the Voice, also contributed their talents as backup singers. (See Appendix A for a list of Elvis's backup singers.)

Vocal Style and Technique

Elvis had a true, clear voice with a distinctly controlled vibrato (quivering or wavering of tone) and the ability to dramatically change his vocal timbre (texture or quality of sound generated) depending on the style of the song. He could sing a ballad with emotion and purity and follow with a snarling blues using a buzzing or roughening of the vocal quality. Elvis's vocal versatility spanned his many style choices, which included blues, Pop, C&W, movie music, light opera, ballads, patriotic music, Gospel, and, of course, Rock 'n' Roll. Only rarely did Elvis use falsetto (upper register singing, often called "head tones"), and he preferred backup singers to overdubbing his own voice. Besides reverb and echo, very little was done to sonically enhance Elvis's voice.

Elvis did occasionally employ narrative, or spoken, sections (recitations) in his songs as early as his 1953 demo recording of "That's When Your Heartaches Begin" and later hits such as "Are You Lonesome Tonight?" Elvis used this device for its romantic and dramatic impact to great success. On songs such as "U.S. Male," Elvis drew on the "talking blues style" heard in the early Folk songs of Woody Guthrie and Pete Seeger.

Elvis's songs featured beautiful harmonies, via his use of backup vocalists and groups ranging from duets with Charlie Hodge, to the Jordanaires and other three- to five-part groups, to a dozen or more singers in the 1970s.

Rehearsal Techniques

Before the final form of a song is realized, it must be rehearsed and refined by private and public performance. Because Elvis had a nearly photographic memory for lyrics and melodies, rehearsing with "the King" was often simply a matter of working out keys, tempos, and arrangements of the material selected.

The Elvis of the 1950s chose his songs from a variety of sources, ranging from Country to Blues, and rehearsed them with Scotty, Bill, and D.J. until all were comfortable. Once Hill and Range Music, the publishing company owned by Elvis's manager Col. Tom Parker, began supplying Elvis with songs (see chapter 3 for more detail on Parker and Hill and Range), Elvis would listen to a stack of demo tapes and select which songs he felt best suited him. After the other musicians became familiar with chord and form structures, rehearsals would commence. Elvis would do a dozen or more takes on each song, and listen back intently—not for mistakes as much as for that "magic" that comes from a cohesive and energetic performance.

When the Jordanaires and other vocal groups joined Elvis, rehearsal would often begin with Gospel singalongs around the studio piano that Elvis often played, where singers and musicians might contribute song ideas and participate freely. After this loose but effective warm-up, rehearsals and then recordings would begin.

By the late 1960s and early 1970s, Elvis's rehearsal style changed. He would rehearse with his rhythm section separately from the orchestra, and then join the combined ensembles for dress rehearsals led by his conductor.

Performance Techniques

Elvis understood the physicality of African-American performers, from declamatory preachers to musical artists like Jackie Wilson, and realized early on that music and movement went hand-in-hand. Elvis's sneer and hip-swiveling sensuality mirrored the upfront sexuality of black R&B performers. His unique style and interpretation of the stage antics of artists such as T-Bone Walker and Louis Jordan made him the physical embodiment of the "spirit" of Rock 'n' Roll as it surged outward upon delighted fans. Whether it was deemed vulgar or a natural musical response, it was exciting beyond anything seen from white musical performers or encountered by American audiences. As Elvis became more Pop music–oriented in the sixties, he toned down the raw sexuality of his performance style, and his frantic leg-shaking gave way to more sophisticated hand gestures and dramatic visual expressions.

The turning point for Elvis as a stage performer came with his introduction to large orchestra performances on the 1968 *Singer Special*. Elvis was a bit leery at first at the size of the ensemble and

Elvis Presley performing in one of his sequined costumes in the early 1970s.
© *Bettmann/CORBIS*

was not sure he could be heard over the sound. After rehearsing and recording "If I Can Dream" with a full orchestra, Elvis found the huge, grandiose sound that earmarked his Las Vegas and touring years of the 1970s. Everyone is familiar with the rhinestone-embossed, Bill Belew–designed jumpsuits that Elvis wore at his shows as he moved like a cat across the stage, adding karate moves and dramatic arm gestures to his movement repertoire. On ballads, Elvis handed out scarves, kissed female fans (sometimes passionately), and moved forward to the front of the stage, touching his audience physically and musically.

Even during his last concert tours, "the King," in his extravagant costumes backed by his huge entourage, was a spectacle that continued to draw hundreds of thousands of fans to cities all over America. The tremendous visual impact of an Elvis Presley performance was exemplified by the 1998 *Elvis in Concert* tour, which sold out arenas nationally. These well-received performances feature a pre-recorded Elvis (shown on gigantic screens within the venues), singing "from beyond" with live stage musicians, including many of his Las Vegas players from the 1970s.

Recording "Suspicious Minds"

Mark James, a member of Chips Moman's writing staff, had previously released "Suspicious Minds" in 1968. (James was also the writer of "Hooked on a Feeling," which Chips produced and which became a hit for B.J. Thomas.) Chips felt Elvis would add the missing ingredient to "Suspicious Minds" that James's voice lacked: passion. History proved him right.

Elvis felt he had something to prove to the world when he entered Chips Moman's American Sound Studios in Memphis during January of 1969. Following the tremendous success of his legendary NBC-TV "comeback" special, which had aired a little over a month earlier, Elvis was eager to record some relevant music to show that his horrible movie soundtrack days were behind him. Elvis decided to work with Moman's hit-making Memphis house band, consisting of guitarist Reggie Young, bass player Tommy Cogbill, Mike Leech, another session bass player who also wrote arrangements, keyboard players Bobby Emmons and Bobby Wood, and drummer Gene Chrisman. Four charting singles came from these sessions—"Suspicious Minds," "Don't Cry Daddy," "In the Ghetto," and

"Kentucky Rain,"—as well as two critically acclaimed albums, *From Elvis in Memphis* and *Back in Memphis*.

Elvis, while initially nervous about recording at Chips Moman's American Studio, quickly became relaxed and invigorated by the atmosphere and top-notch session players. Reports are that outtakes from the session include Elvis swearing on tape several times after making a mistake in his vocal and even staging a karate routine in between takes.

After several nights of intense recording (which included laying the tracks for "Long Black Limousine," "This Is the Story," "Wearin' That Loved On Look," and "Without Love," among others), Elvis began the track that became as much his signature song as "Hound Dog" or "Don't Be Cruel." At around 4:00 a.m., Chips had his session musicians lay down the backing tracks for "Suspicious Minds." An atmosphere of excitement and anticipation ran all the way through the recording, and Elvis achieved the master track in just four full takes.

Elvis was a master at the art of phrasing his vocal to fit the mood of a song. His instincts were invariably dead-on. The tone he established for "Suspicious Minds" was a mix of tenderness and poise, as well as stoicism (at suspected infidelity) and anguish (over impending loss). Elvis worked all night until 7:00 a.m. perfecting the basic tracks of this song, showing his renewed stamina and focus.

Horn and string parts were added in February 1969 to fill out the sound a bit for each of the four charting singles, with "In the Ghetto" being the first to receive this orchestral treatment. Overdubs for "Suspicious Minds" were to follow, but without the benefit (or permission) of Chips Moman, although he held the publishing rights to the song. Elvis still had that grandiose orchestral sound in his head from the 1968 special, and applied it to these songs. (Although Chips maintained a cordial relationship with Elvis in later years, the legal wrangling over releasing his publishing rights, which he refused to do, combined with the fact that the overdubs on "Suspicious Minds" were done without his knowledge, soured him on doing any further business with Presley or Colonel Parker.)

Elvis performed "Suspicious Minds" onstage in the same overdubbed style as the recording. He used a false ending where the volume fades out at the end of the recording, then returned with the same three lines repeated again and again in a four-and-a-half minute coda that is remarkably similar to the ending of "Hey Jude." (Interestingly, Elvis did record and per-

> form his own version of "Hey Jude" around this time.) Bill Porter was the RCA engineer responsible for recording the new "fade out and back" ending for "Suspicious Minds," and since all eight tracks were filled already, he had to record the horns live over the pre-recorded stereo mix, which he then repeated several times over this new mono mix. (This cumbersome feat of engineering is similar to the many overdub techniques the Beatles and George Martin employed on the *Sgt. Pepper's* album.) This final remixed version was quickly released and became Elvis's biggest hit in seven years and his first No. 1 hit since 1962.

Growth and Evolution

Elvis's career is often divided into three phases:

- **Phase One, 1954–1958,** includes his formative years, early Pop, C&W, and R&B hits, and his films through *King Creole.*
- **Phase Two, 1958–1968,** begins with his Army service in 1958 and extends through his last films and the televised 1968 *Singer Special.*
- **Phase Three, 1969–1977,** includes his Las Vegas appearances and continues until his death in 1977.

Elvis Presley's most important period of musical growth may have occurred when he was between the ages of five and twenty-five, when his exposure to C&W and R&B led him to personify Rock 'n' Roll. Elvis's love for black Gospel harmony and Blues gave him unique musical perspective as a white youth in these unique African-American styles, and he utilized "gospelizing" (singing phrases more freely and improvisationally) and "blue notes" (the bent tones culled from the African scale to form the Blues) like no other white artist of his time. He then applied these African American–based musical elements to the Country and Pop songs he enjoyed singing, and thus created a new style: Rock 'n' Roll. His innate ability to synthesize and uniquely reproduce these styles as a new musical form shows his fantastic growth as a performer and musician. Elvis was a young white Southerner singing black music with Country musicians, and the evolution/revolution of Rock 'n' Roll began in earnest.

Between 1960 and 1968, Elvis became almost stagnant, as he was mired in horrible "B" movies that only occasionally produced worthwhile songs such as "Can't Help Falling in Love" from *Blue Hawaii* or "Return to Sender" from *Girls! Girls! Girls!* Even his growth as a competent actor suffered under the mountain of poor scripts with hackneyed plots.

The 1968 *Singer Special* (also known as *The '68 Comeback Special)* marked the next step in Elvis's musical evolution, as he returned to the live performing venue he loved and in which he thrived. He also moved from a small group backup sound to larger orchestras, which paved the way for his future concerts and tours. Elvis grew to some degree when he began touring again in the late 1960s and was released from some of his obligation to record primarily music provided by Parker's Hill and Range publishing company, which was part of his initial contract with Parker (see chapter 3). The lifting of this burden allowed Elvis to sing cover songs by his favorite artists and peers without Parker insisting on a piece of the publishing action. Thus, Elvis broadened his repertoire and his appeal as a contemporary song stylist. Elvis also nurtured his love for gospel music during his lifetime, which eventually won him three Grammy awards for Best Gospel Recording, the only Grammy's of his career.

THE BEATLES

Musical Influences

Coming of age in the 1950s, John, Paul, George, and Ringo all grew up on Skiffle music, the loose British equivalent of American Folk, featuring artists such as Lonnie Donegan and instruments such as the washboard and washtub bass on up-tempo dance numbers. But American Rock 'n' Roll and R&B quickly captured the ears of the young Beatles, with artists such as Eddie Cochran, Carl Perkins, and Buddy Holly providing much of their early repertoire. The Beatles also drew inspiration from the Motown roster and loved soul music. But their main influence was none other than Elvis Presley, as he was the first white performer to signal to mainstream audiences that this new music involved letting go of both personal inhibitions and past, conservative styles. John's first group, the Quarry Men, though based in Skiffle music, included such Elvis songs as "Baby, Let's Play House" in their performances. When John and

> **COLD HARD FACT**
>
> In Britain in 1956, Lonnie Donegan prompted the "Skiffle" craze with his top-ten hit "Rock Island Line." The appeal of Skiffle was that it was simple and inexpensive to play. All that was needed was a Spanish guitar, a snare drum, a stand-up bass made from a broom handle attached to an empty tea-chest, and two chords. One of his hits, which made it onto the charts in the United States in 1961, was titled "Does Your Chewing Gum Lose Its Flavor (on the Bedpost Overnight)?"

Paul first met in July 1957, Elvis was attending the screening of his second film, *Loving You,* and had been a national star since 1956. Elvis's music, fashions, and performance techniques became the foundation, along with American R&B, for the Beatles' early style. Had there been no Elvis, there would have been no Beatles.

The Beatles became enamored of Bob Dylan and Folk Rock music in 1965, with John crediting Dylan's influence on songs such as "I'm a Loser" and "You've Got to Hide Your Love Away." The influence of East Indian music and philosophy on George Harrison particularly is found on recordings such as "The Inner Light" and "Within You Without You." The Beatles soon pioneered psychedelic music along with Jefferson Airplane, the Grateful Dead, and others, and Paul often cites the Beach Boys' *Pet Sounds* album and Frank Zappa's debut album *Freak Out!* as major influences on the *Sgt. Pepper's Lonely Hearts Club Band* album. The San Francisco scene continued to influence Beatles songs, such as "Baby, You're a Rich Man," yet Paul still managed to show his vaudeville upbringing at the knee of his Swing-style bandleader father on "When I'm Sixty-Four" and "Your Mother Should Know." Later Beatles music incorporated avant-garde sounds, symphony orchestras, brass bands, soul saxes, sound effects, and even a return to their roots of Rockabilly and old-time Rock 'n' Roll for the *Let It Be* album.

Instrumentation and Orchestration

There was often a healthy musical competition between John and Paul as to who got the "A" side of a particular single. But after a few years, the Beatles changed their focus from churning out singles to crafting albums. Starting with *Rubber Soul,* they presented each new album as a unique concept and created innovative and colorful packages, including photos and printed lyrics. Beatles releases began to feature techniques, such as "song segues" (moving from one song to another without a pause or break) and unifying musical themes or ideas throughout, as exemplified by *Sgt. Pepper's* and *Magical Mystery Tour.*

The circular nature of their musical growth and evolution (from a purely instrumental and orchestration nature) can be seen in the Beatles' move from guitars, bass, and drums during the early 1960s to ever-increasing additions of woodwinds, horns, and strings in the middle of the decade, then culminating in a return to basic small-band setups by the end of the decade. One can see the trend when comparing early small-group albums such as *Please Please Me* (1963) with the highly orchestrated *Sgt. Pepper's Lonely Hearts Club Band* (1967) and returning to the small group again for *Let It Be* (1970) (prior to its falling into the hands of Phil Spector, who applied his over-the-top "wall of sound technique" to it without the Beatles' knowledge or approval).

By 1956, John Lennon's first group, the Quarry Men, included guitars, washboard, tea-chest bass, banjo, and drums. By the late 1950s the three-guitar and bass lineup (Stu Sutcliffe, an accomplished painter who went to art college with John, played bass) was the sound of the Silver Beetles, Beatals, and finally, by 1960, the Beatles. Pete Best, perhaps the most famous "might have been" in the history of show business, played drums with the Beatles until Ringo Starr replaced him in 1962. With Ringo on board, the magic circle was formed. And with George Martin, a classically trained musician, at the helm as producer, the Beatles' meteoric rise to the top really began. This combination of lead guitar (George), rhythm guitar (John), bass (Paul), and drums (Ringo) was the true essence of the Beatles sound, modeled on the early Crickets musical lineup (with Buddy Holly pioneering solid-bodied Fender electric guitar as a lead/solo instrument).

By late 1963 and through 1964, the Beatles were playing virtually all the instrumental parts on their recordings. All four were extremely capable and adaptable on a wide range of instruments. John Lennon played acoustic guitar, electric guitar, twelve-string guitar, steel guitar, banjo, electric bass, six-string bass, acoustic piano, electric piano, organ, harpsichord, harmonium, clavioline,

Mellotron, harmonica, percussion, comb and paper, saxophone, discordant instruments (which were never specified by the group), and tape loops. Paul McCartney played acoustic guitar, electric guitar, acoustic bass, electric bass, fuzz bass, acoustic piano, electric piano, organ, harpsichord, harmonium, percussion, flute, recorder, flugelhorn, drums, comb and paper, and discordant instruments. George Harrison played acoustic guitar, electric guitar, twelve-string guitar, four-string guitar, electric bass, jazz bass, percussion, sitar, tamboura, harmonica, organ, Moog synthesizer, white-noise maker, comb and paper, violin, xylophone, and discordant instruments. And Ringo Starr played drums, percussion, acoustic piano, organ, harmonica, and discordant instruments.

For one version of "Love Me Do," Martin called in session drummer Andy White, relegating Ringo to the tambourine. Much to Ringo's chagrin, Martin felt a more experienced drummer might suit the song better, as he knew little of Ringo's talent and experience at the time. But after hearing both recordings, Martin realized they were virtually identical, and jettisoned the tambourine version in favor of Ringo's drum performance for the released single, though included the version with White on their first album.

Often called "the fifth Beatle," Martin himself occasionally contributed to Beatles recordings, usually as a pianist, on such songs as "Not a Second Time" and "Money," among others. (See Table 2.1 for a complete list of his contributions as a performer.)

In 1965, the Beatles began using professional string and woodwind players. On songs such as "Yesterday," George Martin arranged a string quartet to accompany Paul's vocals, and a studio flute player was effectively used on the closing "You've Got to Hide Your Love Away." By 1966, the influence of psychedelic substances and Eastern philosophies was reflected in their musical evolution through their use of East Indian instruments such as the sitar on "Norwegian Wood," brass on "Got to Get You Into My Life," and larger groups, including a full orchestra on *Sgt. Pepper's Lonely Hearts Club Band*.

George Martin drew individual instrumental soloists from the finest British Classical and Pop music sources, such as Philip Jones and Ronnie Scott, as contributors to Beatles songs. (See Table 2.2 for a complete list of individuals who performed on Beatles recordings.)

TABLE 2.1 George Martin Plays With the Beatles

YEAR	SONG	INSTRUMENT
1963	Misery	piano
	Baby, It's You	piano
	You Really Got a Hold On Me	piano
	Not a Second Time	piano
	Money	piano
1964	Slow Down	piano
	Match Box	piano
	A Hard Day's Night	piano
	No Reply	piano
	Kansas City / Hey	piano
	What You're Doing	piano
1965	You Like Me Too Much	piano
	The Word	harmonium
	In My Life	piano
	If I Needed Someone	harmonium
	Run for Your Life	tambourine
1966	Good Day, Sunshine	piano
	Got to Get You Into My Life	organ
	Tomorrow Never Knows	piano
	Penny Lane	piano
1967	Sgt. Pepper	organ
	Getting Better	piano
	Being for the Benefit of Mr. Kite	organ
	Lovely Rita	piano
	A Day in the Life	harmonium
	All You Need Is Love	piano
1968	Rocky Raccoon	piano
	Cry Baby Cry	harmonium
1969	Across the Universe	organ
	Maxwell's Silver Hammer	organ
	Sun King	organ

Even the Beatles' personal assistant, Mal Evans, performed on several songs, as did road manager Neil Aspinall and assistant producer Chris Thomas. Other musicians invited to participate on

TABLE 2.2 Individuals Performing with the Beatles

YEAR	PERFORMER	SONG	INSTRUMENT
1965	Mal Evans	You Won't See Me	organ
1966	Mal Evans	Strawberry Fields Forever	tambourine
	Alan Civil	For No One	French horn
	Phillip Jones	Penny Lane	trumpet
		Strawberry Fields Forever	alto trumpet
	David Mason	Penny Lane	piccolo trumpet
1967	Mal Evans	Being for the Benefit of Mr. Kite!	harmonica
	Neil Aspinall	Being for the Benefit of Mr. Kite!	harmonica
		Within You Without You	tamboura
1968	Mal Evans	Dear Prudence	tambourine
		Helter Skelter	trumpet
	Chris Thomas	Bungalow Bill	Mellotron
		Piggies	harpsichord
	Nicky Hopkins	Revolution	electric piano
	Eric Clapton	While My Guitar Gently Weeps	electric guitar
1969	Billy Preston	Don't Let Me Down	organ
		Dig a Pony	organ
		Dig It	organ
		Let It Be	organ
		I've Got a Feeling	organ
		One After 909	electric piano
		Get Back	electric piano
		Old Brown Shoe	organ
		I Me Mine	organ

Beatles songs included well-known symphonic musicians Alan Civil, Phillip Jones, David Mason, and Nicky Hopkins, who was a well-established British studio keyboardist. George Harrison invited Eric Clapton to record lead guitar on "While My Guitar Gently Weeps" and introduced keyboardist Billy Preston to the group as well. His outstanding solo work on electric piano on songs such as "Get Back" and organ on "Let It Be" are but highlights of his contributions to the *Let It Be* recordings.

George Martin served as transcriber and arranger of the musical ideas sung to him by the composing Beatles. He in turn orchestrated and conducted most of the sessions involving outside players. Martin's classical training in music theory and

> ### COLD HARD FACT
>
> When the cameras stopped rolling, the Beatles abandoned mixing the tracks they recorded while filming *Let It Be* for proposed public release, due to the acrimony of their impending breakup. They effectively released control over the final product for the first time since their careers began. In later interviews both John and Paul would complain bitterly about the heavy use of strings and female singers on the Phil Spector–produced *Let It Be* sessions. Paul commented that he would "never [have] put a female vocal on a Beatles record" while John, disappointed in the overall effect as being the opposite of what he originally intended, grudgingly said that at the very least, Spector had taken "a pile of shit" and made it listenable. Two Grammy awards, one for Best Soundtrack and one for Best Song ("Let It Be"), seems to have proven John right in this regard.

orchestration allowed him to transform the Beatles' ideas into written notation and then score out these ideas for specific instruments. For example, when Paul wanted a "noble sounding" instrument to play fanfares on "Sgt. Pepper's," Martin suggested French horn and played Paul recordings of the instrument to refresh his memory. Paul then sang several melodic lines (riffs, or licks, in musician's jargon) to Martin, who quickly transcribed and scored these ideas. Martin then hired the French horn players who were rehearsed by both Paul and Martin before recording. Martin and all the Beatles used this process with great success during the course of their musical collaboration, with Martin writing for everything from solo flute to full orchestra.

Meanwhile, Phil Spector introduced elaborate orchestrations to the Beatles' sound during their *Let It Be* sessions. Spector was the third producer to handle this material, and much to their chagrin, he applied his "wall of sound" production techniques to the Beatles' simple existing tracks. Spector added percussion, choirs, and orchestra to thicken the sound. This resulted in an overly lush texture of horns, strings, and vocal choir that added a Pop sweetening to songs not slated by the Beatles for this musical treatment. In November 2003, the *Let It Be Naked* album was released with the "wall of sound" effect removed, revealing the Beatles' true musical intent for their project. Now the rough edges and raw performances gave listeners a more accurate musical view of the group as they attempted to return to their Rock 'n' Roll roots.

Vocal Styles and Techniques

The Beatles sang all their own songs, with occasional help from such diverse people as Yoko Ono, fans from outside the studio, the Mike Sammas singers, and whoever else might be in the studio or audience and could join an impromptu choir.

The Beatles took many vocal style traits from African-American music, particularly the use of falsetto as heard in the music of Little Richard and other performers. This is true of "She Loves You," "I Want to Hold Your Hand," and many of their earlier recordings. Later, the Beatles used falsetto on occasion in a more humorous and less expressive fashion, on such songs as "Tell Me Why." The Beatles rarely used vibrato, which lent a unique sense of poignancy to their ballad style. By 1963, the Beatles were often double-tracking the lead vocal parts and, by 1966, were employing various studio techniques for vocal enhancement, such as different types and placement of microphones, echo and delay, backwards tapes, and distortion to create new vocal textures.

The Beatles sang their own unique, exquisite style of harmony, including simple two-part textures (John on melody, Paul on harmony, and vice versa), three voices (John, Paul and George), and a wide variety of combinations of personnel. The Beatles used parallel harmony (two voices move together), block harmony (three or more voices move together), contrary motion (one voice moves, one stays the same) and "call-and-response" (lead singer followed by harmonic back-up). Even Ringo lent his rough baritone voice to several Beatles songs, including " With A Little Help from My Friends," and his own delightful "Octopus's Garden."

Rehearsal Techniques

The Beatles' early rehearsal techniques were painstaking, as they spent hours both individually and as a group practicing both singing and guitar playing. Each Beatle was a fervent record buyer and listener, and together they laid much groundwork through their abilities to absorb styles and reproduce them through their own music personalities. This included covering Motown and

The 23-year-old Ringo Starr on June 12, 1964, giving a "thumbs up" sign before leaving Heathrow Airport to rejoin the Beatles touring Australia. © *Bettmann/CORBIS*

Rockabilly and using these influences on their original songs. The simplicity of the Beatles' rehearsal process is remarkable considering how much they accomplished in such a brief career. Whoever wrote the song being rehearsed or sang the lead part on a cover song usually directed the musical elements of the piece, including tempo, solos, and form ideas. But the Beatles as an entity was the result of a fantastic group effort, and everyone's input was welcome regarding intros, endings, and other musical aspects. George Martin often lent his talents during his tenure.

The Beatles' rehearsal process matured as they evolved musically, and soon studio rehearsals and early takes were put on acetate records and given to each Beatle to take home and develop further. They would then meet for the next sessions having listened to this material and practiced or prepared new parts. The amazingly quick learning curve of the four young men assisted in both the efficiency and quality of this very successful process.

Performance Techniques

The Beatles' earliest performances have become legendary, especially their onstage antics and appearance while performing in Germany in the early 1960s. Having modeled their look after Elvis, Marlon Brando, and the British teddy boys, the lads sported greasy, swept-back hair (prior to their famous early 1960s bowl-cut-style coifs inspired by French art students and Stu Sutcliffe's girlfriend, Astrid) tight jeans, and leather jackets both onstage and off. John, always the trickster, might forget to wear his pants to one show or adorn himself with a toilet seat as a neck ornament! They were loose onstage, drinking, swearing at the German sailors who patronized their long shows, and generally having great fun, doing their best to *"Mach schau!"* ("make show"), as the drunken audience members would shout to encourage ever more fury and antics from the boys on stage.

Onstage, they each moved uniquely, with John bowing his legs as he rocked up and down while staring myopically across his nose at the audience (due more to his refusal to wear his glasses on stage than to a pre-planned stage move). Paul looked ever calm and smiling as he sang high notes and played low bass notes, while George often kicked his legs in subtle, dance-like movements as he strummed. Ringo always appeared to be having fun, and smiled as he shook his head back and forth while drumming.

> ## COLD HARD FACT
>
> On July 4, 1966, the Beatles performed at Manila's National Football Stadium in the Philippines for nearly fifty thousand fans. Unfortunately, the President of Manila's wife, Imelda Marcos (notorious collector of women's shoes) felt insulted by the Beatles when they failed to show at her dinner party. Though Brian Epstein insisted he had contacted the palace and informed them that the group needed rest rather than another round of meeting and greeting, palace officials denied his claim, and contacted the local press. Soon the streets of the capital city were lined with angry citizens, and the Beatles and their entourage had to hastily flee the country. But before they were allowed to leave the airport runway, a fight ensued in the terminal, and the group was defended by Mal Evans and others as they sought safety. Adding insult to injury, Epstein was forced to give back all the concert earnings to the Philippine government before being allowed to leave the country.

Soon after signing the group, manager Brian Epstein, always the sophisticate, pushed for their move to matching suits and ties, uniform bows at the ends of songs, and a cordial and professional demeanor. Their new funny haircuts were borrowed from a look French art students had adopted in the early 1960s. John would later say the Beatles "died" because of the change Epstein made in their look, but his snide appraisal is belied by the fact that this was a profitable and successful transformation.

Unlike Elvis, who toured for decades up until weeks before his death, the Beatles abandoned live performances fairly early in their progression. Realizing that their new, more psychedelic music was more complex instrumentally, the group found they were unable to reproduce their recordings live. In addition, the poor sound systems, screaming fans drowning out the music, security nightmares, and an unwelcome (and dangerous) skirmish while in the Philippines made the decision to cease performing live an easy choice, and the Beatles were only too happy to move from the stage to the studio after 1966.

The Beatles did continue to appear "onstage" in some capacity in the many music videos they made to promote their singles.

Brian Epstein, manager of the Beatles, arrives in New York on August 4, 1966 to try to quell the furor aroused in the Untied States by John Lennon's statement that the singing group was "more popular than Jesus." The Beatles began a four week tour of the United States a week later, on August 11th. Epstein said Lennon had been misinterpreted. © *Bettmann/CORBIS*

These ranged from simple stage shots of the group in various outfits performing "Twist and Shout," to the bizarre "I Am the Walrus" video, replete with psychedelic clothing, egg-styled skull caps, and walrus costumes!

The last, and perhaps most famous, Beatles performance took place on the rooftop of the Apple Corp., Ltd., building in London on a cold January day in 1969. Epstein had signed the Beatles to a four-movie deal that included *A Hard Day's Night, Help!,* and *Magical Mystery Tour*. For the fourth movie project, Paul came up with the idea of making a documentary showing the Beatles in the

Recording "Hey Jude"

"Hey Jude" marked the most effective use of orchestra as an added texture on a Beatles single. The song begins with Paul on solo piano and vocals, and eventually builds to a huge orchestral section at the end, which repeats with Paul's ad lib vocals as the highlight. This use of "additive" orchestration has tremendous musical momentum and effectively takes the listener on a musical journey as the song progresses.

On July 31, 1968, recording began at Trident Studios. Both Paul and George had already been involved with some other artists at Trident before this session: George had been busy producing Jackie Lomax, while Paul was doing the same with Mary Hopkin (who had a hit he produced called "Those Were the Days") and James Taylor. (All of these artists were signed to Apple Records.) What attracted the Beatles to Trident was that it was independent, like Apple Records, and had an eight-track recorder, unlike Abbey Road, which was still using the same four-track that had been used for *Sgt. Pepper's*. Sadly, Abbey Road Studios had not moved quickly to acquire the latest recording equipment, so the Beatles looked elsewhere.

Using the Trident eight-track, the Beatles did several takes of "Hey Jude," with Paul on piano, George on electric guitar, John on acoustic guitar, and Ringo on drums. George had wanted to play an answering guitar phrase after each "Hey Jude" vocal line but the idea was vetoed. "Hey Jude" was recorded very quickly in the end. On August 1, overdubs were recorded, with Paul putting down a bass guitar track and a lead vocal, while the other Beatles put down backing vocals.

There were thirty-six instruments used in the orchestra for "Hey Jude": ten violins, three violas, three cellos, two flutes, one contra bassoon, one bassoon, two clarinets, one contra bass clarinet, four trumpets, four trombones, two horns, one "percussion," and two string basses.

During a separate session, George Martin recorded the orchestra for the musical buildup during the song's long refrain.

He also used members of the orchestra to contribute handclaps and backing vocals ("nah, nah, nah"s) for the powerful buildup in the refrain. One person, however, actually walked out of the session, saying, "I'm not going to clap my hands and sing Paul McCartney's bloody song!" (The name of this musician was not noted, which is probably a good thing for him!).

When the final mixes were done, "Hey Jude" became Apple Records' first real release, on August 30, 1968. It sold in excess of 8 million copies worldwide and topped the U.S. charts for nine weeks. Backed with "Revolution," it became the most successful single in Beatles history.

Although recorded around the same time the Beatles were recording *The White Album*, "Hey Jude" was released as a single. Over seven minutes in duration, it was one of the Beatles longest songs. Most Pop singles during the sixties lasted a maximum of three minutes (the standard that was used by radio for airplay to coincide with advertising rates for on-air commercial revenue).

process of writing and recording a new album and ending with a big performance. Their strange choice of a venue for the performance—the Apple rooftop—did not serve the spectators well: No one on the ground could see it. It was a last-minute compromise, as no one could agree on where or when to perform. Nevertheless, the Beatles bundled themselves up in colorful coats (while Ringo borrowed his wife Maureen's red raincoat), to protect themselves from the harsh British winter. And John's now-familiar National Health-issued round glasses and Paul's beard drew attention to the "new look" of the Beatles, who had abandoned their uniformed appearance around the time of *Sgt. Pepper's* to now feature their own individuality while reflecting the Psychedelic sixties look that had become so popular.

Growth and Evolution

The Beatles career is usually divided into four phases:

- **Phase One, 1958–1963,** was their formative years, early tours and U.K. hits.
- **Phase Two, 1964–1966,** was the time when they dominated the U.S. and U.K. Pop charts, produced two films, and toured the world.
- **Phase Three, 1966–1968,** was the Beatles' psychedelic period, when the *Sgt. Pepper's* and *Magical Mystery Tour* albums were created.

> ## COLD HARD FACT
>
> Following the historic "Hey Jude" sessions, the Beatles set another record (of sorts), for the most takes for an unreleased Beatles song. The song was "Not Guilty" by George Harrison, and it required more than a hundred takes. It should be noted that these weren't complete takes of the song (only twenty-one were full takes), but they made eighteen individual attempts on the song's introduction alone. The group felt the song was never quite good enough and withheld its releasse, though it can now be found on bootlegs and the *Anthology* series.

- **Phase Four, 1968–1970,** was the time when the Beatles worked in the studio independent of each other, yet still as the Beatles, with an emphasis on individual styles.

The Beatles grew more significantly during the scant decade in which they existed as a band than did any other group of musicians in history. Society, culture and music were swept along in their evolution. In the late 1950s, Elvis and his musical style invaded Britain, and the young future Beatles were entranced. As lead singer of the Quarry Men, John sang Elvis's version of "Baby, Let's Play House" (with some of his own made-up words, as he had failed to learn the right ones!) as early as the July 6, 1957 performance, at which he first met Paul. Soon the Beatles covered songs by Rockabilly and Soul artists (Carl Perkins, Buddy Holly, Little Richard, and others), putting their own English spin on them.

The biggest step in the Beatles' early evolution came with the advent of their original songwriting, over which Paul and John had the healthiest competition in the history of show business. The growth of both John and Paul (and, to a lesser extent, George) as songwriters between 1962 and 1965 can be seen as a direct reaction to market demands as well as the discovery of their own gifts for composing concise Pop hits. If timing is everything, then the Beatles were perfectly in sync, as they always seemed to be on the leading edge of musical advancement during the 1960s. From 1966 to 1968, the Beatles' lifestyle of drug experimentation was reflected in the psychedelic nature of their music in songs such as "Strawberry Fields Forever" and many of the tracks on the monumental *Sgt. Pepper's Lonely Hearts Club Band* album. Here, musical growth and evolution blossomed, with studio mastery and musical creativity combining to reach an apex still unequalled in Pop music.

During the Beatles' final years, 1968 through 1970, they actually devolved to a simpler style for *The Beatles (The White Album)* and *Let It Be*. The Beatles began to return to simpler musical textures and song forms, and replaced experimentation with stylistic variation and individual songwriting skills. The exception was *Abbey Road,* the Beatles swan song album of 1969, which exemplified the best of both worlds. Elaborate overdubs and studio techniques on songs such as "I Want You (She's So Heavy)" were matched by good old-fashioned Rock 'n' Roll pieces such as "Oh, Darling." Hard-edged songs ("Come Together") were balanced by ballads ("Something.") And the true evolution of the Beatles' real message of "love conquers all" had grown exponentially, yet had remained intact and unchanged. In 1963, the Beatles sang, "She loves you, yeah, yeah yeah," and in 1969 sang, "And in the end, the love you take is equal to the love you make." Through their musical progress also came personal growth and wisdom, which is perhaps why their music remains fresh and timely as the decades pass.

The Beatles were the ultimate ensemble musicians, a synergy of talent and personality greater than the sum of their individual parts. Even though they all eventually enjoyed success as solo artists (particularly Paul) once the group disbanded, the Beatles stand as the first real Rock 'n' Roll band: self-taught and self-contained. As a unique subcultural musical entity, what Wilfred Mellers calls "the magic circle," in his outstanding Beatles book, *Twilight of the Gods*, the band was a phenomenon wholly unto itself, with its own linguistic code words and specific musical identity. Though the group did add the talents of professional symphonic and popular musicians as their own music evolved, the product of the combination of these four singer-songwriter-musicians' talents was always central to the core of the Beatles' innovative sound.

Comparison

The greatest distinction between Elvis and the Beatles is the fact that Elvis focused his career on performing "covers," meaning that he did his own interpretations of songs written by others, while the Beatles performed primarily original compositions. Elvis did co-write "Love Me Tender" and later wrote two other songs with bodyguard Red West, but never went beyond those experiences as a composer. His gift was for memorization, presentation, interpretation, and re-creation, not spontaneity and creativity.

The Beatles, on the other hand, set a standard unequalled in music history in the area of original Pop music compositions, and many of their songs are now considered standards. In fact, the most covered song in history is Paul's "Yesterday," with over 2,500 versions done by other artists. Beatles songs such as "Something," "Got to Get You Into My Life," and "Blackbird" have inspired innumerable musicians and bands to pursue fame and success by either covering (redoing) Beatle songs or building upon their musical foundation. Steven Tyler of Aerosmith claims his band's first demo record was Paul's "I'm Down." One of the Rolling Stones' first hits in 1963 was the Beatles' "I Wanna Be Your Man." Performers as diverse as Aretha Franklin, Frank Sinatra, Joe Cocker, and Phish have recorded Beatles songs. Elvis himself recorded versions of "Lady Madonna," "Hey Jude," and "Something" during the 1970s.

One thing Elvis and the Beatles had in common was their reliance on expanding instrumentation and creative orchestration as they musically evolved. Both Elvis and the Beatles started out in smallish "combos" consisting of simple guitars, bass, and drums and moved through their careers to strings, horn sections, full orchestras, and synthesizers in an effort to bring their musical concepts into focus.

Both Elvis and the Beatles had distinctive vocal styles that they used to great effect in their songs, and both made use of spectacular harmonies. From Elvis, the Beatles took their stage presence, early look, and love of African-American music. One of the songs John and the Quarry Men played live on that fateful day John and Paul met (July 6, 1957) was "Baby, Let's Play House," an Elvis hit. And Paul and John were united by their admiration of the King.

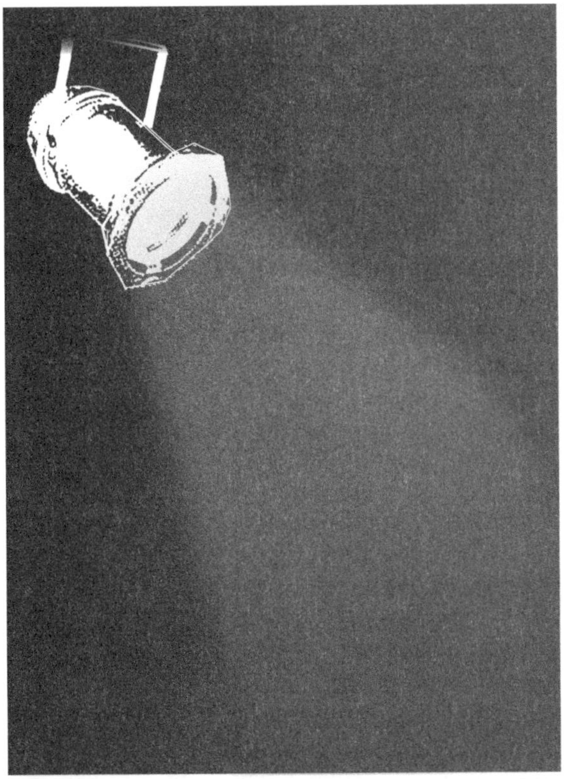

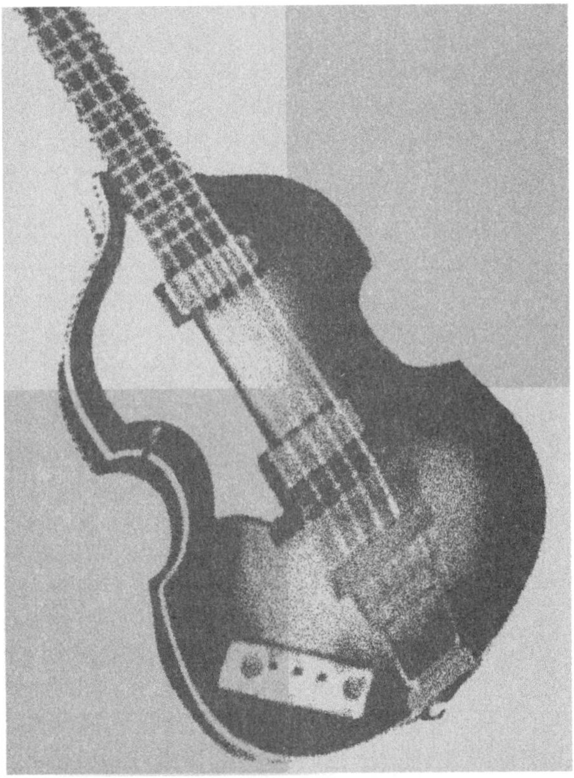

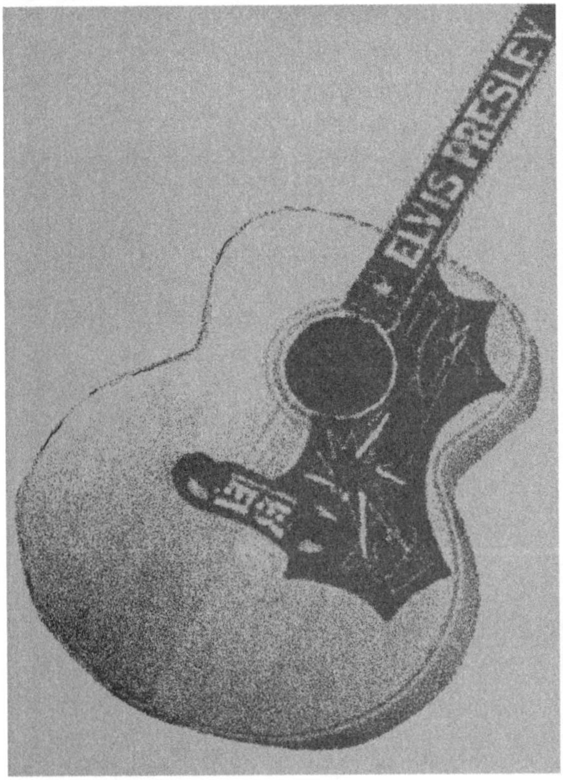
ELVIS PRESLEY

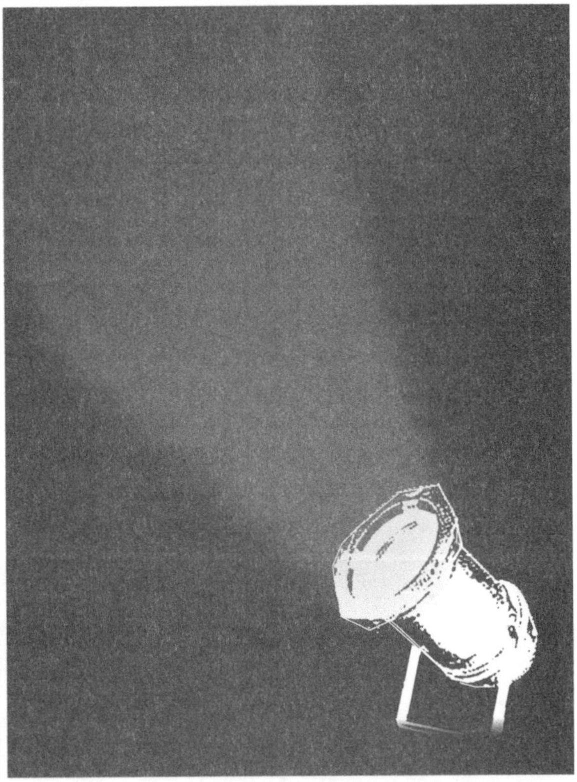

CHAPTER 3

Management and Production

Both Elvis and the Beatles were propelled forward to monumental success by their managers and producers during their musical careers, and thus into popular music history. Because both artists were so unique, many of the management style and production decisions were conceived on the spot. This was necessary to fit the evolution and new musical directions being created by these artists and to adapt to their distinct personal and musical styles. It was also largely due to the fact that both Elvis and the Beatles were breaking new ground. No one had a clue that they would all become larger than life and change the world around them.

Elvis

Manager Colonel Tom Parker

Colonel Tom Parker was never a real colonel, and Tom Parker was not even his real name. Andreas (Dries) Cornelius van Kuijk (pronounced "von Kweek") was born June 26, 1909, in the Netherlands. He illegally entered the United States at around the age of eighteen and served in the U.S. Army from 1929 to 1933 but never

> ## COLD HARD FACT
>
> Colonel Parker never applied for or received his green card (legal U.S. citizenship papers). This aspect of his background influenced many of his decisions later in life, which consequently affected Elvis Presley. For example, Elvis never toured outside of the U.S., and Colonel Parker often turned down lucrative deals involving international travel for Elvis and himself out of fear of being discovered. At one time, a Japanese promoter offered Parker a suitcase containing a million dollars in cash if Elvis would tour Japan. Parker refused! The Colonel also made sure Elvis was the highest taxpayer in America (never taking any form of tax shelter for his client) and that he served his time in the military, again to avoid any type of investigation into Parker's origins.

became a U.S. citizen. There is a distinct probability that Andreas fled Holland after committing a crime. He took his name from the company commander he served under when he was stationed in the army in Hawaii, a Captain Thomas Parker.

Having always enjoyed carnivals and horses as a youth, Parker returned to circus work after his discharge from the military. An ambitious young man, he developed a shrewd and astute business sense early on. His first music management job was in 1939, when he began traveling with a show called Gene Austin's Models and Melodies. In 1940, Parker began working for the Tampa Humane Society—in capacities as varied as dog catcher and pet cemetery employee—but was back managing Country music acts by 1943. His first real management success began in 1944 with singer Eddy Arnold, who made it to No. 1 on the Country & Western charts by 1947. Louisiana governor Jimmy Davis gave Parker the honorary title of "Colonel" in 1948, and Parker proudly took on the moniker from that time on.

Parker next managed Canadian Country singer Hank Snow starting in 1955, and started booking the as-yet-undiscovered Elvis Presley as his opening act. Though DJ Bob Neal was managing Elvis, Parker served as his "special advisor" during this time. By 1956, Parker had convinced Sam Phillips to sell Elvis's contract to a major record label, and RCA offered to pay Sun Records a release fee of $35,000 ($5,000 of which went to Elvis in cash), a large sum of money at that time.

> **COLD HARD FACT**
>
> How much was $35,000 worth in 1956, a year in which the average yearly income was $4,454? The following items give some indication of what Sam Phillips (and Elvis) could buy with the proceeds of their deal.
>
> **1956 Consumer Prices**
>
> New house: $22,000
> Ford car: $1,748–$3,151
> Milk: 97 cts/gal
> Gasoline: 23 cts/gal
> Bread: 18 cts/loaf
>
> Postage stamp: 3 cts
> Eggs: 45 cts/dozen
>
> Coffee: 69 cts/lb
> Beer, six-pack of 12-oz. cans: $1.20
>
> (Source: United States Chamber of Commerce)

In March of 1956, Parker became Elvis's personal manager, and Elvis became Parker's sole client. Parker promised "his boy" that he'd be a millionaire within a year and followed through as promised. (See chapter 8 on Elvis's success in 1956, with hits on the Pop, Country & Western, and R&B charts.) By the end of their first year together, they had grossed nearly $22 million in sales. Parker indeed took Elvis's career by the reins. At the time of Elvis's first national television appearances in 1956, Parker was receiving 25 percent of Elvis's musical earnings and 50 percent of his merchandising, and controlled nearly every aspect of Elvis's career.

Parker and Elvis had a symbiotic relationship (some critics say parasitic on Parker's part), and Parker felt himself to be a "father figure" to Elvis. Parker had already established a reputation in the entertainment industry as a keen businessman and shrewd operator, and both Elvis and his father, Vernon, put their complete trust in the Colonel regarding all business matters. Parker, for his part, saw the tremendous potential in this young Pop singer, and promised Elvis he would get him national exposure and make him millions. Parker did this in an unparalleled fashion in music history, while earning quite a bit for himself along the way. Elvis made no business decisions without consulting Parker, and Parker often did what was best financially for himself (and Elvis on occasion) rather than what Elvis might have wished.

Elvis had always wanted to be an actor and jumped at the chance to accept a seven-year deal with Paramount and producer

After being discharged from the U.S. Army, Elvis grins as he hands his mustering out pay to his business manager Colonel Tom Parker, March 5, 1960. © *Bettmannn/CORBIS*

Hal B. Wallis in April of 1956. Elvis received a rising pay scale for three pictures, moving from $100,000 to $200,000. Parker served as "technical advisor" on every one of Elvis's thirty-plus films, although how much technical advising he did is open to debate. His job, some say, consisted of sitting on the set in a director's chair (on which "Col. Tom Parker" was emblazoned in large letters), smoking expensive cigars and making sure everyone knew to treat Elvis properly. Of course, Parker received much genuflection and a handsome salary in this capacity, as well as numerous perks from the studio.

Parker's influence on Elvis extended to his personal decisions as well. When Elvis's number came up in the draft, he was a bit reluctant to join the army at a time when his popularity was soaring in the late 1950s. But Parker was aware of the negative publicity other stars had received when joining the USO rather than regular duty during the Cold War era. And he had his own personal concerns as well: He did not want the government looking into his own dubious arrival in the United States, as Parker had never secured his green card after arriving from Holland in 1929. Parker himself had served in the U.S. military, and he encouraged Elvis to do his duty as well. Parker also believed that absence makes the heart grow fonder and gambled that the hordes of Elvis fans would long for their hero—and buy even more of his records—while the star was temporarily out of the spotlight.

Elvis returned from the army after his two-year stint (1958–1960) a bit tamed and began focusing on Pop music rather than rebellious R&B–influenced material. Parker saw the lucrative opportunity to steer Elvis toward making lightweight film fare. The thirty movies Elvis did between 1960 and 1969 were tremendous moneymakers for all involved, and starting in 1967, Parker began receiving 50 percent of everything Elvis Presley produced. However, the endless rounds of B movies bored Elvis, took him away from his true love of recording and live performing, and frustrated him at a time when other groups, such as the Beatles, ruled the U.S. charts.

COLD HARD FACT

Columbia Records Pop music division A&R man Mitch Miller, a well-known figure on the music and television scene throughout the 1950s and 1960s, the man who picked hits for Rosemary Clooney, Patti Page, and Tony Bennett, disdainfully let his golden opportunity to sign Elvis slip away. His company offered a maximum bid of $25,000 for Elvis's contract, and Miller refused to go a penny higher. He was one of many record producers at that time who believed Rock 'n' Roll might be a passing fad. RCA came up with $35,000 and the deal was struck.

As Elvis's frustration grew, he became desperate to return to his concert audiences. His opportunity came in 1968 with his successful televised *Singer Special.* It was a triumphant return to music and to center stage for him that might never have happened if Parker had had his way. Parker wanted a special filled with Christmas music instead of the theatrical productions and impromptu band sing-a-longs that made this TV appearance so unique and ultimately successful. When the International Hotel in Las Vegas offered Elvis the opportunity to open its new showroom in 1968, Parker saw gold, and Elvis loved the idea of large rooms filled with adoring fans.

Indeed, the Las Vegas extravaganza Elvis developed—dressing in a white jumpsuit and singing and wriggling in front of a large orchestra—quickly became legendary. Parker maintained several suites at the Hilton from which he publicized Elvis's appearances with zeal. He had him sign for four-week winter and summer stints there. Parker then filled Elvis's time between Las Vegas gigs by booking him on nearly nightly live performances on lengthy nationwide tours. This was a most rewarding time financially for Elvis and the Colonel. Elvis entertained 2.5 million audience members during his over eight hundred Las Vegas shows, and the endless road tours raked in millions in ticket revenue and created a whole new fan base among audiences who could not get to Las Vegas.

As Elvis became increasingly dependent on prescription drugs in the mid 1970s, Parker was seemingly more interested in getting Elvis to keep to his grueling schedule than in receiving rehabilitation. When Elvis was offered the movie role he believed would showcase his acting maturity and reinvigorate him, in Barbra Streisand's remake of *A Star Is Born,* the Colonel asked for an exorbitant salary for his star, abruptly ending any negotiations. Rumor had it that Parker personally disliked Streisand and wanted to control this situation, as well as any other circumstances that involved Elvis. Some critics believe Elvis asked his father to plead with Parker for this film opportunity, but Vernon was afraid of the Colonel and his threats to leave Elvis if he was not in command.

Starting in 1967, Parker began receiving 50 percent of everything Elvis produced. Unfortunately, the Colonel's concern was more for Elvis as a product rather than as a person. In 1973, Parker sold Elvis's entire backlog of RCA material and song catalog for $5.5 million in cash. Even as Elvis poisoned himself with narcotics during his final years, Parker kept him on the road virtually until the last day of his life.

After Elvis died in 1977, Parker became embroiled in heated legal battles with Elvis's family. When the smoke cleared in the early 1980s, Parker received over $2 million in exchange for giving up audio and video rights regarding Elvis's property and estate. But Parker continued to attach himself to anything Elvis after moving to Las Vegas permanently in 1985, often attending ceremonies and other events honoring "the King of Rock 'n' Roll."

Parker passed away from a stroke on January 21, 1997, at the age of eighty-seven, and was survived by his wife, Loanne, leaving behind his legacy as the man who made Elvis Presley.

Elvis Presley could not have made it without Parker's drive and single-minded determination (as well as his many show-biz contacts). Though Elvis certainly had tremendous talent and ambition, perhaps it took the gumption and raw nerve of a brilliant business and marketing man like Colonel Parker to make him into a superstar. Parker always asked top dollar for Elvis when television and movie producers, concert promoters, and magazine reporters came calling, even when the young singer was just a rising star. Parker was notorious for never giving up a fight when it came to his boy or to earning an extra dollar or two. He marketed Elvis like a product and made millions on Elvis merchandise as well as his own salary. His own companies published many of the songs supplied to Elvis and made lucrative side deals for sheet music distribution and songbooks. Parker kept Elvis in the spotlight while the decades passed and in the face of cultural and musical changes, never wavering on the road to success.

Cold Hard Fact

Though Felton Jarvis never seriously pursued a performing career, he did record a song as a tribute to Elvis in 1959 entitled "Don't Knock Elvis."

Producer Felton Jarvis and Elvis

Felton Jarvis came on board as Elvis's producer from 1966 to 1977.

Born in Atlanta in 1934, Jarvis saw Elvis perform as part of Hank Snow's All-Star Jamboree tour in 1955, and was inspired to take up guitar himself.

Felton worked printing sheet music for the National Recording Corporation out of Atlanta. A lucky break came when he was hanging around a recording studio learning about the business and was asked to replace an engineer who had just quit. Jarvis grabbed the opportunity, but he knew that his real skills were producing and promotion.

By 1962, Jarvis produced acts such as Vince Everett (whose name Jarvis changed from Marvin Benefield, after Elvis's character in *Jailhouse Rock*) and Tommy Roe, who had a million-selling single entitled "Sheila." In 1963, Jarvis relocated to Nashville and began working for Paramount Records. In 1965, he switched over to RCA Records, also in Nashville and, the following year, replaced Chet Atkins as Elvis's producer during Elvis's all-night recording sessions. Jarvis had tremendous enthusiasm and admiration for Elvis, and they bonded immediately. Jarvis was open to helping Elvis produce the sounds he wanted, which included a new, more intense, amplified sound. Jarvis proved to be the opposite of Atkins, who was less energetic and did not enjoy the late hours.

Jarvis joined Elvis in Las Vegas during the summer of 1969, when Elvis made his triumphant return to that city (having done poorly there back in the mid 1950s), and soon quit RCA to work exclusively with Elvis. By 1970, Jarvis was producing Elvis's concerts and studio sessions, handling many of the musical details, including rehearsals, arrangements, and contracting musicians.

> **COLD HARD FACT**
>
> One source says that Jarvis was a bit eccentric, had a wild sense of humor, and could be a practical joker at times. His office had a grass hut where his large anaconda snake lived, and he reportedly owned a tiger and an ocelot.

Unfortunately, Jarvis became seriously ill with a kidney ailment in late 1971, and underwent a transplant in 1972 (paid for by the ever-gracious Elvis). Jarvis continued to work with Elvis on and off and also produced such artists as Fats Domino, Carl Perkins, Gladys Knight, and Willie Nelson during his career. Jarvis succumbed to a stroke in January 1981, passing away at the young age of forty-six.

Steve Binder and Elvis

Producer Steve Binder has gone down in television history, if for no other reason than for his contribution to what *TV Guide* has called "the second greatest musical moment on television next to the Beatles' debut on *Ed Sullivan*": namely, Elvis's 1968 *Singer Special,* also known as *The Comeback Special.* This legendary program offered an unplugged session years before the term became in vogue and yielded some of the finest music of Elvis's career. (Chapter 4 covers the *Singer Special* in depth.) Not only was Binder the mastermind behind the special, he also realized that Parker's conservative approach was not in step with Elvis's thinking at the time. Parker believed a Christmas special would be safe, appealing, and lucrative to a point, but Binder and Elvis were looking to the future in setting a pattern for the Elvis of the 1970s. The use of dancers, skits, sets, costumes, large orchestra, and other theatrical elements thrilled Elvis, and foreshadowed and inspired the era of grandiose Las Vegas performances to come.

Binder was a producer and director for Steve Allen at CBS in the 1960s. His interest in music came to the surface with his successful directing of the Rock 'n' Roll television series *Hullabaloo* and his Rock 'n' Roll film *T.A.M.I.* This film, which featured such acts as the Beach Boys, the Rolling Stones, and James Brown, was called "one of the top ten all-time great Rock 'n' Roll films" by Robert Hilburn, music critic for the *Los Angeles Times,* in his interview with Steve Binder for "Town Square 2000", A Factor Concept.

Following the historic *Comeback Special,* Binder produced specials for artists Liza Minelli, Diana Ross, Patti Labelle, Olivia Newton-John, Barry Manilow, and John Denver. His varied background also includes production and direction work with Pee Wee Herman on his successful television series, *Pee Wee's Playhouse,*

Elvis performing in his 1968 *Comeback Special*. © *Bettmann/CORBIS*

Jane Fonda's hugely successful exercise videos, the half-time performance segment of Superbowl XXX (featuring Diana Ross), Disney's *Beauty and the Beast on Ice,* and numerous awards shows and feature films.

In more recent times, Binder has kept active as a professor at the University of Southern California, while maintaining positions on the boards of the National Academy of Recording Arts and Sciences and the Academy of Television Arts and Sciences. Binder has produced or directed more than a thousand hours of media programming, bringing great entertainment to the American public for decades while becoming a multi-Emmy winner along the way.

Steve Sholes and RCA Victor

The story behind how RCA Victor acquired Elvis and his entire catalog is a complicated one. In the 1950s, the major labels rarely ventured into unknown territory without significant reason to do so. For most of the record companies, Rock 'n' Roll was still a new style that had yet to prove itself. In the 1950s, RCA was predominantly a Country & Western and Classical music label, with a large stable of artists, but it lacked talent representatives who could see the next wave of popularity in Rock 'n' Roll, Rockabilly, or the Blues as quickly as could those at Atlantic or Columbia. This is where Steve Sholes came into the picture, and it is also where RCA Victor nearly let the chance to acquire Elvis slip away.

In October 1955, Elvis played the annual Country and Western Disc Jockey convention in Nashville. Among those watching were A&R (artists and repertoire) persons Steve Sholes and Ann Fulchino of RCA Victor. They both agreed that Elvis appeared to be a strange departure from the usual C&W performer, but were equally as impressed by his musicality and showmanship, and the negotiations to sign Elvis to RCA began. Atlantic Records in New York had also expressed an interest in purchasing Elvis's contract, but balked at Sam Phillips's asking price of $18,000, although the owners of Atlantic had been prepared to mortgage their little company to the hilt to buy Presley's contract. Presley's own feelings about signing with RCA are unknown, but he was reportedly upset at leaving Sam Phillips and Sun, possibly because of its "family" atmosphere.

It was a calculated gamble by Steve Sholes, who put his job on the line by signing Presley. No doubt it was Sholes's track record that convinced RCA to back him, as he had signed an outstanding roster of Hillbilly artists and had helped establish RCA's preeminence in the Country market. He had been instrumental in setting up the Country Music Association in 1958 and was one of the first living members voted into the Country Music Hall Of Fame, in 1967. Sholes helped produce Presley's first Nashville sessions and remained active in Nashville until his death in 1968.

While it was true that Sam Phillips at Sun Records did not have enough capital to promote Presley properly and must have realized that Presley would almost certainly leave Sun when his contract expired, it is difficult to overlook the folly of Phillips's lost opportunity in releasing Elvis from his contract early, as he might have made millions had he continued to produce Presley. Some have speculated that Phillips did not want to stand in Elvis's way, given the superiority of RCA's facilities and resources, while others figure he was eager for the infusion of cash. Phillips also believed that one of his other rising Rockabilly stars would eventually eclipse Elvis, as this other singer also wrote his own songs and played a mean piano. But Jerry Lee Lewis would sabotage his own career through drinking and bad marriages (including marrying his own thirteen-year-old third cousin!) and never achieved the stardom he and Phillips had hoped.

RCA reps Steve Sholes and Coleman Tily, along with song publisher Hill and Range's lawyer Ben Starr, Hank Snow, Tom Diskin, and the Colonel, all converged on the tiny Sun studio in Memphis, where the sale of Elvis's contract and all of his Sun masters was formally executed and signed by Tily for RCA, Phillips for Sun, Elvis, Vernon, the Colonel, and Bob Neal, with Gladys Presley proudly looking on. Elvis's contract with RCA of the same date called for a minimum of eight sides per year, two one-year options, and a 5 percent royalty, with the purchase price of the contract recoupable from one half of that royalty, and a $5,000 non-recoupable bonus going to Elvis for back royalties owed to him by Sun Records. Back in the Colonel's room at the Hotel Peabody, a $1,000 bonus was also conveyed from Elvis's music publishing group, Hill and Range, with whom a contract had been worked out to handle song publishing via a 50-50 partnership with Elvis and Parker. Elvis and Vernon signed for receipt of a total of $4,500, with the Colonel taking his 25 percent commission on the full $6,000.

> ## Cold Hard Fact
>
> An interesting detail about Studio A was the design of the walls and ceiling, which employed a series of "polycylindrical diffusers" for acoustics. Peter Guralnick describes Studio A in his biographies of Elvis entitled *Last Train to Memphis* and *Careless Love*. "The studio looked like a set from a 1930s science fiction movie. It was a large rectangular space of acoustical tile walls ribbed with monolithic half cylinders. These ran vertically on the long sides of the rectangle and horizontally on the short sides. The high ceiling rippled with more parallel cylinders and two pipes of fluorescent light. The floor was a series of short strips of wood scaled in a sawtooth pattern of right angles. In the center of the room lay a patch of carpet on which the musicians had placed their instruments." Some of the other musicians who recorded there include Marian Anderson, Harry Belafonte, and Perry Como.

Elvis first went to RCA Victor's New York Studio A on December 1, 1955, soon after signing with the label, but Scotty Moore and the band did not record there until one month later, while in town for their first of two television appearances on the *Dorsey Brothers Stage Show*. Elvis and his band would soon alternate between RCA studios in New York and Nashville, and Radio Recorders in Los Angeles for film music.

Tin Pan Alley in New York City had been a bastion of music publishing and recording since the early 1900s, with Pop music the featured product. By the mid 1950s, RCA Victor had two studios in New York City for recording music, Studio A and B. They were located on the ground floor of the building at 155 East 24th Street, on the block between Third and Lexington Avenues. The building had originally been built as a seven-story stable in 1907 for Fiss, Doer & Carroll, who at the time supplied many of the horses for use in the transit system and later for World War I. Many of New York's earliest buildings became music houses for the burgeoning entertainment industry.

Elvis did not use the New York studios for very long. He recorded there for the last time on July 2, 1956, the day after appearing on *The Steve Allen Show*. The session yielded the hits

"Hound Dog" and "Don't Be Cruel." It was the first time Elvis and his crew actually went into a studio with a song ("Hound Dog") they had first sung live with the purpose of making into a successful single release. It was also the first time they recorded with all four of the Jordanaires (Gordon Stoker, Neal Matthews, Hoyt Hawkins, and Hugh Jarrett).

For the remainder of Elvis's recording career, RCA Victor acted merely as a studio booking agent for wherever their most famous client wished to record, certainly not the typical arrangement between an artist and recording studio. In 1956, companies such as RCA Victor and CBS were all-powerful and controlled virtually every aspect of a musician's career, from the style of songs recorded to the publicity campaigns to performance contract negotiations. But Elvis and Colonel Parker rewrote the book on that relationship to such an extent that it changed the "typical" method forever. Elvis rehearsed the musicians, worked out the arrangements, warmed up the singers at the piano with Gospel songs, and basically called all the shots regarding the song productions, rather than a representative from RCA or in-house studio producer being in charge.

RCA was virtually a prisoner of Colonel Parker throughout the 1960s. During this musically explosive time period, the label was able to sign only one other major Rock act, the Jefferson Airplane. Ostensibly, this was due to Parker's belief that Elvis provided all the revenue RCA could ever want. But, in reality, he had made it clear that if RCA were to sign any other competing music acts, he would walk away with Elvis in his pocket. This effectively shut RCA Victor out of the burgeoning Rock music industry at a time when domestic artists, such as the Beach Boys, the Grateful Dead, Steppenwolf, Jimi Hendrix, and others, were making millions of dollars for their respective labels.

The Colonel first held Elvis in abeyance from RCA beginning when Elvis was in the army in 1958, and refused to allow him to record new material until RCA had re-signed Elvis's contracts at a higher royalty rate. As a result of this musical blackmail, RCA was forced to reissue familiar Elvis songs again and again, frantically coming up with new schemes to resell the same music catalog in different packages. This method worked well as long as Elvis was unchallenged on the charts, but the surge of new Rock music spearheaded by the Beatles in late 1963 doomed it to eventual failure, although the last laugh was to be RCA Victor's.

RCA eventually purchased Elvis's entire back catalog in 1973 for $5.5 million, almost entirely in what the industry called "now money." The term implied that it was believed that there was not much to be gained from the future royalty rights to Elvis's catalog, and Parker was willing to take money "now" in lieu of any future returns. In retrospect, it was an incredible deal for RCA and a huge loss for Elvis, as the record company will continue to make money for the foreseeable future on Elvis's entire song catalog. Unreleased and deleted songs from past Elvis albums continue to be released on various collections, aimed mainly for die-hard Elvis fans craving outtakes and any new Elvis material.

Hill and Range

Parker had worked closely with brothers Jean and Julian Aberbach, owners of Hill and Range music publishing (established by them in 1943 to publish C&W songs) in supplying his client Eddy Arnold with songs in the late 1940s. After becoming Elvis's manager in 1956, Colonel Parker helped Elvis establish his own publishing company, Gladys Music (named after his mother), as a subsidiary of Hill and Range to handle song royalties. He also insisted that all songs given to Elvis for consideration, and/or released and recorded by Elvis go exclusively through Hill and Range Music. The Aberbachs worked a deal through Colonel Parker to transfer publishing of Elvis's songs from Sun to Hill and Range, splitting the profits among all involved. Songwriters knew that to get a song to Elvis, it had to go through Hill and Range, and Elvis (meaning also the Colonel) would receive one-third of the publishing royalties. This procedure was in force until the early 1970s, when Elvis departed from the Hill and Range catalog (which basically handled studio recordings only) to perform live covering music by artists such as Mac Davis and Jerry Reed, who had representatives handling their own publishing interests.

Elvis rarely, if ever, had any interest in the publishing or distribution (or even merchandising) end of his career. He felt that if he had a million dollars in his checking account at all times, he was rich. Needless to say, Colonel Parker made piles of money on Elvis the product, including his music, films, and likeness on shirts and hats, splitting these earnings fifty-fifty with Elvis. Eventually,

Parker had to sell these interests to Priscilla Presley and her Elvis Presley Enterprises (EPE), which now handles almost all commercial Elvis items.

Though Elvis earned many millions of dollars during his lifetime, he left an estate valued at less than $7 million. Elvis had managed to save only one dollar for every $5,000 he'd made, according to Sean O'Neal's text, *Elvis Inc*. Currently, EPE generates nearly $100 million annually from Graceland visitors and merchandise sales.

THE BEATLES

John, Paul, George, and Ringo became the greatest band in Pop music history, but they didn't do it alone. Even during the early days of the 1960s, the Beatles added two personal assistants. Neil Aspinall (later the managing director of their company, Apple) drove them from gig to gig in his van, and Mal Evans (road manager) helped load and unload equipment and guarded the stage during breaks. As the 1960s unfolded, former record store owner Brian Epstein, who became their manager, George Martin, their producer, and Dick James, their music publisher, helped the Beatles immeasurably on their road to mega-stardom.

The Beatles had spent the late 1950s making their first amateur recordings (including a now-released version of Buddy Holly's "That'll Be the Day," from 1958) and playing various clubs (such as the Casbah), and on local Liverpool television performing as Johnny and the Moondogs. With Stu Sutcliffe joining on bass in 1960, the group continued touring England, Scotland, and then Germany. Their name changed from the Beatals (Stu's suggestion) to the Silver Beetles and finally the Beatles (courtesy of John's wordplay), reflecting the new "beat" music of British Pop and Rock the U.K. teens enjoyed. Richard Starkey (Ringo Starr) met the group during a German recording session that year and attended their club performances as an audience member while they were abroad. The group spent 1961 playing many lunchtime sessions at the Cavern Club in Liverpool and other local venues as their notoriety increased. In November of that year, Epstein met the group and became enamored with John in particular (Epstein admitted to this in his book *A Cellarful of Noise*). He signed on as their manager in early 1962.

Manager Brain Epstein

Brian Samuel Epstein was born in Liverpool, England, on September 19, 1934. His father, Harry, was the owner and proprietor of a very successful family furniture business. Harry soon bought the business next door, the North End Road Music Stores (NEMS), which, coincidentally, was where Paul McCartney's father, James, a musician and bandleader, purchased his pianos.

Brian entered the British workforce in 1950 and was drafted into the military within two years. He was discharged after only ten months, suffering from emotional problems related to the early stirrings of his then unrecognized homosexuality. By 1954, Epstein was working at Clarendon Furnishing, another family business, where he was extremely successful. His educated, soft-spoken demeanor and conversational prowess made him a natural-born salesman. But Epstein had always hoped for a career in the theater, and briefly joined the Royal Academy for Dramatic Arts for acting training before returning to the business world.

Epstein was soon relocated to the NEMS branch in Whitecastle, where he continued to sell pianos and took special interest in the expanding phonograph recordings area. NEMS outlets had been carrying a local music newspaper, *The Mersey Beat,* since July 1961, and Epstein asked its editor, Bill Harry, if he might write a record column for it. By the end of the summer of 1961, Epstein was a regular contributor.

According to Epstein, a regular NEMS customer named Raymond Jones came in to the store on October 28, 1961, and requested the 45 rpm record of "My Bonnie" by Tony Sheridan and the Beatles. Epstein, who prided himself on having the latest records available at all times, had never heard of the Beatles, and so he began investigating them. He ordered a box of the records from Hamburg and soon heard the band live at the Cavern Club in Liverpool just down the road from his store.

Epstein says in his autobiography, *A Cellarful of Noise,* "I hadn't had anything to do with management of Pop artists before that day I went down to the Cavern Club and heard the Beatles playing, and this was quite a new world, really, for me. I was immediately struck by their music, their beat, and their sense of humor onstage. And even afterwards when I met them I was struck again by their personal charm. And it was there that it really started."

> ### COLD HARD FACT
>
> Brian Epstein would later admit in candid interviews that it was his personal emotional and physical attraction to John Lennon, beginning the moment he first saw the Beatles onstage in 1961 that really sparked his interest in the group. Epstein struggled his entire life with his homosexuality and the consequent public scrutiny during a time when alternative lifestyles were not widely accepted, even in the world of Pop music. Brian never officially "came out" to anyone, but it was a poorly kept secret in London entertainment circles.

However, this entire account is disputed by Bill Harry, who was a personal friend of John Lennon's. In a 2000 interview, Harry said that Epstein already knew about the Beatles in October 1961 and that "Raymond Jones" never existed. "Not only had I been talking to Epstein about the Beatles for months, not only were the Beatles in his record shop all the time [as customers], not only were they on the cover of *Mersey Beat* [Harry was its editor] all the time, which he was writing and reviewing records for, but he was even selling tickets for the Beatles' promotions at the Tower Ballroom [a massive Liverpool venue] and he was getting a cut of the money!" Harry believes that "Epstein wanted to claim that he created the whole thing himself," according to John Hester's Bill Harry interview for *Beatle Folks*. Though there is no listing of when the Beatles first appeared in Harry's magazine, John did have an article published in the first issue (July 6, 1961). There is also a photo featuring the group on the cover of *Mersey Beat* a week before Epstein signed as their manager (Jan. 8, 1962). (It is interesting to note that Paul's last name was misspelled as "McArtrey" in the photo's caption!)

On December 10, 1961, Epstein and the Beatles decided he should become their manager. John later stated that the group hoped Epstein's wealth might bail them out of sticky personal or business situations, so they agreed to his hiring. A formal contract was signed on January 24, 1962, at drummer Pete Best's house.

Epstein's first point of business was to literally clean up the Beatles' act. He forbade the leather jackets and replaced them with matching smart suits and ties. He told them to behave onstage, and not to drink, smoke, or curse while performing. He insisted they appear as complete professionals, even bowing in a uniform

The Beatles have their famous hair-dos tidied up before going on to the set at Twickenham Studios to begin filming, March 13, 1964. *(Photo by Keystone/Getty Images)*

fashion at the end of each song or set. Paul readily agreed to this overhaul in appearance and demeanor, but John was reluctant and later quipped that he felt the Beatles "were tamed" or "died" when they adopted this new direction. John rebelled against the suits by undoing his top button and pulling his tie slightly askew, which can be seen in many of the early promotional photos of the band. Epstein correctly realized that the more professional demeanor was a necessary step forward if the Beatles were to progress to national and international performances and television appearances.

Sometime around the summer of 1961, Astrid Kircherr, Stu's German girlfriend, suggested the group cut their hair in the style the French art students at the university were wearing. John, Paul, George, and Stu adopted this new look, later called the "Beatle cut." Only Pete Best declined to follow suit.

Epstein's next important job was to shop the demo recordings the Beatles had made at Decca Records to the major record labels in Britain, in hopes of acquiring a contract and a producer. He was turned down by every major label in London, including Decca (whose A&R people felt that "guitar groups were on the way out," though they later signed the Rolling Stones). But Epstein eventually connected with producer George Martin at Parlophone, a small subsidiary of EMI Records. Epstein's enthusiasm convinced the skeptical Martin that the Beatles should be judged on the basis of their potential. The timing was perfect, as Martin was looking to produce something new and exciting in an effort to break away from comedy records and light classical recordings.

Epstein next task, an unpleasant one, was to fire drummer Pete Best and replace him with Richard Starkey (Ringo Starr). John, Paul, and George had been together since 1958, and Pete simply did not gel musically or personally with the other three. Pete, who was called "moody and magnificent" by *Mersey Beat,* was an average drummer with a bit of an attitude of superiority. He simply did not have the sense of humor and fun the others did, and relished the role of "outsider" even within the context of a band. His extremely poor playing on the first take of "Love Me Do" that the group recorded on June 6, 1962, is audible proof of his lack of skill as a drummer. The truth was Pete did not complete the "Magic Circle," of which Wilfred Mellers speaks in his Beatles book *Twilight of the Gods,* that would form the basis of the group's synergistic energy. That man would be Ringo Starr.

Epstein proved to be a dedicated and hard-working manager, securing performances throughout the U.K. in 1962, culminating with the Royal Command Performance for the Queen in 1963 and the complete domination by the Beatles of the British Pop charts by that year's end. Epstein also managed a number of other British groups with moderate success, even appearing as a guest and music commentator on U.K. television shows. But his first and

> **COLD HARD FACT**
>
> Pete Best later cashed in on his early connection with the Beatles through interviews and tours fronting his own band. The release of the Beatles *Anthology* series of videos and recordings in the mid 1990s brought him back into the limelight and garnered him a new source of performance royalties to boot.

foremost love was the Beatles. Perhaps Epstein's greatest triumph was securing the Beatles' first U.S. tour and their appearance on *The Ed Sullivan Show* on February 9, 1964. These events propelled the Beatles to international stardom. Epstein planned their subsequent U.S. and world tours through 1965 and 1966, accompanying them on the road and always at their disposal.

As it turned out, those years were the highlight of Epstein's too-short life. As the Beatles ceased touring in late 1966 to concentrate on studio projects, Epstein found his role diminished. At around this time, he began fighting bouts of depression stemming from his unsatisfying situation with the Beatles and his unresolved issues concerning his homosexuality. Brian believed he needed to keep his sexual orientation a secret. He didn't want to shame his wealthy parents in front of their social peers, and he specifically did not want it to affect the Beatles in any adverse way. The gay lifestyle was not as widely accepted in the 1960s as it is today, and the stigma attached was hard for Brian to bear.

Like many people involved in the world of Pop culture, Epstein drank and took recreational drugs. He also found it necessary to take sleeping pills on occasion, as well as other pills to wake him in the morning. One night he took too many. Epstein was found dead in his home on August 27, 1967, from an overdose of sleeping pills, and speculation remains to this day that it might have been a suicide. But the Beatles and Epstein's family believe it was an accident, and no medical evidence was found to indicate otherwise.

During the scant six years during which Epstein was their manager, the Beatles enjoyed the most meteoric rise and the greatest success of any act in show business history. The band was never quite the same after Epstein's death, as he was also a referee between the often cynical, acerbic John and the sometimes overbearing, demanding Paul. Epstein was also a rudder for the band's direction and an impartial, non-musical outside observer whose insights and comments regarding the Beatles were often right on the mark. The Beatles did continue to make outstanding music without him, but their business relationships soon fell apart, eventually leading to the breakup of the band in 1970.

Producer George Martin

If anyone deserves to be called "the fifth Beatle," it is producer George Martin, as he made so many significant contributions to the band's musical growth. He arranged and conducted strings and horns, played keyboards when needed, contracted musicians, chose song orders for albums, and, perhaps most important, helped the Beatles to musically realize what they heard in their heads as they evolved creatively.

George Martin was born January 3, 1926 (fourteen years before the oldest Beatle, Ringo) in North London. The son of a carpenter, Martin did not come from wealth and taught himself to play music by ear. By the age of sixteen, Martin was playing piano with his own dance band, George Martin and the Four Tune Tellers, and served as a lieutenant in the air force arm of the British Royal Navy from 1943 to 1948.

After his military duty, Martin studied music at the prestigious Guildhall School of Music in London, where he excelled in composition and orchestration. Martin was working at the BBC Music Library in 1950 when he took a job with EMI's Parlophone label, a very minor branch of the huge company. In 1955, at age twenty-nine, Martin became the youngest manager of an EMI label. That same year, Capitol Records in the U.S. became an associated "sister company" to EMI (and would later release many Beatles albums).

When he first met Brian Epstein, Martin had produced fairly successful comedy records (Peter Sellers, Dudley Moore, and the Goons) and light Classical music and Jazz (Judy Garland and Stan Getz). He recognized the arrival of Rock 'n' Roll as the next big thing and was looking for something along these lines to spark the musician in him and as a diversion from his usual work. Martin actually signed the Beatles even before hearing them, simply to take on a fresh endeavor to make his life more interesting.

Martin was not initially impressed with the four lads from Liverpool, as they came into Abbey Road Studios in awe of and unfamiliar with the recording process. William Dowlding reports in his excellent book, *Beatlesongs,* that on June 26, 1962, after the Beatles auditioned with raw renditions of such songs as "Love Me Do," Martin warned them of the bleak musical future that might lie ahead. He then asked them if there was anything they didn't particularly like, George Harrison looked up and dryly responded, "Well, for one thing, I don't like your tie." That glib remark broke the ice for everyone, and the personal and professional relationship among the five men developed smoothly over the next sessions. The three most important elements of the Beatles' remarkable

> **COLD HARD FACT**
>
> Paul McCartney is quoted as stating that Martin's military service gave him his sense of responsibility and composure. According to Phillip Norman in his book *Shout,* Paul said, "He pulled it all together—you're ultimately responsible, you're the captain. I think that's where George [Martin] got his excellent bedside manner. He'd dealt with navigators and pilots . . . he could deal with us when we got out of line."

success—their ability to grow, their attention to detail, and their sense of humor—were all nurtured by George Martin's personality and strengths, and their combined synergy made for perhaps the greatest musical offering in Rock 'n' Roll history.

In their early days, the Beatles would play their songs live in the studio for Martin, and he would make suggestions as to form, tempo, and other musical or production elements. They would then record as if performing for an audience. Some Beatles historians suggest that it was Martin who convinced John, Paul, and George to fire Pete Best, whose drumming was below par, but it was the group and Brian who made the final decision.

In the beginning, Martin was also not convinced that the group's original songs were particularly good. He commented to *Melody Maker* magazine that "as composers, they didn't rate. They hadn't shown me they could write anything at all. 'Love Me Do' I thought was pretty poor, but it was the best we could do." Martin was also unsure who the "front man" in the band was, John or Paul, as most groups had one individual who literally stood out in front. This made Martin a bit unsure as to whom to speak with as the actual "leader" of the group. It quickly became apparent that John and Paul were a team and more than just as songwriters. John seemed to be the spokesperson for the group regarding wants and needs, and Paul seemed to be the musical director during rehearsals.

Despite Martin's doubts, in 1962, "Love Me Do," the Beatles first single on the U.K. Pop charts, rose to No. 16. (It got there with a boost from Brian Epstein, who personally bought 10,000 copies!)

In February 1963, the Beatles recorded "Please Please Me," a Lennon original penned in the style of Roy Orbison. Martin suggested speeding up the tempo, convinced that this recording would reach No. 1 on the charts with this adjustment. He was correct: The song reached No. 1 within a month.

He quickly brought the group back from touring to record their first album, also entitled *Please Please Me,* in a one-day marathon session. "There can scarcely have been 585 more productive minutes in the history of recorded music," according to Mark Lewisohn, the foremost Beatles technical expert, in his fine book *The Complete Beatles Recording Sessions.* Martin basically asked the group to recreate the excitement of a live Beatles performance and even considered recording at the Cavern Club. The results were extraordinary: a raw but unique and honest representation of the Beatles at that time. Lennon's screaming performance on the final album track, "Twist and Shout," became a Rock 'n' Roll classic.

The year 1963 was a stellar one for Martin, as he would spend thirty-seven weeks at No. 1 on the U.K. charts as producer for the Beatles and several other acts, including, most notably, Gerry and the Pacemakers. By June, Parlophone Records was dominating the British Pop charts, a scant year after the Beatles first auditioned.

In September 1963, John and Paul brought Martin a new original song, and Martin suggested they also use the song's chorus—the catchy lyrics, "she loves you, yeah yeah yeah"—as an introduction. What emerged as the classic "She Loves You" was the culmination of Beatles magic (talent, inspiration, and timing) at that stage of their development. It sold faster than any other single in British history and became the group's first million-selling record.

By 1964, Martin realized that his contribution to the Beatles success was not being recognized by EMI in the form of direct financial compensation, so he formed his own production company, Associated Independent Recording (AIR). He supervised the design and construction of AIR Studios, which became one of the most successful venues of its type in the world.

Prior to 1965, Martin's musical (non-production) job consisted mainly of suggesting song structures, introductions, endings, harmonies, arrangements, or solos. With McCartney's "Yesterday," Martin departed drastically from the usual Pop-band format, adding a classical string quartet. Martin also continued to participate as a musician-sideman (hired outside performer) on Beatles recordings, playing various keyboards while acting as producer and arranger. He also contributed orchestral scores to the Beatles films *A Hard Day's Night, Help!,* and *Yellow Submarine,* as well as to Paul McCartney's later works, including his album *The Family Way* and his single "Live and Let Die."

With the Beatles' 1965 album *Rubber Soul* came the advent of new and innovative recording techniques, including overdubbing and layering of tracks. Using these techniques, Martin helped the Beatles carefully craft each song in the studio. This process set a new course for music production in Pop music. He also brought in top-flight studio musicians to augment and enhance the Beatles' ever-increasing musical sophistication. For example, Martin's arrangement for a double string quartet on Paul's "Eleanor Rigby" is elegantly simple and understated compared to their earlier efforts, such as "Love Me Do."

After their 1966 world tour (their last), the Beatles' musical emphasis turned to studio productions of original songs. George Martin's skills truly came to the forefront during this period. In addition, with the *Revolver* album, the Beatles' music began to reflect the "trips" they experienced while using mind-altering drugs. The final song on this album, John's "Tomorrow Never Knows," is unlike any piece they had ever produced. With lyrics inspired by the Tibetan *Book of the Dead,* John asked Martin to make his voice sound like "the Dalai Lama singing from a high mountain top with four thousand monks chanting in the background," says Dowlding in *Beatlesongs.* Martin achieved this unusual effect by routing John's voice through a rotating Leslie speaker, often used with Hammond organs. Tape loops at various speeds and a hypnotic drumbeat signaled the Beatles' new musical direction in this piece.

The epitome of the new musical direction for the Beatles was the song "Strawberry Fields Forever," with its unique combination of Pop and Psychedelic musical elements. John started writing it while serving as an extra in the film *How I Won the War* (1967) by Richard Lester, the director of the Beatles' early films. He performed an early version of this song in the studio for George Martin—a lovely, acoustic ballad rendition. Martin added trumpet and cellos, but John then recorded a heavier, more Psychedelic version featuring electric guitars. He ended up liking the beginning of the second version and the end of the first, and wanted them joined without a break. A technical problem arose when Martin realized

> **COLD HARD FACT**
>
> John's character in the film *How I Won the War* (1967), Private Gripweed (is there an implied marijuana connection in this fictitious name?), wore military-issue round spectacles. John soon started wearing this style of frame all the time (he needed prescription lenses), and it became a trademark "look" for him in his later years.

that they were at different tempos and a half step apart in key. Using the variable tape speed available on the four-track machines EMI used at the time, Martin brilliantly sped up one version and slowed down the other, then spliced them together seamlessly. Many Rock 'n' Roll historians believe that George Martin was the first to truly use the studio itself as a musical instrument—a device for creating music much like a keyboard or guitar.

Both "Strawberry Fields," which was released as a single in the U.K. in February 1967, and its flip side, Paul's "Penny Lane," were Psychedelic nostalgia pieces and musical precursors to the monumental *Sgt. Pepper's Lonely Heart's Club Band* album, which was released a few months later. Martin's contributions on *Sgt. Pepper's* alone would have earned him the title "the fifth Beatle." He used a wide variety of studio techniques to make this recording a Psychedelic masterpiece of sonic innovations. His musical imprints are on almost every song. For the opening title track, Martin dubbed in audience sounds and scored brass parts for four French horns based on musical lines Paul helped conceive. For John's "Lucy in the Sky With Diamonds," Martin sped up the track and added a variety of reverbs and echo effects to the voices specifically. On songs such as "She's Leaving Home," Martin used strings and harp, and on "When I'm Sixty-four," Martin cleverly arranged four clarinets to create a vaudeville sound.

John had composed "Being for the Benefit of Mr. Kite" using lyrics taken directly from an old Victorian circus poster. He told Martin that he wanted to "smell sawdust in the ring," says Dowlding in *Beatlesongs*. So Martin used sections of steam organ recordings on tape pieces of various lengths spliced together at random (actually thrown into the air and joined in whatever fashion they landed, some even backwards). This "aural wash," as Martin put it, was used as background to more conventional live organ tracks played by himself and John. For effect, Martin also recorded a Hammond organ at half-speed, increasing it later to create a whooshing sound.

After George Harrison became fascinated with East Indian instruments and philosophy, Martin helped him conceive the song "Within You, Without You." Martin combined both traditional Western violins and strings and East Indian strings and percussion. The resulting sound is hypnotic and mesmerizing. For John's "Good Morning Good Morning," Martin put together a track of animal noises (under John's direction) that segued directly from the sound of a chicken clucking to the sound of an electric guitar so similar in tone and texture that Martin later called it one of his best edits.

The pinnacle of creativity on the *Sgt. Pepper's* album may be on the song "A Day in the Life," a true Lennon and McCartney collaboration. John had written the verses in a slow, moody, dreamlike style, and Paul wrote a middle section with an up-tempo narrative (storytelling) approach. According to Dowlding, Paul suggested to Martin a "freakout, " and John wanted "a sound like the end of the world" to fill the twenty-four bars separating these two sections. Martin scored parts for a forty-one-piece orchestra to create this "organized chaos," in which each musician played the first note of this musical "swell," or "rush," on his instrument's lowest note and then slowly slid upward harmonically until the highest note possible was achieved twenty-four bars later. Paul suggested that this orchestral recording session be festive, so he handed out party hats and fake noses and mustaches to these usually reserved symphonic performers. One violinist clutched his bow wearing a gorilla's paw! Celebrities, including Mick Jagger, Mike Nesmith, and Donovan Leitch, were also on hand as observers to this unique moment in recording history.

Brian Epstein's death after the success of *Sgt. Pepper's* left the group rudderless and searching for something musical that might compare with that monumental release. The next project was the film and associated album, *Magical Mystery Tour,* which fans seemed to enjoy but critics blasted as amateurish and self-indulgent. John was becoming increasingly indifferent and a bit resentful, as Paul basically conceived and created this project by himself and took control of all production aspects. To some extent, Martin was also relegated to a subordinate role, as Paul commandeered the sound booth and instructed the engineers as to what he wanted.

John had largely relinquished his leadership role, finding both relaxation and lethargy in his ever-increasing use of marijuana and diversions with his new love Yoko Ono, whom he had met in June of 1966. This allowed Paul to step in and take the reins of the band.

During the recording sessions for the Beatles' double album (*The Beatles "White" Album*), John and Paul worked separately on their own songs, using others in the band as sidemen when necessary. This was a huge departure from the teamwork and camaraderie that had marked their earlier days. George Martin also became more detached from the goings-on and pursued outside projects. As the Beatles, and particularly Paul, became more adept at studio production themselves, Martin often found himself a mere spectator and arranger rather than a contributor of ideas. Meanwhile, Martin was fighting with EMI for a well-deserved raise, feeling a bit resentful of everyone else's tremendous financial success while he was still on salary.

The Beatles *Let It Be* project (filmed in 1969, album released in 1970) was meant to be a return to their earlier days of band jams and Rock 'n' Roll songs, with less reliance on studio techniques. Unfortunately, John was at his worst during the earlier morning filming sessions, and Paul appears bossy and narcissistic during the film. As the group, particularly John and Paul, bickered continually over every aspect of the recording process, Martin divorced himself from the proceedings as much as possible. The recordings for *Let It Be* were shelved while the Beatles worked on *Abbey Road* and eventually fell into the hands of producer Glyn Johns, who listened to the many hours of rough takes. John eventually passed the tapes on to Phil Spector, who applied his famous "wall of sound" production technique (which he had used on the Ronettes, Crystals, and other Girl Groups in the late 1950s) to the raw tracks, adding strings and choir. Both Martin and the Beatles were dismayed by the result. Martin felt he had established a particular style of arranging and producing the Beatles sound that Spector did not follow.

Martin was surprised when the group asked him to produce their final album, *Abbey Road,* with the same production process and techniques employed on their earlier releases. So, for *Abbey Road,* the Beatles' magnificent swan song album, Martin once again produced in the fashion of *Sgt. Pepper's* and earlier days, though with less textural complexity regarding overdubs and effects.

Martin spent his post-Beatle days of the 1970s and 1980s producing albums for Paul McCartney and other artists, including Kenny Rogers, Neil Sedaka, Jeff Beck, America, Cheap Trick, and the Mahavishnu Orchestra. In the mid 1990s, Martin worked on the release of the much-touted *Beatles Anthology* series of recordings and videos, and was knighted in 1996 (becoming "Sir" George Martin in the U.K.). Martin produced Elton John's huge hit "Candle in the Wind" in 1997, a charity recording honoring the deceased Princess Diana that became the bestselling single of all time.

In 1999, Martin retired from recording, with a final Beatles tribute album entitled *In My Life,* featuring such diverse performers as Robin Williams, Jim Carrey, Phil Collins, and Goldie Hawn performing Beatles hits. That same year, Martin was inducted into the Rock 'n' Roll Hall of Fame.

Beatles historian Mark Lewisohn says of George Martin "[He] was, as ever, a vital ingredient in the process, always innovative himself, a tireless seeker of new sounds and willing translator of the Beatles' frequently vague requirements." During his fifty-year career, Martin produced thirty No. 1 hit records in the U.K. and over seven hundred recordings in a wide range of musical styles. Most critics agree that he may be the most influential and important Pop record producer in music history.

EMI (Capitol)

The Beatles needed a major record company to press, distribute, and market their product. George Martin's association with EMI (Electric and Musical Industries) through its subsidiary Parlophone gave them the business platform from which to launch their international career.

EMI was formed in 1931 in Britain when the British Gramophone Co. and the U.K. branch of Columbia Records merged. Parlophone started as a German record label, purchased by Columbia around the time of World War I. Parlophone was a smaller division that focused on comedy and novelty recordings when the Beatles came on board, and was already fairly successful in this arena. When the Beatles signed to Parlophone Records in 1962, the label's parent company, EMI, was perhaps the largest record company in Britain, producing over 30 percent of all records in the U.K.. Prior to the 1950s, Decca Records, which had allowed the Beatles to record a demo at their facilities but did not sign them to a recording contract, split control of the U.K. market with EMI.

EMI handled the release of all U.K. Beatles recordings, with Capitol handling their U.S. releases after 1964. Prior to that, early Beatles albums had been released on small U.S. labels such as Swan, Tollie, and Vee Jay. Capitol, as EMI's American "sister" company, should have welcomed the Beatles' music with open arms, but executives were hesitant to bet on a foreign band making it in the U.S. No British act prior to the Beatles had done extremely well in the U.S. Pop market. After the Beatles' great success with "I Want to Hold Your Hand" and earthshaking performances on *The Ed Sullivan Show,* Capitol jumped on board, but often changed the song lineup on albums prior to *Sgt. Pepper* and released many compilation and collection albums not released in the United Kingdom. EMI officially released only thirteen Beatles LPs, whereas Capitol released sixteen. (See Table 3.1 for a complete album discography.)

Since 1964, Parlophone and Capitol have released a number of collections, compilations, box sets, and other special packages for Beatles fans.

Apple Corp, Ltd.

In 1968, the Beatles started their own label, Apple Corp., Ltd. They announced its formation when they appeared on *The Tonight Show* (guest-hosted that night by Joe Garagiola) on May 15.

John and Paul had grandiose plans for the company, but only the recording end turned out to be successful. The group rented office space on a fashionable London street, but they ran into problems trying to be businessmen and musicians at the same time. Richard DiLello, in his book *The Longest Cocktail Party,* tells of John and Yoko often sitting in an office eating caviar and baked potatoes and hearing wild schemes such as elaborate sound systems made up of dozens of tiny speakers from peddlers like Magic Alex, who frequented the headquarters.

But the Beatles did demonstrate an ability to spot talent by developing new stars such as Mary Hopkin, Badfinger, and James Taylor. And they continued to release their own terrific songs on the Apple label, including their most successful single as a band, "Hey Jude," backed by "Revolution." EMI handled the pressings for Apple, as they had for Parlophone.

TABLE 3.1 Beatles Album Discography

YEAR	TITLE	COMPANY
1963	Please Please Me	Parlophone
1963	With the Beatles	Parlophone
	Introducing . . . the Beatles	Vee Jay
1964	Meet the Beatles	Capitol
	The Beatles Second Album	Capitol
	A Hard Day's Night	Parlophone
	A Hard Day's Night	United Artists (U.S.)
	Something New	Capitol
	Beatles '65	Capitol
1965	Help!	Parlophone
	The Early Beatles	Capitol
	Beatles VI	Capitol
	Help!	Capitol
	Rubber Soul	Parlophone
	Rubber Soul	Capitol
1966	Yesterday and Today	Capitol
	Revolver	Parlophone
	Revolver	Capitol
1967	Sgt. Pepper's Lonely Hearts Club Band	Parlophone
	Sgt. Pepper's Lonely Hearts Club Band	Capitol
	Magical Mystery Tour	Parlophone
	Magical Mystery Tour	Capitol
1968	The Beatles (White Album)	Parlophone
	The Beatles (White Album)	Capitol
1969	Yellow Submarine	Parlophone
	Yellow Submarine	Capitol
	Abbey Road	Parlophone
	Abbey Road	Capitol
1970	Let It Be	Parlophone
	Let It Be	Capitol

The least profitable Apple endeavor was its clothes boutique on Baker Street in London, which closed within two months of opening, with the majority of the stock given away.

Northern Songs, Ltd.

In 1963, Brian Epstein and Dick James, an established U.K. music publisher, formed Northern Songs, Ltd. (named after London, "the northern city"), to handle the royalties and licensing for the Beatles' music and merchandising. James was the majority shareholder of the company, with a 49 percent share. John owned 19 percent, Paul 20 percent, and NEMS (Brian Epstein's company) 10 percent. Within a couple of years after Northern's formation, the shareholdings were restructured, with both John and Paul reducing their shares to 15 percent. NEMS went down to 7 percent, with the remainder of the shares going public, while George and Ringo, neither of whom had much interest or involvement in the business end of the Beatles at this stage, shared just 1.6 percent between them.

The arrangements between Paul and John and their publishing company bound them to Northern Songs through 1973. Unfortunately for John and Paul, they had also sold their own copyrights, held, by Lenmac Music, to Northern Song's Maclen Music (James's and the Beatles' joint company for handling Beatle song royalties, with anagrams and wordplay used in naming the companies), and eventually received only 15 percent of all Northern Songs' earnings on their own musical creations, but James and Maclen received more than 60 percent! They did this to raise funds, and paid the price, literally.

Eventually, with the creation of Apple, John and Paul were able to take over 20 percent of Maclen Music, which entitled them to 80 percent of the remaining earnings. Part of this deal required Lennon and McCartney to provide Northern Songs with at least six songs a year. The problem remained, however, that Maclen Music had assigned the copyright of songs to Northern in ex-

> **COLD HARD FACT**
>
> George expressed his resentment toward the company and the entire situation in his 1967 composition "Only a Northern Song," which he wrote as a throwaway. It was a poorly written, disjointed piece of nonsense meant to convey his distaste and frustration at not owning his own songs, such as "If I Needed Someone" and "Don't Bother Me."

> **COLD HARD FACT**
>
> Paul and Michael Jackson were actually quite close before 1985. They teamed up in 1981 for the song "The Girl Is Mine," and for "Say, Say, Say" in 1983. Paul blames himself for giving Jackson financial advice by telling him to invest in the purchase of musicians' song catalogs, as Paul had done quite successfully. The difference was that Paul bought only the catalogs of deceased musicians, such as Buddy Holly. Sometime after the takeover, Paul did approach Jackson hoping to negotiate an increase in his royalty rate, but he was turned down.

change for royalty payments. So John and Paul were receiving composer's royalties but had lost control of the rights to their own songs to Northern, which retained control over how and to whom the songs were licensed for use.

Dick James sold his 49 percent shares in Northern Songs in the late 1960s to Sir Lew Grade and ATV Music. Allen Klein had just stepped in to manage the Beatles' affairs. He, John, and Paul were unhappy with the sale, even though John and Paul had received a substantial cash bonus.

Later, ATV Music itself underwent a takeover battle. In 1985, Pop megastar Michael Jackson was the high bidder at a reported $47 million when ATV sold its music catalog. Jackson's acquisition included the publishing rights to between 160 and 260 Beatles songs, which was his specific target. In 1995, Jackson merged ATV with Sony's publishing branch. The end result is that Sony/ATV now owns most of the Beatles' catalog. By excluding some songs from his initial deals with Northern Songs in the Beatles' early days, Paul was able to retain the rights to several titles, including "Please Please Me," "Love Me Do," "Tell Me Why," and "P.S. I Love You." But, sadly, Paul had to ask permission from Jackson to use his own song, "For No One," on his album *Give My Regards to Broadstreet*. Meanwhile, media venues, particularly television commercials and some films, are now saturated with Beatles covers and remakes, many produced without the remaining Beatles' input.

In 2005, Jackson faced a slew of financial and legal problems. In June of 2005 Sony reported that Jackson had taken out a substantial loan using half of the Beatles' catalog as collateral, and many observers predicted that he would eventually find it necessary to sell his rights to the Beatles' songs. After Bank of America sold the loan to Fortress Investments (April 2005), Jackson continued to miss payments on the loan. As of December 20, 2005, Fortress had the right to foreclose on the loan, allowing Sony Music the first right to buy Jackson's share of the loan. However, Fortress extended the loan, allowing Jackson time to get his finances in order. In late 2005, after being acquitted on child molestation charges, Jackson put his Neverland Ranch up for sale and went on extended vacation to the oil-wealthy Persian Gulf country of Bahrain. Following the untimely death of Jackson in June of 2009, unsubstantiated rumors circulated that his will specify the Beatles catalogue be left to Paul. This is not likely, though, as Sony/ATV owns 50% of said catalogue, and the remaining Beatles or their benefactors would most certainly have some input regarding distribution.

Comparison

Elvis's manager Colonel Tom Parker and the Beatles' manager Brian Epstein were very different people, yet both were extremely devoted to their respective clients. Each man's undying faith in the abilities of his artists, coupled with financial acumen, provided a platform for tremendous success, as neither Elvis nor any of the Beatles were businessmen in their own right.

Elvis had no interest whatsoever in the business machinations of his musical product, and this neglect cost him millions in merchandising funds that went to Colonel Parker and manufacturers and distributors of these goods. Elvis also lost potential earnings due to the Colonel's insistence that he tour incessantly rather than make quality films in the 1970s; Elvis was offered several meaty roles which Parker refused on his behalf. Elvis invested little of his vast earnings and had more wealth tied up in jewelry, guns, and a huge assortment of winged and wheeled vehicles than he had in real estate or retirement holdings. Elvis did own a large parcel of land directly across the state border in Mississippi called the Circle G Ranch from 1967 through 1974, but sold it after losing interest in ranching. Elvis also invested in a string of racquetball clubs near the end of his life, but this proved to be a financial boondoggle and he quickly abandoned the project. Elvis was a simple man who lived an extravagant life, and his money was a tool for enjoyment rather than a foundation for his future.

The Beatles, like Elvis, relied on management and business people to handle their financial affairs. The circumstances surrounding their sale of personal song copyrights as part of a deal to generate income has become famous in the lore of musical business woes, and an example of what not to do. John, who already tended to be a bit cynical, accepted this as part of the great conspiracy "the suits" (well-dressed, pretentious executives) were known for, and even the gentle George became irate at losing his song rights. Had the Beatles had proper legal representation (Brian Epstein was gone, Allen Klein joined too late), they would have protected their interests with ferocity.

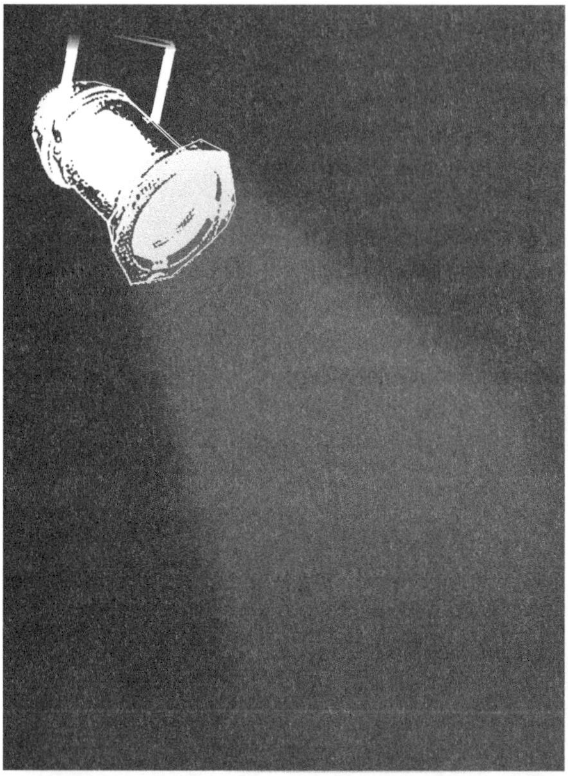

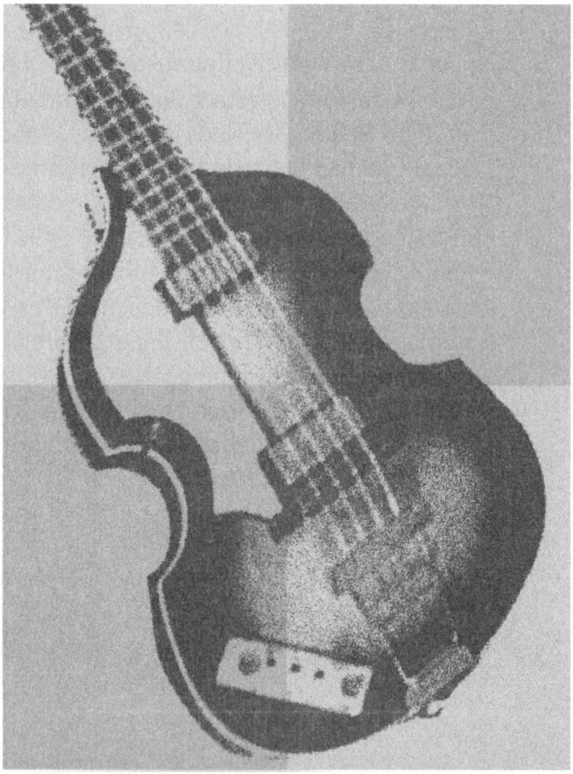

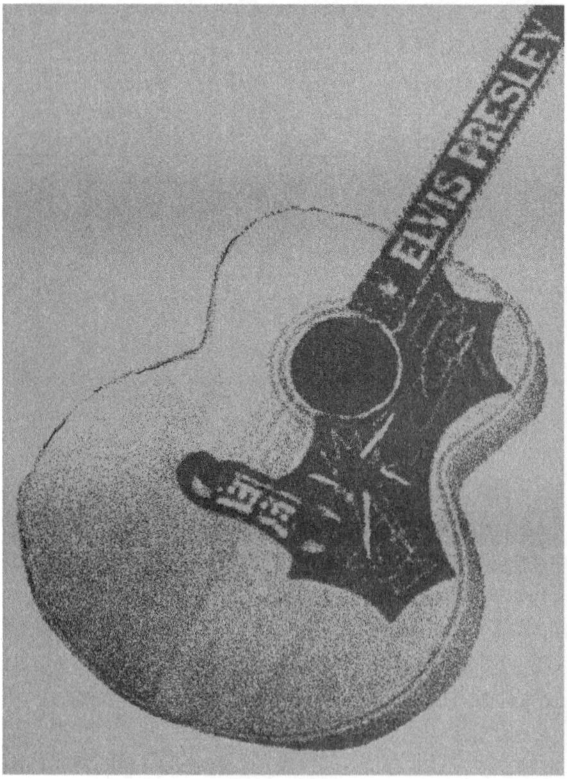
ELVIS PRESLEY

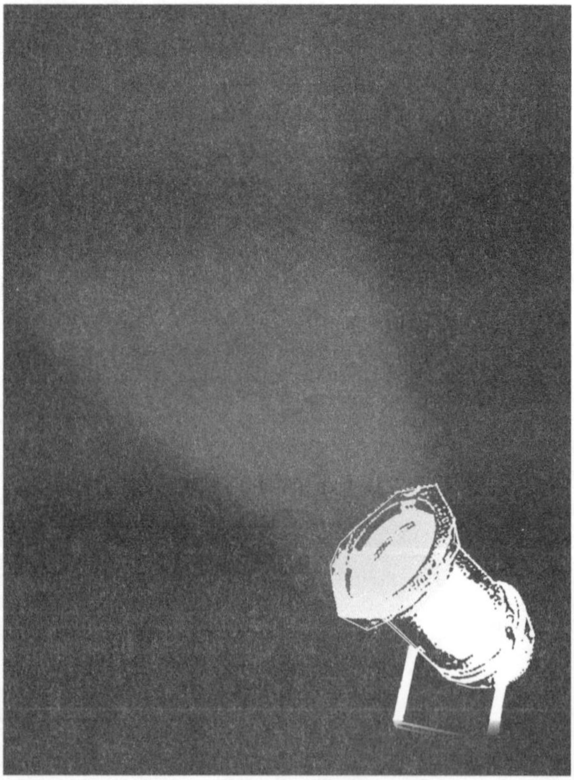

CHAPTER 4

Elvis and the Beatles in Film and Television

In the 1950s and early 1960s, Rock 'n' Roll musicians dreamed of becoming not only Pop stars but also movie stars. Both Elvis and the Beatles felt that the pinnacle of stardom for them, and what would best ensure their longevity in show business, would be their immortalization on the silver screen. In interviews of the day, both Elvis and the Beatles are quoted as stating that being famous musicians was not of primary importance and that they would like to make films. Elvis, in fact, had the blood lust for the big screen, and his thirty Hollywood films attest to his legacy in that field. Ringo alone among the Beatles proved himself a durable actor in several films and television appearances. Today, both Elvis and the Beatles are remembered chiefly for their music—but it is important to remember that in the beginning of their careers, they all felt that the road to truly lasting fame and stardom led through Hollywood.

ELVIS

Elvis's Films From 1956 to 1964

In the 1950s, Elvis's films were loosely biographical, with the obvious exception of *Love Me Tender* (1956), a Civil War–era period piece. This film was originally written without any songs by Elvis, but through the urging of Colonel Parker, this was amended. Elvis cowrote the title song, which was adapted from the Civil War song "Aura Lee." Reviewers generally praised the King's acting, though Elvis's initial reaction to seeing himself on the big screen was to ask, "Who is that fast– talking hillbilly son-of-a-bitch?" Elvis received $100,000 in salary for his work on this film, and his fans attended the movie in droves across the country.

Loving You (1957) was the first of nine films Elvis would make with producer Hal Wallis. It was specifically written for Elvis and drew closely on his real life story, with its southern roots, Country and Rockabilly music, flashy clothing, and tale of poor-boy-makes-good. It is notable because it was the first of his films shot in Technicolor, allowing fans to see Elvis on the big screen in all his multi-shaded glory rather than just in black-and-white.

When Elvis began filming *Jailhouse Rock* in May 1957, he commanded the then-unheard-of sum of $250,000 plus 50 percent of the profits, making him one the highest paid actors in Hollywood. With a great title song by Jerry Leiber and Mike Stoller that frames a wonderfully choreographed segment, this film is considered one of Elvis's best works.

King Creole (1958) was filmed just before Elvis joined the army in March. Elvis plays Danny Fisher, a high school dropout who gets a job as a dishwasher at a New Orleans nightclub. Given the chance to perform one night, Danny displays his considerable musical talents, and the club's sleazy crime-boss owner (Walter Matthau) realizes he has a hit on his hands. Danny initially tries to steer clear of the obviously illegal goings-on but discovers that saying no isn't always so easy. Widely believed to be Elvis's best film, *King Creole* has an incredible supporting cast that includes Matthau, Vic Morrow as a gangster hoodlum, and Carolyn Jones (who later played Morticia on the television show *The Addams Family*).

Cold Hard Fact

Elvis's parents, Vernon and Gladys, both appear in the film *Loving You,* with Gladys most visible during Elvis's performance of "Teddy Bear." After his mother's death, Elvis could not bear to watch this film for years.

Elvis Presley in *Jailhouse Rock,* 1957. © *John Springer Collection/CORBIS*

The soundtracks for Elvis's 1950s films were strong and varied. *Loving You* offered the Country side of the King, *Jailhouse Rock* his Rock and ballad side, and *King Creole* his raw, bluesy side. The only weak link was *Love Me Tender* (a story set in the Civil War era), in which, at the insistence of Colonel Parker, several songs by Elvis were included in the soundtrack, and the storyline was adjusted for their inclusion. The result is tepid at best, with Elvis (who dies in the film) singing "Love Me Tender" as the credits rolled to appease his fans who might otherwise have disliked the film enough not to attend it at all. Yet the strength of these soundtracks is very apparent when contrasted with the formula Pop soundtracks chosen for Elvis's later films (though the latter sold well into the millions).

After his discharge from military duty in March 1960, Elvis fell into a formulaic film rut designed by Parker and the studios to keep the soundtrack albums selling and fans in the theater seats. Elvis's first film after serving his military duty was *G.I. Blues* (1960). It casts Elvis as Tulsa, a U.S. Army specialist stationed in Germany. While dreaming of opening his own nightclub, Elvis accepts a lucrative bet from his army buddies to break the ice that surrounds a notoriously chilly, but beautiful, local cabaret singer, played by Juliet Prowse. When the bet turns into real romance, Tulsa gets more than he bargained for. *G.I. Blues* features ten acclaimed songs, including "Blue Suede Shoes" and "Pocket Full of Rainbows."

Aspiring to become a well-respected actor, Elvis next appeared in two serious films (with few songs). Though fans appreciated this side of Elvis, and he enjoyed these roles, sales slumped without album and singles tie-ins. The first film, *Flaming Star* (1960), was a box-office disappointment, largely because Elvis died at the end of the picture and it featured only two songs. The second film, *Wild in the Country* (1961), based on a fine screenplay by Clifford Odets, was a slow-moving, well-acted moody melodrama, but it failed to set the box office on fire. Instead of drama, Colonel Parker, the studio, and the fans wanted breezy movies chock-full of songs.

In *Blue Hawaii* (1961), Elvis played Chad Gates, returning home to Hawaii after a stint in the army. Rather than reporting for work at his parents' pineapple plantation, Chad takes a job as an island tour guide, freeing up his time to entertain Hawaii's most beautiful women. His parents, of course, have other plans for their

> **COLD HARD FACT**
>
> During an early audience screening of *Love Me Tender,* fans were so upset by the ending, with Elvis's character dying, that producers quickly shot an additional scene. The film was revised with a ghostly transposition shot of Elvis singing the title song over the original footage. His image, seen in the clouds singing "Love Me Tender," emphasized his star image over his film character, thereby reassuring his fans that the King would "never die."

boy, and a hilarious string of complications ensues. With Angela Lansbury miscast as Chad's domineering mother (she seemed far too young for this matronly role), *Blue Hawaii* features the beautiful and famous ballad, "Can't Help Falling In Love." With fantastic location shots, catchy songs, beautiful girls, and a trim and tanned Elvis, this film grossed over $14 million. Its soundtrack was Elvis's biggest selling record during his career and remains one of the most popular soundtrack albums of all times.

In *Follow That Dream* (1962), Elvis teamed with Arthur O'-Connell as southerners taking care of orphan children. *Kid Galahad* (1962) was a boxing remake featuring a strong supporting cast, including Gig Young and a soon-to-be-superstar, Charles Bronson. Actress Stella Stevens played Elvis's love interest in *Girls! Girls! Girls!* (1962), which features Elvis as a singing sailor and a fine performance of the hit "Return to Sender." *It Happened at the World's Fair* (1963) was an enjoyable, family-orientated production with a pleasant soundtrack and amusing scenes, including great location shots in Seattle. This was also the film debut of young Kurt Russell (he kicks Elvis in the shins!), who would go on to play Elvis in the critically acclaimed television movie, *Elvis* (1979), and in the violent and plot-muddled heist caper *3000 Miles to Graceland*.

TABLE 4.1 Elvis's First 15 Films (and the Charting Songs from Their Soundtracks)

- *Love Me Tender* (20th Century-Fox, 1956) - title song "Love Me Tender"
- *Loving You* (Paramount, 1957) - "(Let Me Be Your) Teddy Bear"
- *Jailhouse Rock* (M-G-M, 1957) - "Treat Me Nice"
- *King Creole* (Paramount, 1958) - "As Long As I Have You"
- *G.I. Blues* (Paramount, 1960) - "Wooden Heart"
- *Flaming Star* (20th Century-Fox 1960) - title song "Flaming Star"
- *Wild in the Country* (20th Century-Fox, 1961) - title song "Wild in the Country"
- *Blue Hawaii* (Paramount, 1961) - "Can't Help Falling In Love"
- *Follow That Dream* (Mirisch, 1962) - title song "Follow That Dream"
- *Kid Galahad* (Mirisch, 1962) - "King of the Whole Wide World"
- *Girls! Girls! Girls!* (Paramount, 1962) - "Return to Sender"
- *It Happened at the World's Fair* (M-G-M, 1963) - "They Remind Me Too Much of You"
- *Fun in Acapulco* (Paramount, 1963) - "Bossa Nova Baby"
- *Kissin' Cousins* (M-G-M, 1964) - title song "Kissin' Cousins"
- *Viva Las Vegas* (M-G-M, 1964) - title song "Viva Las Vegas"

Fun in Acapulco (1963) offered nothing new in its plotline, but this didn't matter thanks to its glorious scenery and Latin-flavored soundtrack, as well as beautiful actress Ursula Andress. With this production, Elvis's film characters started becoming a bit absurd. Elvis portrays an ex-trapeze artist who is a singing sailor and lifeguard! *Kissin' Cousins* (1964) truly stretches the audience's credulity as Elvis plays a dual role as identical cousins in this hillbilly comedy, which also features actor Jack Albertson.

Elvis soon became notorious for his offstage flings with many of his leading ladies. The 1964 film *Viva Las Vegas* was the pinnacle of such behavior. Elvis's character, Lucky Johnson, becomes involved with the lovely Ann-Margret, and the chemistry between these two actors bursts from the screen. When not filming, Elvis and Ann-Margret spent most of their free time together riding motorcycles and being seen. Priscilla continued to play the real-life role of the patient bride-to-be back in Memphis while Elvis made no secret of his affairs. But he ultimately ended this relationship with Ann-Margret after the actress told the press of her upcoming wedding to the King! The film itself put Las Vegas back on the map, some say, and foreshadowed Elvis's return there in 1969 (he had been there once in 1956 with little success) to live out his successful Las Vegas years in showrooms.

In *Roustabout* (1964), Elvis's character, Charlie Rogers, is a wandering karate man and motorcycle-riding bad-boy singer who takes a job at a carnival run by Maggie Morgan, played by Hollywood legend Barbara Stanwyck. Stanwyck, who was put off by her brash costar at first, soon became quite close to Elvis and was even spotted riding around the set on the back of his motorcycle. While on the job, Charlie encounters an equal share of hard work, romance, and the jealousy of a sleazy rival. Joan Freeman plays Cathy Lean, Charlie's love interest, with Leif Erickson costarring as her overprotective father. *Roustabout* also features early appearances from Raquel Welch and Teri Garr and includes the hit tune "Little Egypt." Its soundtrack songs had a total playing time of just over twenty minutes. Red West, Elvis's longtime bodyguard and an original member of Presley's "Memphis Mafia," appears in a small role (see Table 4.5 for West's other appearances in Elvis films), and the film features carnival attractions, such as Billy Barty as Billy the Midget, and seven-foot-tall Richard Kiel, who went on to play Lurch on the television show *The Addams Family*.

The huge box-office success of *G.I. Blues* and *Blue Hawaii* convinced the film studios and Colonel Parker that Elvis did not need any more dramatic challenges. The simplified strategy became as follows: place Elvis in an exotic locale surrounded by beautiful women, have him punch out his rival, sing a few unmemorable songs, and get the girl, all in less than seventy-two minutes running time.

Elvis's Films From 1965 to 1969

The formula continued to prove highly profitable until 1965 when the decline in box-office receipts became noticeable. The Beatles' *A Hard Day's Night* came out in 1964, followed by *Help!* in 1965, and Elvis was now competing with the Fab Four at the box office as well as for radio time. *Girl Happy* (1965) features Elvis and costar Shelley Fabares in a Miami Beach romp highlighted by the beautiful song "Puppet on a String." This film proved lighter and more accessible than the Beatles' films to some and was extremely popular with Elvis's ever-aging fan base.

Elvis was paid $750,000 plus 50 percent of the profits for *Tickle Me* (1965), one of his flimsiest and most criticized films, but one that saved Allied Artists from immediate bankruptcy. The *New York Times* reviewer wrote, "This is the silliest, feeblest and dullest vehicle for the Memphis Wonder in a long time." Because of the scantily clad girls who populated films like this, some critics and fans made comparisons to soft-core pornography. One exception to the rule in this period was the 1965 film *Harum Scarum* (originally titled *Harem Holiday*), which actually had decent costuming and a reasonably listenable soundtrack.

Frankie and Johnny (1966) featured Donna Douglas (who later played Ellie Mae on the television show *The Beverly Hillbillies*) and Harry Morgan (Colonel Potter on TV's *M*A*S*H*) in a nineteenth-century riverboat setting with period costumes to dramatize this famous song. *Paradise, Hawaiian Style* (1966) was a poor attempt to repeat the success of *Blue Hawaii,* while *Spinout* (1966) featured singing race-car driver Elvis fighting off the advances of three female costars. More low-quality films followed, such as *Easy Come, Easy Go* (1967) and *Double Trouble* (1967). These films came to symbolize the three- to four-week shooting schedules of late '60s Elvis films (earlier films had been shot over several months). *Double Trouble* (1967) has the distinction of including the absolute all-time low of

Elvis's film songs, including a corny rendition of "Old MacDonald's Farm" (better known as "Old MacDonald Had a Farm"). The long but steady decline of the quality of Elvis's films can be seen as his early, meaty action roles with fine songs and well-established costars devolved into song-filled sexy romps with poor scripts and modest budgets. His later films often featured great location shots such as Hawaii, Mexico, and Las Vegas rather than well-worded scripts or interesting plots of the earlier days of Elvis in Hollywood.

Recording the soundtracks for his B movies by singing at least six or seven quickly composed songs in each film but with hardly any time to properly rehearse was a tedious process that Elvis dreaded. He would complain about how awful these songs were to everyone around him—everyone, that is, except Colonel Parker, the only person who had the power to change the situation. By 1967, production values for Elvis's films declined even further. Location shooting often replaced studio shoots for cost-cutting purposes, and the quality of scripts was variable. Similarly, the songs chosen for each movie generally were mediocre at best. For most fans, however, they were still great and worked quite well within the plotline. Parker knew that these films were simplistic but necessary diversions for fans, who hadn't seen Elvis perform live in years. In those days before music videos, the only way for fans to see their idol's stage act was either on television or at the movies.

In assessing the worth of Elvis's B movies, it is important to remember that their intended audience and purpose was to entertain Elvis's fans. They were never intended to be blockbusters with huge budgets. The studio's financial goal was that each Elvis film earn back two and a half times its cost. Compared with other examples of the mid-1960s teenage genre (beach party and biker movies), Elvis's films have higher production values. If kept within the parameters of having Elvis basically portray himself, most of the Elvis films worked very well, and every one of them made money for all involved.

By the late 1960s, however, Elvis's films began to show declining box-office receipts. At around this time, his weight began to go up and down (a portent of things to come), and his hair was a lacquered black pompadour completely unlike the long, unkempt locks favored by teens and the current Pop idols, such as the Beatles and the Rolling Stones.

In *Clambake* (1967), Elvis played, most appropriately, a rich, bored southerner, alongside comic sidekick Bill Bixby. *Stay Away,*

TABLE 4.2	Years in Which Elvis Ranked Among the Top Ten Movie Stars

1957 - No. 4
1961 - No. 10
1962 - No. 5
1963 - No. 7
1964 - No. 6
1965 - No. 6
1966 - No. 10

(From *The Top Ten of Film* (DK Publishing, 2003) compiled by Russell Ash)

TABLE 4.3	Top-Selling Elvis Film Songs in the U.K. (according to *Melody Maker* magazine)

1. "Jailhouse Rock," 1957
2. "Wooden Heart," 1960
3. "Return to Sender," 1962
4. "Can't Help Falling In Love," 1961
5. "Teddy Bear," 1957
6. "King Creole," 1958
7. "Let's Have a Party," 1957
8. "Hard Headed Woman," 1958
9. "I Just Can't Help Believing," 1970
10. "Always on My Mind," 1972

TABLE 4.4	Top-Selling Elvis Film Songs in the U.S. (according to Billboard & Cashbox ratings)

1. "Love Me Tender," 1956
2. "Jailhouse Rock," 1957
3. "Teddy Bear," 1957
4. "Return to Sender," 1962
5. "Can't Help Falling In Love," 1962
6. "Hard Headed Woman," 1958
7. "Bossa Nova Baby," 1963
8. "One Broken Heart For Sale," 1963
9. "Follow That Dream," 1962
10. "I'm Yours," 1965

Joe (also that year) was a Western formula film elevated by actors Burgess Meredith, Joan Blondell, and L. Q. Jones but marred by the deplorable song "Dominick," which Elvis sings to a bull! *Speedway* (1968) teamed Elvis with Nancy Sinatra, Bill Bixby, Gale Gordon, and a number of famous race car drivers and featured funkier grooves on songs such as "Let Yourself Go."

Elvis always had the ability for light comedy, which showed clearly in *Live a Little, Love a Little* (1968). The song "A Little Less Conversation," a funky track that was quite modern in groove and instrumentation and ahead of its time, also highlighted this film. *Charro!* (1968) was a solid spaghetti western with a strong music score (but only one Elvis song), good central characterizations, and a tough, adult script, but Elvis turned in a curiously wooden performance, and the film failed to attract a large audience. *The Trouble With Girls (and How to Get Into It)* from 1969 was Elvis's last comedy. It featured the superb song "Clean Up Your Own Backyard." Elvis gave a very decent performance. It was initially panned but has since been seen in a more favorable light.

Change of Habit (1969) was Elvis's final non-documentary film. At the time, it was a fine attempt at a contemporary, socially aware film. Despite good performances by Elvis and costar Mary Tyler Moore, the film is offbeat (Elvis as a doctor in the barrio!), predictable (Elvis gets the girl), and perhaps laughable by today's standards, and seems destined to remain on lists of the 100 worst films.

By the late 1960s, Elvis fans were turning away from his films, and, despite some admirable attempts at changing the direction of his film career, neither fans nor critics were willing to sanction Elvis's attempt to move in the direction of more serious, less song-filled productions. Since the bottom line for film studios is profits, the studios were not interested in giving the new direction time to develop and attract a substantial audience. Furthermore, Elvis felt he needed a change. He wanted to return to live performing and the adrenalin rush of being in front of an adoring audience.

It is unfortunate that Elvis did not persist with a non-documentary film career in the 1970s, including Barbra Streisand's remake of *A Star Is Born*. A balance might have been struck between commitments for live performing and the making of one movie every twelve months or so. At best, continued filmmaking might have provided a greater creative spark for Elvis and, at worst, it might have slowed his physical and psychological decline throughout the 1970s—a decline that seemed to have begun in earnest when he finally realized that his dream of being a "real" actor was never going to be fulfilled.

The final phase in Elvis's film career consisted of his two concert documentaries: *Elvis: That's the Way It Is* (1970) and *Elvis On Tour* (1972). The superb re-edit and digital remastering of *Elvis: That's The Way It Is* (2000 edition) is bringing a vibrant Elvis to a whole new generation. Both films showcase Elvis at his dynamic best, doing what he really loved and being showered with adoration by the fans. It is a pity that his feature films could not capture the depth and essence of the performer and instead focused only on the surface of the star. The film *The New Gladiators*, a mid-'70s Karate documentary that Elvis had conceived and financed, was released in 2002. Many Elvis-related fictional and documentary-style films have followed since his death in 1977.

Elvis on Television

In 1956, Elvis came to New York for a series of six television appearances on the Dorsey Brothers' variety series *Stage Show,* produced by entertainer Jackie Gleason, quickly followed by two appearances on *The Milton Berle Show*. Although his detractors decried Elvis's "hip swiveling" as vulgar, that didn't lessen his appeal to a growing audience of young fans. The success of the Dorsey and Berle appearances encouraged Steve Allen to risk having Elvis on his program (despite network protests) provided he would tone down his aggressive body movements and dress in comically square white tie and tails.

Even Ed Sullivan, who had initially announced that he was not a fan of Elvis's, succumbed to popular opinion and invited him for a series of three appearances on *The Ed Sullivan Show,* assuring critics that the camera would be carefully manipulated to prevent Elvis's gyrations from shocking the audience. But examination of archival video of these performances shows that such restricted camera framing did not actually happen: Elvis is seen from head to toe, gyrating madly throughout the performance.

After his army tour in Germany, Elvis appeared on *The Frank Sinatra–Timex Show* in 1960, in what was to be his last television performance for eight years. He spent the intervening years pursuing his cinematic career in B (and lower quality) movies, but returned triumphantly to television in 1968.

TABLE 4.5 Elvis Films 1956–1969

YEAR	TITLE	ELVIS AS	FEMALE STARS	MALE STARS	+ RED WEST
1956	Love Me Tender	Clint Reno	Debra Paget Mildred Dunnock	Richard Egan James Drury	
1957	Loving You	Deke Rivers	Delores Hart Lizabeth Scott	Wendell Corey James Gleason	
	Jailhouse Rock	Vince Everett	Judy Tyler Jennifer Holden	Mickey Shaughnessy Dean Jones	
1958	King Creole	Danny Fisher	Carolyn Jones Delores Hart	Walter Matthau Dean Jagger	
1960	G.I. Blues	Tulsa McLean	Juliet Prowse Letitia Roman	Robert Ivers James Douglas	
	Flaming Star	Pacer Burton	Barbara Eden Delores Del Rio	Steve Forrest L. Q. Jones	
1961	Wild in the Country	Glenn Tyler	Tuesday Weld Hope Lange	Gary Lockwood Jason Robards, Sr.	X
	Blue Hawaii	Chad Gates	Joan Blackman Angela Lansbury	Roland Winters Howard McNear	X
1962	Follow that Dream	Toby Kwimper	Anne Helm Joanne Moore	Arthur O'Connell Alan Hewitt	X
	Kid Galahad	Walter Gulick	Joan Blackman Lola Albright	Gig Young Charles Bronson	
	Girls! Girls! Girls!	Ross Carpenter	Stella Stevens Laurel Goodwin	Jeremy Slate Gary Lockwood	X
1963	It Happened at the World's Fair	Mike Edwards	Joan O'Brien Vicky Tui	Robert Strauss Kurt Russell	X
	Fun in Acapulco	Mike Windgren	Ursula Andress Elsa Cardenas	Alejandro Ray Paul Lukas	X
1964	Kissin' Cousins	Josh Morgan Jodie Tatum	Glenda Farrell Yvonne Craig	Arthur O'Connell Jack Albertson	
	Viva Las Vegas	Lucky Johnson	Ann-Margret Teri Garr	William Demarest Ceasare Danova	
	Roustabout	Charlie Rogers	Joan Freeman Barbara Stanwyck	Leif Erickson Pat Butram	X
1965	Girl Happy	Rusty Wells	Shelley Fabres Mary Ann Mobley	Harold J. Stone Gary Crosby	X

Year	Film	Character	Co-stars	Supporting	
	Tickle Me	Lonnie Beale	Julie Adams Jocelyn Lane	Jack Mullaney Bill Williams	x
	Harum Scarum	Johnny Tyronne	Mary Ann Mobley Fran Jeffries	Michael Ansara Jay Novello	x
1966	Frankie and Johnny	Johnny	Donna Douglas Sue Ann Langdon	Harry Morgan Robert Strauss	
	Paradise, Hawaiian Style	Rick Richards	Suzanna Leigh Irene Tsu	James Shigeta Robert Ito	x
	Spinout	Mike McCoy	Shelley Fabares Deborah Walley	Carl Betz Jack Mullaney	x
1967	Easy Come, Easy Go	Ted Jackson	Dodie Marshall Elsa Lanchester	Pat Harrington, Jr. Skip Ward	
	Double Trouble	Guy Lambert	Annette Day Yvonne Romain	John Williams Chips Rafferty	
	Clambake	Scott Hayward	Shelley Fabares	Bill Bixby Gary Merrill	x
1968	Stay Away, Joe	Joe Lightcloud	Joan Blondell Katy Jurado	Burgess Meredith L. Q. Jones	
	Speedway	Steve Grayson	Nancy Sinatra	Bill Bixby Gale Gordon	
	Live a Little, Love a Little	Greg Nolan	Michele Cary	Dick Sargent Sterling Holloway	x
	Charro!	Jess Wade	Ina Balin	Victor French Paul Brinegar	
1969	The Trouble With Girls	Walter Hale	Lynn Kellogg Marilyn Mason Anissa Jones Mary Tyler Moore	John Carradine Vincent Price	
	Change of Habit	John Carpenter	Barbara McNair	Edward Asner A Martinez	

Elvis (a.k.a. The Singer Special or The '68 Comeback Special)

In 1968, Steve Binder had just finished producing and directing a prime-time television special starring Petula Clark and Harry Belafonte that generated a huge controversy because it included a scene in which a black man and a white woman touched each other. At that point in American history, the backlash this innocent gesture caused made Binder feel as if he would never work in the industry again. However, that feeling lasted only until he got a call from NBC and executive producer, Bob Finkel, who told him that they needed to find a young rebel to get involved with the upcoming Elvis special. According to Finkel, even though he had a deal with Colonel Parker, there was no one Elvis could relate to—who was close to his age or reflected his true musical tastes—and therefore he balked at actually showing up and doing the special.

When Binder first met Elvis and Parker, the Colonel informed Binder that Elvis would simply sing twenty or so Christmas songs, say hello and goodbye to the audience, and that would be the special. Upon hearing this, Binder told Elvis that if he did what Parker had described, his career would be finished for good. Elvis listened. In 1968, his career was in freefall. The Beatles, the Rolling Stones, and wilder rock acts, such as Jimi Hendrix and the Doors, were dominating the charts. The raw sexuality and energy of Elvis's early Rock 'n' Roll performances had given way to his post-army Pop crooning. He had not had a hit in years, had grown tired

> **COLD HARD FACT**
>
> When Binder first met Elvis, he was not particularly fond of the King's music, although he enjoyed classic songs like "Blue Suede Shoes" and "Hound Dog." "When I started working with him and really 'tuned in,' I really began to appreciate what a great artist he was . . . and aside from the lousy movie songs that he was obligated to sing, per contract . . . I really realized what a great producer he was . . . his abilities to select great material like 'Can't Help Falling in Love' for example."

of churning out increasingly bad B movies, and was primed for the meeting with the dynamic young producer. He and Binder set out to create a special that Elvis would be comfortable with and, most important, would turn Elvis on creatively. Binder recalled that Elvis said he knew how to make records but was afraid of television. "I told him: Let's make a record and I'll put pictures to it."

The Singer Special, as it was officially titled (it was sponsored by Singer Co., the sewing-machine makers), but which came to be more commonly referred to as *The '68 Comeback Special,* was a well-planned script that had elements of stage-show performance in front of a live audience (similar to what Elvis would begin to do in Las Vegas later that year). It wasn't until after the fact that Binder and Howe came up with the idea of an acoustic version that was later shown on HBO in 1984 under the title *One Night With You.*

Binder further commented on what he and Presley later shared in a documentary about the *'68 Comeback Special* that was released to DVD in 1998. "When Elvis saw the edited special, before it aired on NBC, he told me he would never sing a song or make a movie that he didn't believe, and I told him that I heard what he said but that he would have to break away from the 'inner circle' of friends and especially Colonel Parker, who for some reason really had a hold on him. Unfortunately, I never saw Elvis pursue his dreams after we parted. I personally feel what really probably killed him, other than drugs, was the fact that he was so bottled up and never had a chance to climb any new mountains."

And as far as the Colonel's influence on Elvis's career and life, Binder stated, "I think the Colonel did a brilliant job promoting and publicizing Elvis, as many businessmen do with a product, but there is a thin line between knowing what the public really wants and I think Elvis even doubted his own talent when we met . . . wondering whether it was all the hype and publicity that really made him a star."

Aloha From Hawaii

Elvis's *Aloha From Hawaii* performance and broadcast was a huge event in the history of the entertainment business. Just after midnight on January 14, 1973, Elvis (dressed in one of his

TABLE 4.6 The Original Credits as they Ran on Elvis's Singer Special in 1968.

Executive Producer: Bob Finkel
Producer & Director: Steve Binder
Writers: Allan Blye, Chris Beard
Music Production: Bones Howe
Musical Direction & Arrangements: William Goldenberg
Special Lyrics & Vocal Arrangements: Earl Brown
Choreography: Jaime Rogers, Claude Thompson
Additional Musical Arrangements: Jack Elliot
Art Direction: Gene McAvoy
Associate Producer: Norman Morrell
Costume Design: Bill Belew
Production Assistant: Patricia Rickey
Assistant to Producer: Ann McClelland
Assistants to Choreographers: Yonko Inone, Eddie James
Production Coordinators: Joe Esposito, Lamar Fike, Tom Diskin
Associate Director: Tom Foulkes
Stage Managers: Glen Huling, Jerry Masterson
Makeup: Claude Thompson
Technical Director: Karl Messerschmidt
Lighting: John Freschi
Audio: Bill Cole
Senior Video: Jerry Smith
Videotape Editors: Wayne Kenworthy, Armond Poitras
Featured Cast: The Blossoms—Fanita James, Jean King, Darlene Love, Buddy Arett, Barbara Burgess, D. J. Fontana, Alan Fortas, Susan Henning, Charles Hodge, Lance LeGault, Tanya Lamani, Scotty Moore, Jaime Rogers, Claude Thompson
Unit Manager: Gene Marcione
A Production of Teram, Inc. Production and Binder/Howe Productions, Inc.

now-familiar white, rhinestone-encrusted jumpsuits), his rhythm section, and a full orchestra took the stage at the Honolulu International Center Arena in Honolulu. The show was beamed live via satellite to over ten countries and was eventually seen in over thirty European countries. This concert was the first worldwide satellite broadcast by a Pop musician. The concert itself was tied in with Elvis's benefit work involving the U.S.S. *Arizona,* and quite a bit of the funds from this concert went to charity.

> ## Cold Hard Fact
>
> In interviews in 1989 Steve Binder shared some interesting tidbits about his impressions of Elvis during production of the 1968 *Singer Special*:
> - Binder watching in amazement as Elvis rehearsed while curled up "in a fetal position" in a pitch-dark studio.
> - Seconds before the opening number of the show, Elvis hid in the studio parking lot, "shaking with fear" at the prospect of performing live for the first time in seven years.
> - Elvis begged Binder to "send the orchestra home" when he turned up to his first rehearsal, because he had never sung along with "trombones and stuff."
> - Binder broke the golden rule in his first meeting with Elvis by telling him he thought his movies and his music at that time were "going nowhere."
>
> Binder and his business partner, Bones Howe, pitched the idea of an *Unplugged* series to MTV bosses years ago but were turned down only to see MTV launch their own successful *Unplugged* format later.

Elvis had arrived in Hawaii on January 9, with rehearsals commencing January 12 (both rehearsals and performance are available on DVD and CD as *Elvis: Aloha from Hawaii*). After the broadcast on January 14, Elvis and his musicians returned to the arena and recorded five additional songs for an expanded version of the show to be shown on U.S. television by NBC on April 4. In total, over one billion people viewed *Aloha From Hawaii*. The accompanying album went platinum and was Elvis's only No. 1 album of the 1970s.

Elvis's career was more than simply Rock and Roll; his early film catalog alone justifies his popularity as an artist, at least up to 1963. His real dream was to be seen as an "all-around entertainer" rather than just a singer of teenage dance songs, and according to his fans he succeeded more than he could have hoped.

TABLE 4.7 Elvis's Radio and Television Appearances

Louisiana Hayride

Elvis performed regularly on this Country music radio program, beginning when he was nineteen. In his first appearance on Hayride, he sang "That's All Right, Mama," the song with which he made his recording debut in 1954. *(Radio, 1954; 5 minutes)*

Stage Show

Elvis made his television debut and five subsequent appearances on *The Dorsey Brothers Stage Show*, produced by entertainer Jackie Gleason, hosted by Jimmy and Tommy Dorsey, between January and March 1956. He performed "Shake, Rattle, and Roll," "I Was the One," "Blue Suede Shoes," "Money Honey," and "Heartbreak Hotel." *(January–March 1956; 15 minutes)*

The Milton Berle Show

Berle's ratings shot up when Elvis Presley appeared (and caused a sensation) on his show. Elvis performed "Hound Dog," and Berle did an Elvis imitation and asked the singer for advice about women. In a record store skit, Elvis performed "I Want You, I Need You, I Love You." Berle presented Elvis with a Billboard award for "Heartbreak Hotel." *(June 5, 1956; 15 minutes)*

The Steve Allen Show

Steve Allen, promising to do a show that "the whole family can watch and enjoy," introduced "the new Elvis Presley" in white tie and tails. Elvis performed "I Want You, I Need You, I Love You" and sang "Hound Dog" to a basset hound. "Tumbleweed Presley" appeared with Allen, Imogene Coca, and Andy Griffith in a western variety-show skit. *(July 1, 1956; 15 minutes)*

The Ed Sullivan Show—September 9, 1956

Ed Sullivan, who had declared that Elvis was "not my cup of tea," bowed to popular pressure and paid him $50,000 for three appearances. In his first appearance, guest host Charles Laughton congratulated Elvis on his unprecedented success and introduced him to his largest audience to date. Elvis, appearing from a studio in Hollywood, performed "Don't Be Cruel," "Ready Teddy," and "Love Me Tender," the title song from his first movie. *(September 9, 1956; 15 minutes)*

The Ed Sullivan Show—October 28, 1956

Sullivan himself hosted Elvis's second appearance on the show. Elvis sang "Don't Be Cruel," "Love Me Tender," the just-released single "Love Me," and "Hound Dog." *(October 28, 1956; 15 minutes)*

The Ed Sullivan Show—January 6, 1957

In his third Sullivan Show appearance, Elvis performed songs including "Don't Be Cruel," "Too Much," "When My Blue Moon Turns to Gold Again," and "Peace in the Valley." *(January 6, 1957; 15 minutes)*

The Frank Sinatra-Timex Show: "It's So Nice to Go Traveling: Welcome Home Elvis"

This special welcomed Elvis back from his eighteen-month stint in the army. Frank Sinatra, his daughter Nancy, Joey Bishop, and Sammy Davis, Jr., recapped the events Elvis missed while he was away in Germany. Elvis sang "To Know That You Love Me Brings Fame and Fortune My Way" and "I'm Stuck on You." In a once-in-a-lifetime duet, Elvis and Frank Sinatra sang "Love Me Tender" and "Witchcraft." *(May 12, 1960; 60 minutes)*

Elvis (Later known as *The '68 Comeback Special, The Singer Special,* and *Singer Presents Elvis*)

This special was Elvis's first television appearance since the 1960 Sinatra show, and one of the most significant events of his career. Having completed more than twenty-nine films and receiving fifty gold records, Presley proved that he was still a vital and exciting live performer and illustrated the importance of his contribution to the contemporary music scene. *(December 3, 1968; 75 minutes)*

Aloha From Hawaii: Dress Rehearsal

Elvis sang "Can't Help Falling in Love" to an audience of excited fans during a rehearsal the day before the live concert, broadcast by NBC *(January 13, 1973; 3 minutes)*

Elvis: Aloha from Hawaii

Following his popular and critical success on television in 1968, Elvis returned to live performing, becoming the toast of Las Vegas and a major attraction at concert arenas around the country. On January 14, this special was the first live television performance to be broadcast via satellite. *(April 4, 1973; 80 minutes)*

Elvis in Concert

Produced by Gary Smith and Dwight Hemion, this special was taped during Elvis's last concert tour and shows what tragically turned out to be his very last live performance. It was broadcast on CBS after his death in August 1977. Interviews with his fans and his father, Vernon, are interspersed with clips of Elvis performing and talking to the audience. *(October 3, 1977; 60 minutes)*

TABLE 4.8 Song Lineup from *Aloha From Hawaii* Show

1. Also Sprach Zarathustra
2. See See Rider
3. Burning Love
4. Something
5. You Gave Me a Mountain
6. Steamroller Blues
7. My Way
8. Love Me
9. Johnny B. Goode
10. It's Over
11. Blue Suede Shoes
12. I'm So Lonesome I Could Cry
13. I Can't Stop Loving You
14. Hound Dog
15. What Now My Love
16. Fever
17. Welcome to My World
18. Suspicious Minds
19. I'll Remember You
20. Long Tall Sally / Whole Lotta Shakin' Goin' On
21. An American Trilogy
22. A Big Hunk o' Love
23. Can't Help Falling in Love

THE BEATLES

The Beatles did not have a movie career comparable to that of Elvis, for one very good reason: They were too busy making incredible music while Elvis was churning out his lightweight location films. During the time that the Beatles were a functioning band, they did five officially released film projects: *A Hard Day's Night, Help!, Magical Mystery Tour, Yellow Submarine,* and *Let It Be. A Hard Day's Night* (1964) and *Help!* (1965) were the first two of a three-picture deal that the group had entered into with United Artists as a result of Brian Epstein's negotiations. Finding a third film that all four Beatles could agree on was difficult, partially because the search for it came during their final touring years, when the band was ready to shed the lovable moptop image that had been portrayed in the first two films.

From left to right, Paul McCartney, George Harrison, Ringo Starr, and John Lennon run down an empty London street in a scene from the movie *A Hard Day's Night*. © *Bettmann/CORBIS*

A Hard Day's Night

A Hard Day's Night, released in 1964, marked the Beatles' debut on the silver screen. This black-and-white documentary-style film follows them through a day of early "Beatlemania" and their journey to do a television performance. Along for the ride is Paul's (fictional) troublemaking grandfather, constantly referred to in the film as being "very clean." Throughout the movie, the group has to dodge screaming fans, avert the press, disobey their managers, and try to keep Paul's grandfather in check. The film ends with the Fab Four giving a wild television performance and moving on to the next show. Chock-full of great songs and energetic performances, fans and critics alike hailed this film, some comparing the young Beatles to the Marx Brothers, with Ringo specifically standing out as a likely actor in days to come.

Help!

In 1965, the Beatles returned to the big screen with *Help!* This action/adventure spoof begins when Ringo gets the sacrificial ring of a Far Eastern cult, known as Kahili, stuck on his finger. While the cult members of Kahili set out to get their ring back, Professor Foot and Algernon, a pair of mad scientists, are also in pursuit of it. The Beatles are chased throughout the world, as both Kahili and the scientists fall over each other trying to get at Ringo and the ring. This was the first Beatles film in color and was much more scripted than *A Hard Day's Night,* with location shots around the globe as they "vacationed" while filming. The Beatles themselves were not as pleased with this movie, due to the simplistic characterizations of them as written by Alun Owen. (For example, John is the "smart" Beatle, Paul is the "cute" Beatle, etc.) John said later, "We were like guest stars in our own film."

Both *A Hard Day's Night* and *Help!* were directed by an industry outsider named Richard Lester, whom John had sought out after seeing a short film Lester had made called *The Running, Jumping and Standing Still Film.* This experimental movie, starring Peter Sellers and Spike Milligan, combined jump cuts with broad, quick comedy. The Beatles were huge fans of this film and of Lester's work with cast members of *The Goon Show,* and they jumped at the chance to work with Lester.

A Hard Day's Night expanded on the techniques Lester used in *The Running,* with its refreshing mix of surrealism, slapstick, and *cinema verité*. Lester's use of hand-held cameras and his quick cutting style proved to be highly influential on the next generation of directors. Steven Soderbergh (*Erin Brockovich* and *Traffic*) and Danny Boyle (*Trainspotting*) both credit Lester as having had major influence on their work.

Lester's love of both movies and the Beatles comes through loud and clear in *A Hard Day's Night,* from the resounding open-

The Beatles, in costume and on location for the film *Help!*, in Obertauern, March 17, 1965. *(Photo by Keystone/Getty Images)*

ing guitar chord of the title track to the unbridled joy in the montage of the band running and jumping (there's not much in the way of standing still) and the strains of "Can't Buy Me Love." Musical sequences like that and Lennon singing "I Should Have Known Better" in a train's luggage compartment led MTV to dub Lester the "father of music video." Lester modestly (or astutely) declines that designation, saying he was merely trying to make the images and music successfully interact. But he managed to accomplish that in a way that captured the spirit of the time, the charisma of the Beatles, and the insanity that was beginning to envelop the band.

Magical Mystery Tour

In 1967, the Beatles concentrated on producing *Magical Mystery Tour,* which debuted on the BBC on December 26, 1967, a huge national holiday known as Boxing Day. It was customary for advertisers, artists, and businesses to show their best on this day to a captive audience of Brits. Because the Beatles chose this moment to unveil their new film, it was a watershed in the public's perception of the group as being infallible.

First shown in black-and-white, the hour-long psychedelic home movie baffled the largely conservative TV audience, while giving critics the much-needed ammunition to try to deflate the egos of the Beatles. Initially lambasted by critics, this film has come to be seen as the harbinger of MTV and video music in general, is still viewed in film classes for its visual techniques and imagery, and is revered by fans as a cult video.

Much has been made of the fact that *Mystery Tour* was the Beatles' first creative venture after Brian Epstein's death. Fans still debate whether the film would have been better if Brian had remained alive due to his input and ability to rein in both Paul's overexuberance and John's negativity or if it might never had been made at all. But this argument is moot. When the group stopped touring in 1965, Epstein became removed from every function and came to serve only as a figurehead in their lives, albeit still an important one. George Martin had taken over the creative care of the band, and they tended to run their own affairs.

The failure of *Mystery Tour* to initially attract a wide audience notwithstanding, it came to be regarded as a pivotal breakthrough in Pop musical filmmaking. Even John Lennon, who was harshly critical of the entire "Magical Mystery Tour" concept Paul had

> **COLD HARD FACT**
>
> The animation of *Yellow Submarine* has sometimes falsely been attributed to the famous psychedelic Pop art artist of the era, Peter Max. He was originally hired to work on the film, but he produced only a few concept drawings before he became too busy with other projects. Max's style, however, heavily influenced the work of many of the artists and animators who worked on the film. Heinz Edelman supervised the film's artwork, while British animation producer George Dunning directed the movie.

concocted, later said he enjoyed the casual atmosphere of the film, with its variety of skits filmed on location in the U.K.

Yellow Submarine

In 1968, work began on *Yellow Submarine,* a full-length animated feature film. The Beatles were not enthusiastic about participating in a motion picture at the time, partly because they were experiencing personal stress (the band was already beginning to break apart), and partly because they were still under critical fire for *Magical Mystery Tour.* Actors were hired to imitate the Fab Four's voices in the film. However, after seeing the finished film, the boys did agree to make a cameo appearance in the final scene of the film just before the closing credits. The cameo was originally supposed to feature psychedelic colors, but due to time and budget constraints, it was left in the normal form. (The black background was meant to be replaced with hand-drawn images.) Over the years, *Yellow Submarine* proved to be a groundbreaking children's film, delighting audiences worldwide for its wild imagery and interwoven musical themes. Even more than thirty years later, it consistently placed high on lists of favorite films.

Let It Be

The year 1970 brought a close to the Beatles saga and one final film, *Let It Be.* Shot in 1969, the film was intended to be a documentary of the rebirth of the Beatles but turned out to be a portrait of the band's slow demise and all its associated acrimony. The original idea was to film the band rehearsing and then performing a live concert in front of an audience. Initially planned as a TV documentary, the Beatles released it as a feature when they realized this would satisfy the terms of their three-picture deal with United Artists. What they committed to film were countless hours of seemingly aimless jam sessions, arguments, and a hurried yet remarkable final concert on the roof of the Apple building in London. The film ends with the London police attempting to shut the rooftop performance down and John's witty remark "I'd like to thank the group and ourselves, and I hope we passed the audition!" It is the one Beatles film that won an Academy Award (for Best Score), and the title song, composed by Lennon and McCartney, won a Grammy for Best Song in 1970.

Besides appearing in all the official Beatles films, each member of the band participated in individual film projects, with two Beatles pursuing acting and the other two composing soundtracks. In 1966, John played Private Gripweed in Richard Lester's film *How I Won the War*. That same year, Paul composed music for the film *The Family Way*. George supplied the music for the feature film *Wonderwall* in 1967, and Ringo, the Beatle who got the best reviews for his natural acting ability, appeared in the films *Candy, The Magic Christian,* and *Caveman,* and did some television work, including on the children's show *Shining Time Station* in the early 1990s. The 1988 documentary *Imagine: John Lennon* was an insightful look into the life of John and Yoko, complete with unreleased demos such as "Real Love" and marvelous domestic footage from their UK home. A 2007 musical film entitled *Across the Universe* featured over thirty Beatles songs as a backdrop for a fictional love story, and received nominations for both a Golden Globe and a Grammy.

Beatles Films That Might Have Been

The Beatles had a number of opportunities to make additional films, but for various reasons these projects did not come to fruition. Much of this can be attributed to the beginnings of the dissolution of the group, as each individual member of the band began to explore his own vision rather than a shared one.

The Yellow Teddybears

A year before *A Hard Day's Night,* the Beatles were offered a cameo role in the 1963 film *The Yellow Teddybears*. The plot revolved around a group of teenage girls who wore yellow teddy bear pins as their badge of carnal knowledge. Since 1963 was the year that Beatlemania originated, it's not surprising that the band turned down involvement in a film in which they would not be the stars. Also, the possibility of performing other people's songs probably killed serious consideration.

A Talent for Loving

The Beatles considered experimenting in the genre of the American Western. *A Talent for Loving* was based on a novel with the same title by Richard Condon (author of *The Manchurian Candidate).* The story was based on a real horse race in the 1870s in which the prize was a wealthy girl! The Beatles would play pioneers in the old West who had traveled from Liverpool (to get around the problem of their distinctive accent). The Beatles' fascination with the Old West was evident when the group decked out in cowboy attire in various photo shoots from 1954 to1964 (and on the back of their *Rubber Soul* album). Although they acquired the rights to the film, the Beatles finally rejected it and someone else released it in 1969.

The Jungle Book

Brian Epstein and Walt Disney met in late August 1965 to discuss the Beatles appearing in and/or supplying some music for Disney's next film, *The Jungle Book.* However, John was already bitter due to lack of creative control over the *Beatles* cartoon series that was set to premier on the ABC television network in September, and when Epstein mentioned the Disney idea to him, he exploded, being in no mood to hear of yet another animation project. An incarnation of the Fab Four did appear in *The Jungle Book,* as four friendly vultures with moptop hair and British accents sing to the Mowgli character a song titled "We're Your Friends," but the real Beatles had nothing to do with it.

Lord of the Rings

John wanted the Beatles to do a version of *Lord of the Rings* and intended to cast himself in the most attention-getting role. The Beatles' version would have had John playing the grasping, thieving creature Gollum, Paul as the hero Frodo, George as the wise wizard Gandalf, and Ringo playing Frodo's devoted sidekick, Sam. The plan fell flat when the author J.R.R. Tolkein, who still had the film rights, rejected the idea of the group's doing it. Also, the possibility of John's playing the starring role might not have sat well with the other Beatles.

The Three Musketeers

The Beatles also turned down a comedy version of Alexander Dumas's classic novel *The Three Musketeers*. Supposedly, Brigitte Bardot would have starred as Lady de Winter, which was probably a big selling point for the Bardot-obsessed Lennon. There had already been three versions of *The Three Musketeers* filmed before the group considered it. The Beatles eventually rejected the idea. Richard Lester, the director of *A Hard Day's Night* and *Help!* went on to direct the 1974 version of *The Three Musketeers,* which is very similar to the kind of wild chase and deadpan humor that characterized the Beatles' first two films.

Shades of a Personality

At the end of 1966, producer Walter Shenson announced a project in which the Beatles would, for a change, not play themselves or four characters who look, think, and talk like the Beatles. Tentatively titled *Beatles 3* (it would have been their third movie), the storyline was similar to that of the *Quadrophrenia* project realized by the Who in 1973. The script called for a man (to be played by John) suffering from a three-way split personality, with the remaining Beatles playing each of these personalities. Since schedule conflicts prevented Richard Lester from directing it, Michelangelo Antonioni was announced as a possible director. The project wasn't rejected outright but simply fell through the cracks in the group's hectic schedule of 1967.

Up Against It

At the same time that *Shades of a Personality* was being considered, Joe Orton was approached about writing a screenplay for the Beatles. The Beatles and Epstein probably considered the up-and-coming new playwright the logical choice to write a "serious" third movie. In addition McCartney had invested in one of Orton's plays.

Orton received a $12,000 advance from producer Walter Shenson for a screenplay and set about writing. Although he took the basic idea from *Shades of a Personality,* he adapted it using elements of two of his novels, *The Silver Bucket,* published in

1953, and his 1961 novel *Head to Toe*. The final title became *Up Against It*. As Orton described it, "with its political assassination, guerilla warfare, and transvestitism, it might have been designed with the Beatles in mind!" Orton delivered the script in late February 1967, and it was returned from Epstein's office in April without a reason for its rejection.

Years later, McCartney explained why *Up Against It* was rejected: "We weren't gay and really that was all there was to it. Now, it wasn't that we were anti-gay, just that we, the Beatles, weren't gay." Richard Lester reasoned, "I don't think that it would have worked at all. I don't think they possessed the acting skills to deal with those linguistic acrobatics that Orton demanded."

Comparison

Elvis and the Beatles will always be remembered as rock stars above all, but their ventures into cinematic production were also very interesting aspects of their careers. For Elvis, moviemaking was a huge part of his life, as he starred in many films from the late 1950s through the late 1960s, but for the Beatles filmmaking was just another venue for selling records.

Elvis enjoyed acting, whereas the Beatles (save for the ever-enthusiastic Ringo!) merely tolerated being on-screen. Elvis earned more in the movie houses than did the Beatles, as his films were money-making machines. The Beatles' songs were always highlights of their theatrical endeavors, whereas some of Elvis's later film songs were downright bad! Ultimately, both Elvis and the Beatles lost interest in filmmaking to pursue making music. Elvis ended his moviemaking on a high note with *Change of Habit* in 1969 and moved into the final live-performance phase of his career. Luckily for fans, Elvis was just beginning his drug dalliances at this time, and even later films, such as *Elvis on Tour* (1972), mask any signs of this pervasive problem from his adoring public. The Beatles film *Let It Be* was released last (1970) and was the unfortunate document of a band's breakup, but the group had lost interest in filmmaking as early as 1967, even as they worked on *Magical Mystery Tour,* and showed only peripheral participation in the animated *Yellow Submarine* project. While fans do return to Elvis and the Beatles films with nostalgic interest, it will be their fine recordings and musical performances that stand the test of time.

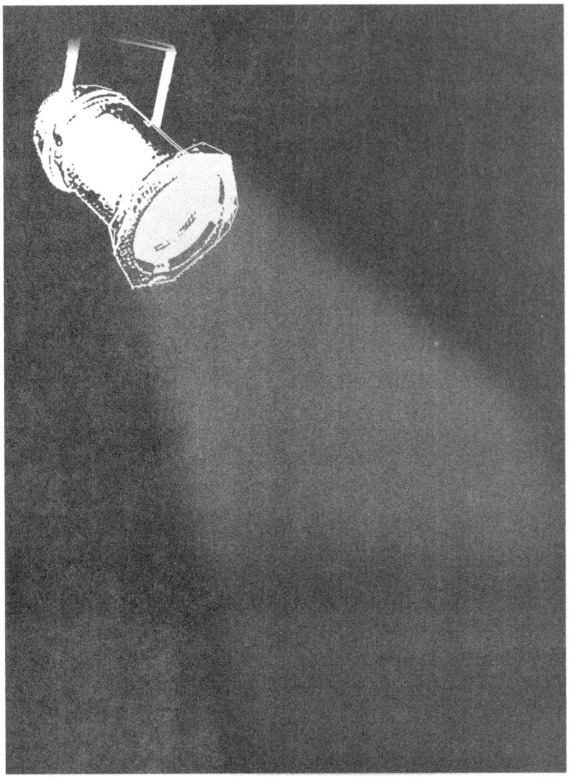
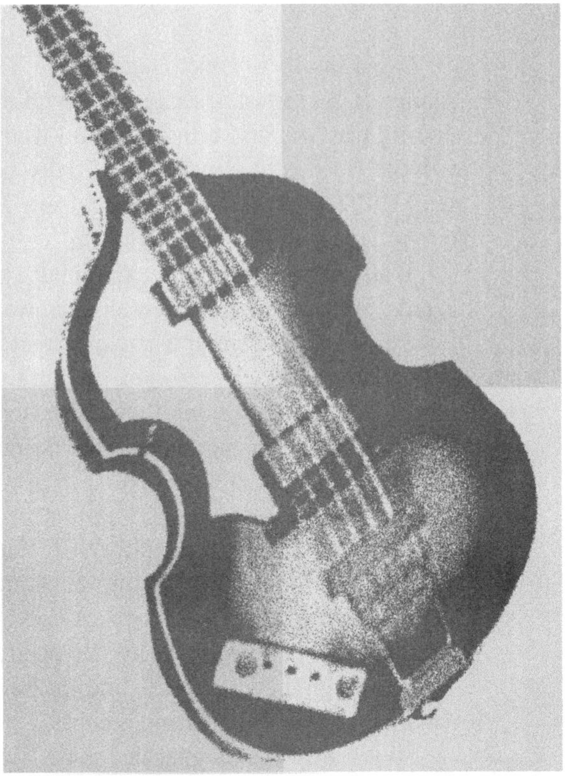
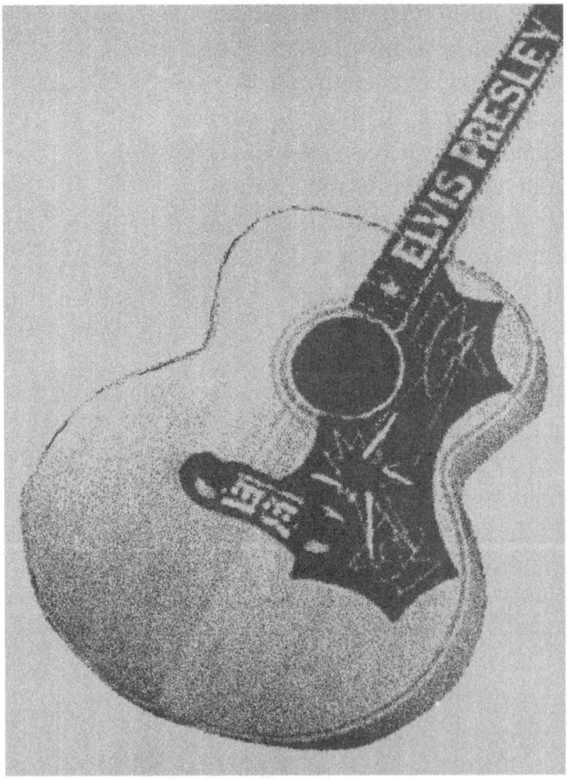
ELVIS PRESLEY
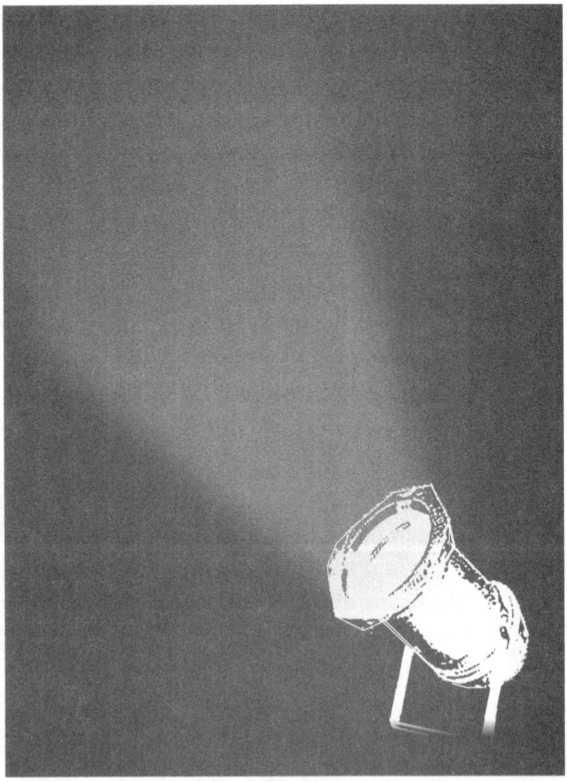

Chapter 5

Drugs and Alternative Lifestyles

The prevalence of drug and alcohol abuse in the history of Pop music dates back to the use of marijuana by early Jazz players who were searching for ways to enhance their expressive abilities. Even the "Father of Jazz," Louis Armstrong, admitted to using "mezz," an early slang term for marijuana. More potent drugs, such as heroin, soon became the drugs of choice for such artists as vocalist Billie Holiday and Bebop sax player Charlie Parker. The great Jazz innovator Miles Davis struggled with drug addiction, and young pianist Kenny Kirkland, who recorded frequently with Sting in the 1990s, succumbed to heroin abuse.

The period from the late 1960s through the 1970s is often referred to as the "feel good" years, when drug use was no longer confined mainly to "hippies" and counterculture types but had become accepted behavior among mainstream Hollywood actors and studios. Cocaine soon became the favored drug of the movie stars, while pot (marijuana) and LSD remained choice among musicians. Some doctors freely prescribed medications for patients and even touted the benefits of pills in everyday life. The Pop music world, in particular, carried drug abuse to scandalous extremes. Artists such as Frankie Lymon (lead singer of the Teenagers, whose debut single was "Why Do Fools Fall In Love"), Jimi Hendrix, Janis Joplin, and Kurt Cobain suffered from drug addictions that ruined their careers and ended their lives prematurely.

The drug histories of both Elvis Presley and the Beatles are especially well known because of the magnitude of their celebrity.

Living in the spotlight has both advantages and disadvantages, and the intense scrutiny of personal habits and choices (whether right or wrong) fall in the latter category. What both Elvis and the Beatles shared in this regard was a penchant for experimentation and the financial ability to indulge themselves to a far greater extent than ordinary people could. Whether the results made up for the risks is for history to decide.

Elvis

Elvis Presley was probably introduced to prescription drugs while in the U.S. Army, where he served from March 1958 to March 1960. His back problems were treated with painkillers, his insomnia with sleeping pills, his anxiety with depressants, and his lethargy with stimulants. Unlike the Beatles, Elvis did not start out using drugs in a "recreational or creative" fashion. Elvis took drugs to feel better, out of boredom and frustration, and to simply escape unpleasant situations in his life.

According to Elvis's close friend Lamar Fike "Elvis was the kind of guy who would dodge reality. He didn't like to face things." David Stanley, Elvis's stepbrother, had a similar take on the situation: "Drugs were Elvis's escape from reality. He didn't take them to get happy. He took them to get unconscious. He often said, 'I'd rather be unconscious than miserable.'"

One might ask why someone as great as Elvis, with such immense fame, fortune, and popularity, would need to escape from reality. But when one examines his life more closely, it becomes clear that his unique career was characterized by a stressful roller-coaster pattern of effort, success, defeat, and comeback. Sadly, the defeats often led to an increase in drug intake. Then, his comebacks typically involved desperate efforts to "get it together" before pending concerts, movies, or tours.

Elvis returned from his military service a changed man, not only musically but also personally. His career soon took a new turn, as he transformed himself from a rebellious Rock 'n' Roller into a Pop crooner and movie actor, and his life at Graceland soon included the presence of his bride, Priscilla Beaulieu. However, after making an endless string of B movies throughout the 1960s, Elvis became bored and frustrated, and turned to drugs as a means of relaxation and escape. Wanting desperately to return to live performing, he cleaned up his act prior to his 1968 *Singer Special* (also known as *The '68 Comeback Special*), in which he appeared slim and healthy.

Just What the Doctor Ordered

During the late '60s and into the early '70s, Elvis justified his continued use of pills because they were prescribed for him, which meant they were "legal." Elvis's personal physician, Dr. George Nichopoulos, was his chief supplier, though Elvis often visited dentists while touring various cities in order to obtain premium narcotics.

When Elvis imbibed, he clearly wasn't seeking "spiritual awakening" or musical growth and creativity through mind-expanding substances. He was just becoming comfortably numb. Though musicians prior to Elvis had used drugs for various purposes, Elvis was quite conservative in his upbringing, and did not dabble in drugs "recreationally" but saw himself using them only for "medical reasons." Whether or not Elvis ever tried to "expand his mind" in a creative fashion through all his pill-popping is open to debate, though his lack of musical growth stylistically and his inability to create original music are possible signs that he was simply out of it, for the most part, rather than inspired. Elvis looked to books for enlightenment rather than drugs, and was quite open in his criticism of illegal drugs in Rock 'n' Roll.

In fact, one of the ironies of Elvis's turbulent life lay in his sincere belief that the Beatles, the Rolling Stones, and other "drug-oriented" Rock bands were promoting rampant drug use and subverting the youth of America, and that he personally had a responsibility to do something about it, even though he was hooked on pills himself! In December 1970, Elvis flew to Washington, D.C., to discuss America's drug problems with then-president Richard M. Nixon. Afraid for his safety without his entourage, he quickly returned to Los Angeles, but just as quickly gathered up several of the Memphis Mafia and returned to the nation's capitol on a mission. On the way, Elvis hand-wrote a six-page letter to the president, on American Airlines stationery, requesting a personal meeting to discuss his desire to join the crusade against illegal drugs by becoming an official Drug Enforcement Agency special assistant. Nixon agreed to honor his request.

After receiving his prestigious badge and identification, Elvis returned to Graceland and enlisted the services of his stepbrothers, Ricky and David, who were still in high school, to fill prescriptions written out to them and then turn the pills over to Elvis while also acting as undercover narcs at the school. And as is the case with most addicts, having those around him participate in his habit, including the members of the Memphis Mafia, was essential to Elvis. To help him assuage his own guilt, he would claim that he wasn't really a drug addict, because (1) drug addicts use needles, and he only took pills at the time, and (2) he was a deputized government agent and needed to be closely involved in the drug world. Elvis was extremely serious about his personal war on drugs, stressing to anyone who would listen that he was now a deputized U.S. federal narcotics officer directly linked to the president, with all his personal weapons at his disposal to support his crusade.

Nevertheless, as the 1970s unfolded, Elvis's drug use increased dramatically, though documentaries from this period, such as *Elvis: That's the Way It Is* and *Elvis: On Tour,* were deliberately shot to mask any appearance of "the King" as less than sober. Meanwhile, though Elvis appeared easygoing to the public during this period, his personal life was in turmoil. Priscilla had reached her limit with his cheating, drug dependence, and neglectful treatment of her, and filed for divorce. Elvis's career was also in a downturn, as younger Pop groups, such as the Beatles and the Rolling Stones, came to rule the world over which he had once reigned. His dreams of touring the world and appearing in quality films had been quashed by Colonel Parker for reasons discussed earlier in this book. Thus, with many aspects of his life in turmoil, Elvis escaped into a world of narcotics.

Gaining Weight, Losing Control

By the mid 1970s, telltale signs of Elvis's self-destruction were appearing to fans and critics. Elvis had always eaten more than he should of the wrong kinds of foods, but several of his prescriptions also served as appetite stimulants, and he quickly gave in to this hunger with noticeable results. By 1975, the year Elvis turned forty, his weight had become a topic of public discussion, with comedians and talk-show hosts regularly getting laughs at his expense. The drugs' effects also became apparent onstage. Elvis was touring smaller venues on a grueling schedule arranged by Colonel Parker to keep the money coming in. But Elvis was no longer reliable. Sometimes he didn't even bother to show up. When he did make it onstage, he would often forget song lyrics or mumble incoherently, split the pants of his ill-fitting jumpsuits, or simply sit or lie down while performing.

Offstage, Elvis, who had always exhibited a quick temper, became more violent and threatened those around him both physically and verbally while under the influence. He was frequently hospitalized for a variety of ailments, from ear, eye, and throat infections to intestinal problems that had plagued him since childhood. But it was common knowledge that these visits were often detoxification periods for Elvis, with only short-term positive results evident.

Elvis's drug use and resulting changes in behavior were bad enough to drive away his steady girlfriend, Linda Thompson. He quickly replaced her with a Priscilla-lookalike named Ginger Alden. However Elvis was always careful to hide his drug use from Lisa Marie, who remained unaware of this aspect of her father until many years after his death.

In his final two years, Elvis rarely recorded outside the confines of his den at Graceland. Stanley describes this sad period of his life as a time of constant drug use and marked decline in his 1994 book *The Elvis Encyclopedia*.

> *At the end, Elvis had a trailer in the back of Graceland where a full-time nurse lived. And in that trailer was a drug store. Every night about 12 or 1 we'd give Elvis what we called Attack 1. It was a package of eleven drugs, including three shots of Demerol. Then Elvis would eat. And you had to stay with him for that, because sometimes he was so stoned that he'd choke on his food. Then, after he fell asleep, you'd have to sit there and watch him. And about three or four hours later, he'd wake up and take another package of drugs which we called Attack 2. After several more hours of sleep, Elvis would wake again and take Attack 3. One of us would have to be with him 24 hours a day. It was bad craziness, and no one knew how to break the cycle.*

Even though Dr. Nick prescribed over five thousand pills and vials for him in the six months leading up to his death, Elvis did not die from a drug overdose. When Elvis passed away, on August 16, 1977, at age forty-two, an autopsy was performed immediately. Tennessee's chief medical examiner, Dr. Jerry T. Francisco, held a press conference to report the possible causes of the King's death. They

Elvis, at 42 years old, performing in Lincoln, Nebraska, just two months before his death on August 16, 1977. © *Bettmann/CORBIS*

included clogged arteries, high blood pressure, and an enlarged heart, with the official cause listed as "cardiac arrhythmia," an irregular heartbeat. Some skeptics speculated that Elvis gave himself a massive heart attack while attempting to relieve his bowels, a painful situation exacerbated by drug use leading to severe constipation. Interestingly, no mention was made of the presence of any drugs in Elvis's bloodstream, though subsequent reports indicate the following substances were found: Ethinamate, Methaqualone (sedatives), barbiturates, codeine (painkillers and depressants), Placidyl, Valium, Demerol, Meperidine, Morphine (painkillers and tranquilizers), and Chloropheniname (antihistamine).

THE BEATLES

The Beatles' introduction to drugs came about as a perceived necessity during their performances in Hamburg, first at the Indra

> **COLD HARD FACT**
>
> All of the Beatles did their share of pranks both on and off the stage, but John was the one responsible for their most memorable moments. Appearing onstage with a toilet seat around his neck, engaging in fistfights with drunken audience members, and swearing at and haranguing patrons while pretending to be Hitler were just a few of the antics he was known for.

Club and later at the more upscale Kaiserkeller and the Top Ten Club. These performances required them to play grueling two-hour sets, four sets a night, seven nights a week. Even their youthful energy could not keep them up, so they began to take amphetamines, specifically Preludin, which they nicknamed "Prellies." Paul has stated that the pills were cheap and legal and, if consumed with alcohol, would keep the user awake and energetic for hours. In addition, the German audiences were composed mainly of German and English sailors, prostitutes, and bikers, who demanded that the Beatles "*Mach schau*!" ("Make a show!"). Naturally, the lads complied, and the stories surrounding their antics onstage and in Hamburg—largely fueled by their drug taking—are legendary.

As the decade of the sixties went into overdrive, the Beatles were leading the charge, and their experimentation in the name of creativity knew no bounds. As a result, various myths sprung up regarding the lyrics to a number of their songs from this period, beginning with the *Rubber Soul* and *Revolver* albums. Many discographers consider these two LPs to be a matched pair, and both were said to have been conceived while the Beatles were smoking marijuana, which was introduced to them in 1965 by Bob Dylan and Al Aronowitz, a Rock journalist and Dylan's biographer.

Aronowitz described the Beatles' first pot-smoking experience (in a *Washington Post* article titled "The Rock Journalist at a High Point in Music History," published August 3, 2005) as follows:

> *[The Beatles] wanted to know how the marijuana would make them feel, and we told them it would make them feel*

good. I still hadn't learned how to roll a joint in those days, so when the Beatles agreed to try some, I asked Dylan to roll the first joint." In later years, Ringo related that marijuana initially made him laugh uncontrollably, which is confirmed by Aronowitz: *"John [commanded Ringo to try it first]. That act instantly revealed the Beatles' pecking order. Obviously, Ringo was the low man on the totem pole. When Ringo hesitated, John made some sort of wisecrack about Ringo being his royal taster. . . . Soon, Ringo got the giggles. In no time at all, he was laughing hysterically. His laughing looked so funny that the rest of us started laughing hysterically at the way Ringo was laughing hysterically. Soon, Ringo pointed at the way Brian Epstein was laughing, and we all started laughing hysterically at the way Brian was laughing."*

It was also reported that Paul exclaimed that he could, for the first time, finally "think" after first trying pot, and that he asked Mal Evans, the Beatles' assistant, to write down everything he was saying. The Beatles were quite enamored with marijuana and its mild hallucinatory effects.

The immediate result of the Beatles' initiation into marijuana was the new musical direction it took them in, as they thought more and more along the lines of creative experimentation in their productions, and it permanently changed them from a "singles" band to a "studio" band. You can hear the echoes of Dylan in Lennon tracks like "Norwegian Wood," a moody and introspective

COLD HARD FACT

In 2000, Cherri Gilham, a journalist who wrote for *The Daily Mail, The Guardian, The Observer,* and other British papers, disputed the story that Bob Dylan and Al Aronowitz were the first to introduce John Lennon to marijuana. She wrote, "I don't wish to be a killjoy . . . but I know for certain that it wasn't [the first time] for John Lennon. Lennon took his first puff or two of pot a few months earlier; in the spring of '64, in a basement flat in Bayswater. Not only did he smoke his first joint, or 'reefer,' as it was called then, but he also threw up. I know this because I was there."

> ## COLD HARD FACT
>
> Because of the weird images in the song, and the initials in the song title, it's widely believed that the song "Lucy in the Sky With Diamonds" is about the drug LSD. The Beatles maintained for many years that the song was not about drugs at all. They maintained that John's son Julian, a four-year-old at the time, inspired the title. He brought home a picture he drew in nursery school, and when John asked him what it was, he told John it was his friend, Lucy, in the sky, with diamonds. John also said in interviews that the "Wool and Water" chapter in Lewis Carroll's *Through the Looking Glass* inspired the lyrics of the song, specifically the part in which Alice is taken down a river in a rowboat by the queen, who has suddenly changed into a sheep. Additional images came from things like the plastic ties worn on *The Goon Show*, one of John's favorite British television programs.
>
> However, in a 2004 interview in *Uncut* magazine, after insisting that the song had indeed been named for the drawing by Julian, Paul also acknowledged that, "it's pretty obvious" that "Lucy in the Sky" is about an acid trip.

number that was a long way from "Do You Want to Know a Secret." (Dylan, for his part, would put more Rock in his Folk, performing with an electric guitar for the first time in 1965. Bob Dylan was impressed with how quickly the Beatles assimilated new musical styles—including his own acoustic guitar style—and later joked about regretting that he had turned the Beatles on to marijuana, according to the *Washington Post* article cited earlier.)

The maturity of the songs on both *Rubber Soul* and *Revolver* is astonishing. From John's "Nowhere Man," a song about alienation and lack of self-confidence, to Paul's "Drive My Car," about a smug, self-righteous Pop star, these songs revealed a new depth and vision that took a listener's breath away. New instruments were introduced, not only to the Beatles but also to the music world at large. These include a number of "firsts," such as George's playing sitar on "Norwegian Wood" (first use of this instrument on a Rock album), and Paul's playing fuzz bass with a distinctly distorted tone on "Think for Yourself."

Subsequent albums displayed the influence of mind-altering chemicals, from *Sgt. Pepper's Lonely Hearts Club Band* ("With A

The Beatles and friends meet with the Maharishi Mahesh Yogi, September 4, 1967. From left to right: Paul McCartney, Jane Asher, Patti Harrison, Ringo Starr, his wife Maureen, John Lennon (1940–1980), George Harrison (1943–2001) and Maharishi Mahesh Yogi. *(Photo by Keystone Features/Hulton Archive/Getty Images)*

COLD HARD FACT

Both Roger McGuinn and David Crosby of the Byrds met with the Beatles (John and George in particular) many times during 1965 before the songs for *Rubber Soul* were recorded and written. McGuinn was already an experienced user of LSD; the Beatles had taken the drug but hadn't experienced its full impact. The Beatles took LSD and played around with guitars alongside McGuinn and Crosby. George borrowed heavily from the Byrds for his composition "If I Needed Someone." McGuinn and Crosby introduced George to Ravi Shankar and John Coltrane.

> **COLD HARD FACT**
>
> Not everyone associated with the Beatles was taking drugs or enamored by their use of drugs. Speaking at the Association of Chief Police Officers (ACPO) conference in June 1998, Sir George Martin recalled his anguish and frustration when John began experimenting with drugs in the late 1960s. Martin said the Beatles knew he disapproved of their taking drugs, and he said his relationship with them was a bit like that of a teacher with his class. He stated that John often looked "under the weather" during recording sessions and that his condition deteriorated over time. The veteran record producer said he was "sickened" by the extent of drug abuse in the music industry, stating, "Everybody does it. That is what frightens me."

Little Help From My Friends," "Fixing a Hole," and "A Day in the Life"), to *The White Album* ("Bungalow Bill," "Yer Blues"), to *Abbey Road* ("I Want You [She's So Heavy]," "Come Together"). The incredible diversity of musical styles, instrumentation, and recording techniques has never been equaled. The Beatles' drug experimentation undoubtedly helped advance the art of music production as a whole. By taking chances with their musical image, they continually pushed themselves to be creative and produce quality work. According to Ken Townsend, the general manager of Abbey Road Studios (where the Beatles recorded most of their work), because of the Beatles' massive success, they gained clout with the music studios and were able to pioneer new studio techniques. Equipment improved drastically due to the demands the world began placing on the recording industry.

The Beatles were the first Rock musicians to experiment with meaningful lyrics and incorporate orchestral instruments, as well as the more unusual instruments, into traditional Rock style. In their own words over many years, they attributed their explosion of creativity largely to their experimentation with drugs. While they have all collectively and individually gone on record as stating that drug use is not for everyone, it clearly played a role in their development as artists.

Comparison

While the great debate regarding the impact of drugs on music and popular culture rages on, the passing of time helps put some of this activity in perspective. During the heyday of drug activity among American youth, with 1967 perhaps the high point (pun intended), Elvis was already thirty-two and singing Pop songs in above-average films, while the Beatles had just released their psychedelic masterpiece, *Sgt. Pepper's Lonely Hearts Club Band*. Drugs undeniably played a role in both Elvis's and the Beatles' lives and in their development as artists, but to the eventual detriment of their talents as writers and performers. Elvis did not have an intimate support group like the four Lads from Liverpool. He was solo, and his "Memphis Mafia" were sycophants more than supporters. They did whatever he wished them to do and did not curtail Elvis's drug addiction in any meaningful way. Also, unlike the Fab Four, Elvis was truly an addict and remained in denial about his addiction until the day he died, and his artistry clearly suffered due to his habit.

The Beatles' music, some say, became more flowery and ornate with their use of drugs. Marijuana seemed to unleash creative juices in the Fab Four, particularly in the writing styles of John and Paul, unseen to that point in music history. The wave of "psychedelic music" initiated in the United States by the Warlocks in 1965 (soon to become the Grateful Dead) and other drug-oriented groups, such as the Doors and the Jefferson Airplane, can also be seen in the Beatles' albums of the mid 1960s. This process of using drugs to get a creative "high" was captured in the Beatles' unique creations, from "Strawberry Fields Forever" to "Lucy in the Sky with Diamonds," all reflecting their new perception of the world through a drug-altered experience.

The Beatles admitted to using LSD as well as pot (but did not openly encourage youth to participate). Perhaps, had the Beatles known of the physical and psychological dangers posed by heavier drugs, they would have approached things differently. But the Beatles' fortuitous timing was perhaps their greatest talent, and their use of drugs as a creative tool was part of this historic synchronicity. Had they not participated, one has to wonder if they still would have been "The Beatles" as people came to know them, on the leading edge of the alternative lifestyles of their era.

Over time John, Paul, George, and Ringo reexamined their reliance on drugs to promote their creativity and eventually stopped using chemicals altogether. All four men publicly stated that they felt drugs were not necessary to spark their creativity.

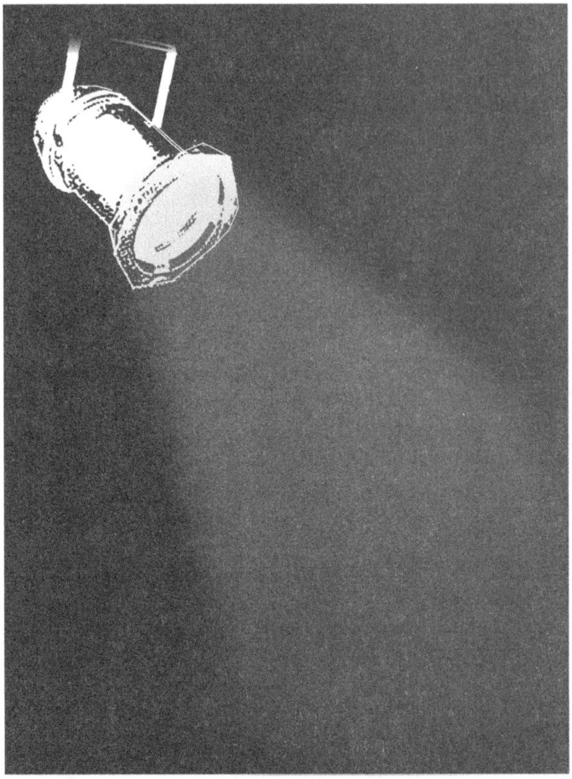

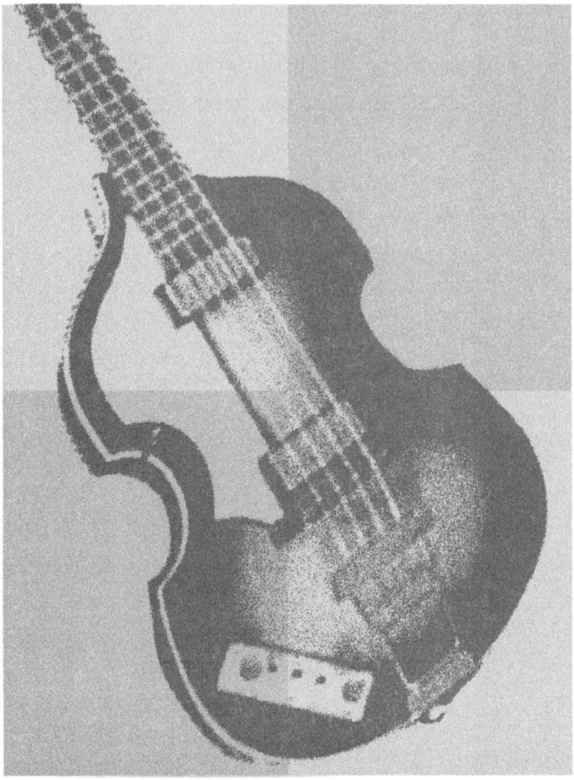

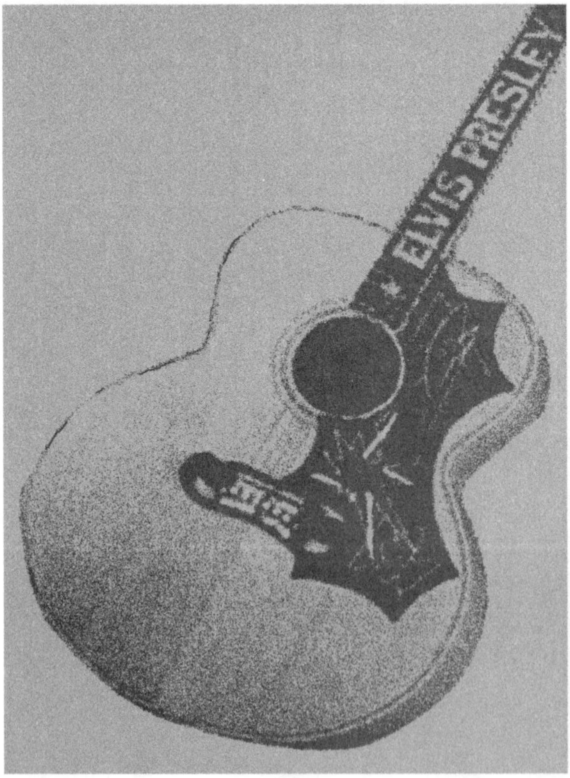
ELVIS PRESLEY

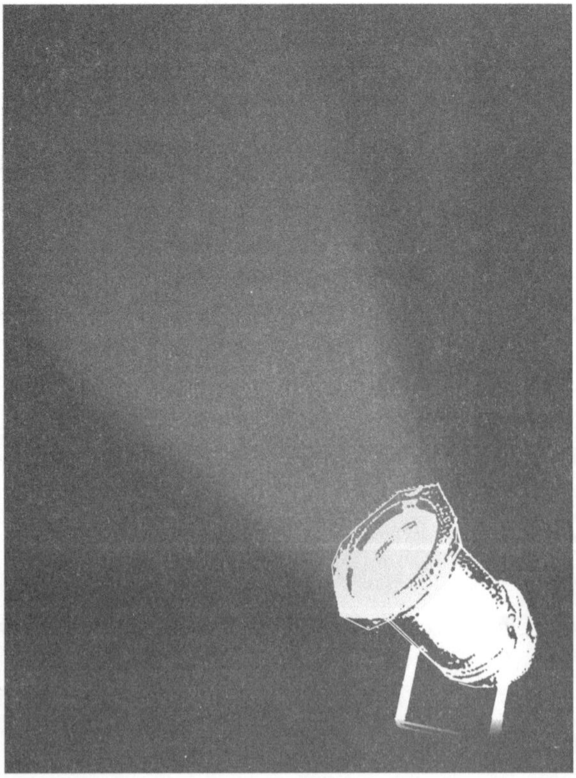

CHAPTER 6

The Business of Being a Pop Star

Elvis was the King of Rock 'n' Roll, and the Beatles ruled the Pop charts for over a decade, but none of these individuals excelled at the business end of music. For Elvis, it was a combination of lack of formal education, a poverty-stricken upbringing, and a love for extravagance over substance that led to his lack of personal savings. Elvis lived for the moment, and spent accordingly. The Beatles enjoyed the trappings of wealth—fine houses, luxury trips, expensive belongings—but only Paul seemed to have any knack for keeping a flush savings account. This may have largely been due to the times. IRAs, 401Ks, and other extended, high-interest-yielding investments were the domain of bankers, not Rock stars, and neither Elvis nor the Beatles trusted banks. Goods and possessions and ready cash seemed more important than bankbooks with many zeros.

ELVIS

Elvis was a great singer and a wonderful performer, but he was certainly not an astute businessman or forward-looking financial planner. For the most part, he was unconcerned about his finances once his success was assured, and left many of his business affairs to his father, Vernon, to handle. Elvis once remarked that, with his

Elvis and Liberace performing as each other . . . Liberace gave up his piano and gold-sequined jacket to Elvis for his guitar and striped sports coat in an impromptu jam session backstage after Liberace's appearance at the Riviera Hotel in Las Vegas, November 16, 1956. © *Bettmann/CORBIS*

newfound financial freedom, he could buy all the cheeseburgers and Pepsi he wanted. His extravagances ranged from his buying an entire fleet of cars for his friends to his giving many thousands of dollars to various charities throughout his life. (In 1968, he donated a Rolls Royce to a Hollywood woman's charity benefiting retarded children, raising $35,000 for that cause.)

> **COLD HARD FACT**
>
> In his later years of performing, Elvis handed out extravagant gifts of costly jewelry to his fans from the stage. In one infamous act of largesse, Elvis gave away nearly $35,000 worth of jewelry to fans during one concert in 1976.

Elvis spent money like water, showered his friends (and even strangers on occasion) with expensive gifts, and he was the best friend of every car dealer in Memphis when his urge to buy vehicles hit. He was charitable and generous to a fault, and filled Graceland with luxurious (some say tacky) furnishings and decorations, including many pricey personal belongings, such as guns, jewelry, and a variety of musical instruments. Elvis's money was tied up in dozens of cars, motorcycles and jets, as well as houses in Los Angeles, Memphis, and Aspen. He traveled extensively, taking his entourage with him, and always picked up the bill for everyone. The Memphis Mafia (his group of close friends, hangers on, and sycophants) rarely received salaries, but the fringe benefits were outrageous–cars, horses, houses, trips, and the like.

The King's Estate

When Elvis passed away at Graceland on August 16, 1977, he had a little over $1.5 million in his personal checking account. His will appointed his father, Vernon, as executor and trustee. Other beneficiaries included Elvis's grandmother, Minnie Mae Presley, and his daughter, Lisa Marie, then nine years old. Additional provisions included a moderate sum for Priscilla and child support for Lisa Marie. The will stipulated that Vernon Presley could, at his discretion, provide funds to other family members as necessary. When Vernon passed away in 1979 and Minnie Mae Presley in 1980, Lisa Marie Presley became the sole heir to Elvis's estate. The will specified that her inheritance be held in trust for her until her twenty-fifth birthday (February 1, 1993).

On June 7, 1982, Priscilla and investment manager Jack Soden, who together had formed Elvis Presley Enterprises, Inc. (EPE) to conduct business and manage the estate's assets, opened

> **COLD HARD FACT**
>
> Within days of his death, Elvis's records began to be reissued in various collector's sets and compilations, which for years generated a tremendous amount of "silent income" to EPE's merchandise inventory. This included rarities, interviews, bootlegs, alternate takes, unreleased concert songs, European releases, and fan club collections.

Graceland to the public, with Priscilla becoming chief executive of Elvis's estate. EPE currently holds all of the merchandising rights to Elvis products and name and likenesses.

In 1983, EPE acquired the shopping center plaza across the street from Graceland under a long-term lease agreement. After Elvis's death, this urban strip mall had quickly become an outlet for cheap Elvis souvenirs and bootleg items, none of which were licensed by EPE. Once acquisition of this property was secured, EPE began to upgrade the facilities and crack down on the sale of non-licensed items. The property was finally purchased in 1993 and became known as Graceland Plaza.

As early as 1979, Probate Judge Joseph Evans ordered an investigation into Parker's relationship with the Presley estate, and by 1981 the Shelby County, Tennessee Probate Court issued a cessation of all payments to Parker, and suggested that Presley's estate (Priscilla and family) bring suit against Parker and RCA for improper activities. This suit was settled via an undisclosed payment from RCA, and in 1983, litigation ended, business affairs ended, with Colonel Parker giving up all of his audio and video rights for a large financial settlement. In 1984, Elvis's airplanes were purchased back from their second owners and displayed at Graceland, while the automobile museum featuring many of Elvis's famous vehicles opened in 1989. After that, a wide variety of Elvis-related endeavors sprang up in the area surrounding Graceland, including luxury hotels and restaurants. Graceland and EPE Enterprises generated $100 million a year in earnings from visitors and merchandise sales in 2005.

In January 1992, the Rodgers & Hammerstein Organization took over exclusive North American administrative rights to Elvis's music catalogue, and RCA and the RIAA presented his estate with 110 gold and platinum records for his career sales in August of that year. On the twentieth anniversary of his death, (August 1997), EPE exhibited the 135 gold and platinum records Elvis had by then amassed. When Lisa Marie turned twenty-five in 1993, the aforementioned trust automatically dissolved and she chose to form a new trust, the Elvis Presley Trust, to continue the very successful management of the estate. Her mother and the National Bank of Commerce continued to serve as co-trustees.

In February 2005, Robert F.X. Sillerman, founder of SFX Entertainment, acquired an 85 percent interest in EPE in a $100 million deal with Lisa Marie and EPE, including purchasing all physical and intellectual properties. Lisa Marie retained a 15 percent ownership in the publicly traded company CKX Inc. and continued to be involved, as did Priscilla. Lisa Marie also received $53 million in cash and absolution of $25 million in debts owed by the estate. As of early 2006, she held shares in this new company worth more than $20 million. Thus, Lisa Marie retained 100 percent sole personal ownership of Graceland Mansion, including the thirteen-acre original grounds and her father's personal belongings. These items include clothes and costumes, musical instruments, lavish pieces of furniture, pictures, awards, trophies, recording collections, televisions, statues and sculptures, guns and other firearms, many cars, horses, motorcycles, golf carts, and the two airplanes that were the property of the estate. Priscilla received $6.5 million and a ten-year consultation agreement with CKX at over $500,000 per year and was appointed to the company's board of directors. Proposed plans for the renovation of Elvis Presley's Palm Springs home as "Graceland West" home include a large complex with a recording studio, theater, museum, bowling alley, wedding chapel and guesthouses.

Merchandising Elvis

Elvis may be the most merchandised person in history. And as much as he and Colonel Parker earned from this end of the business during Elvis's life, posthumous sales figures outdo those earnings by a landslide. To put it crudely, Elvis was worth more dead than alive, earning ten times as much posthumously.

As early as February 1956, Colonel Parker began increasing his personal staff and upgrading his offices in preparation for the onslaught of interest in Elvis songs and soon-to-be-released merchandise. At that time, Colonel Parker astutely commented that after Elvis received his first army haircut in 1958 he should have saved some hair to sell to fans.

Soon the kinds of items fans could purchase were as varied as T-shirts, bumper stickers, mugs, teddy bears, pictures, key rings, lunch pails, dolls, buttons, posters, books, magazines, jewelry, pens, old concert tickets, commemorative plates, license plates, bubble gum packs, Christmas tree ornaments, statues, wrist watches, belt buckles, bath products, broken guitar strings, replicas of Elvis's army dog tags, and clumps of grass from the grounds of Graceland.

Shortly after Elvis's death, Parker made an agreement with Factors Etc., Inc., giving them exclusive marketing rights to all things Elvis. Parker was then getting more than 50 percent of all earnings on Elvis merchandise. However, this would change when Parker sold his holdings in 1983.

In 1999, a three-day auction of Elvis items in Las Vegas brought in $5 million. Two thousand of the King's personal belongings were up for bid, including his sixth-grade report card, his 1956 Lincoln Continental Mark II (valued at $250,000), the beaded cape from the 1973 Aloha From Hawaii concert, his first piano, his army fatigues, and his first RCA contract signed in 1955. Lisa Marie used much of the proceeds from this auction to fund Presley Place, a transitional housing development in Memphis.

EPE sold millions of dollars worth of Elvis merchandise via the Internet and through catalogues—over $50 million between 1984 and 1987 alone. Elvis became one of only a dozen artists or bands with his own category on eBay, the well-established online auction site. A single visit to that site in 2005 showed over 18,000 items listed for sale in the "Elvis" category, including records, CDs, cassettes,

COLD HARD FACT

In January 1989, retired airline pilot Ed Leek was offered $1 million for his acetate of the 1953 recording of Elvis singing "That's When Your Heartaches Begin" and Elvis's first version of "My Happiness." Sun Records signed the deal with Leek in April of that year. Leek and Elvis shared a homeroom in the twelfth grade at Humes High and hung out together for a year or so. Leek had acquired this ultimate collectible from Elvis because, as a youth, his grandparents owned a record player and the Presley family didn't.

Elvis surrounded by his enthusiastic teenage fans, 1956. © *Bettmann/CORBIS*

music accessories, musical instruments, wigs, DVDs, memorabilia related to his music, movies and television performances, autographs, decorative collectables, trading cards, advertising, knives, swords, blades, postcards, paper, tobacco-related items, photos, barware, kitchen items, arcade games, and jukeboxes. In 2007, Elvis' wedding ring was auctioned off for over $150,000 and in October of 2009, a clump of his hair sold at auction in Chicago for $15,000.

Elvis Presley purposefully avoided any personal financial responsibility during his hugely successful and lucrative career. Once he had deep pockets, he simply told any retailer he visited to "send the bill to Daddy" (Vernon), who often blanched at the enormous amounts of money Elvis relinquished so freely. Financial independence to Elvis meant he could give with open hands to friends, relatives, car dealers, fans, hangers-on, strangers, charities, and anyone else upon whom the King wished to bestow gifts. He said he felt that if he had a million dollars on hand, he was always rich. Elvis rarely saved or invested, he just spent.

THE BEATLES

When interviewed early in their careers, the Beatles each told British Beatles fan club president Freda Kelly what their goals were. Paul said, "ambition, money, etc."; John said, "money and everything"; and George said, "to retire with a lot of money." Ringo's goal was more modest: He said he thought he might like to own a string of women's hair dressing salons some day. The Beatles did wish to earn money as performers, but the youthful exuberance of reaching an audience with their original songs was satisfying enough in those early days.

Real spending money did not come the Beatles' way so quickly, as they were paying their dues on the road from 1960 through mid 1963, sometimes earning as little as 80 pounds sterling (at the time, about $240) a week to be shared by all four members. The group's financial situation started to improve dramatically in late 1963 after the success of the *Please Please Me* album, the hit U.K. single "She Loves You," the Royal Variety Performance, the release of their second U.K. album, *With the Beatles,* their U.K./U.S. crossover single "I Want to Hold Your Hand," and the massive attention from fans and the British press, who quickly coined the term "Beatlemania."

As band manager, Brian Epstein was the man who set up the initial contracts that affected the Beatles and their financial picture for years to come. He made mistakes along the way and later came in for substantial criticism, even after he was no longer around to give his side of the story. As he was learning on the job, Epstein often low-balled the band's wages for the sake of publicity and exposure in the early stages of the game. Then, even as their fame and success grew, Epstein and the Beatles felt obligated to honor several lower-paying contracts already in place, sometimes barely covering expenses incurred. But Brian knew his boys' worth and potential earning power, and astutely negotiated their appearance fees in his silver-tongued, erudite manner so that they increased dramatically as the group became more successful. Brian often paid all of the group's expenses before any money came in because his belief in the boys' potential earning power was so firm.

When the Beatles were scheduled to play for seven weeks in Germany starting in April 1962, Epstein publicized this as a "European Tour" and even paid out of his own pocket for the band to fly to Germany. Brian's unwavering faith in the group was equaled only by his persistence and work ethic, as he peddled the Beatles early demos around the U.K. and purchased multiple copies of their first single as an unabashedly enthusiastic fan as well as their manager. He made deals with whomever was necessary to get things rolling.

In late 1963, Brian made a publicity deal with British European Airways that involved the Beatles carrying merchandise that tied in to both their success and the airline's name: BEA(tles) bags. Fees and perks included three weeks unlimited air travel between Paris and London, but the pay was so meager that the fees for the Paris shows didn't even cover the expenses.

In 1963, the Beatles received only one farthing (one quarter of a penny!) per double-sided disc, and millions of records were sold under this skimpy original Parlophone contract. When the Beatles started out in show business, they were in the 94 percent tax bracket, as the British tax system collected heavily from successful artists and performers. The Beatles were just working-class lads, with very little experience or education regarding money matters, and for years all they received was the 50 pounds a week apiece doled out to them by Brian as salary. This amount was later increased to 100 pounds a week. And Epstein and EMI picked up all of their expenses, so none of the boys wanted for material items.

The Beatles also relied on "Uncle Walter" (Dr. Walter Stratch), a senior executive with a local accounting firm, to serve as their treasurer and secretary. He would receive their bills for apartments and living expenses. His other job was to collect money in reserve to pay future taxes the group might incur once their salaries as performers ceased; thus, much of their liquid assets were held in bank accounts. A limited partnership, Beatles Ltd., was also established to equally divide any concert earnings during 1963.

Epstein oversaw the group's business affairs so that the lads could enjoy a relatively worry-free existence. Any items they wanted, from cars to houses, they simply charged to NEMS, which paid the bills without question. The Beatles themselves made very few personal financial investments during their peak years.

Few question Epstein's enthusiasm for the Beatles or his hard work on their behalf. Beatles historians question, however,

> **COLD HARD FACT**
>
> Overzealous Beatles fans cost the group some money early on. Publicist Alistair Taylor tells of a bill he received from Heathrow Airport after the Beatles had landed when returning from a tour. Damage claims included a number of vehicles crushed by fans anxious to see the Fab Four.

whether Epstein was always truthful with his famous clients about his own take of their financial success. When Brian renegotiated their royalty deal with EMI (and with Capitol in the United States), he wrote in a 25 percent earnings clause that he kept hidden from the group. This new provision guaranteed that 25 percent of all Beatle record royalties would continue to go to NEMS (Brian's own company) for nine additional years, even if the Beatles didn't renew their management contract with him. The Beatles were never much for reading contracts and had signed without scrutinizing the fine print. But the Beatles themselves weren't overly concerned early on and didn't "care too much for money," as the song stated. One interview from *Beatle Money Dot Com* reports "the boys carry very little cash; there isn't much opportunity for them to spend it casually. Neither are their houses riddled with safes, as you might suppose. John's attitude is, 'You [the Beatles handlers] worry about that, I never carry any'."

Losing a Fortune

Unfortunately, the Beatles' lack of business acumen ended up costing them a great deal of money. In February 1963, Northern Songs, Ltd., the Beatles publishing company, was registered, with owner Dick James, an established U.K. music publisher, retaining 50 percent, John and Paul splitting 40 percent, and Epstein receiving 10 percent. James had impressed Brian with his contacts in the British entertainment industry, helping him secure television appearances immediately for the group, and Brian struck this unusual deal that favored James without proper review. His legal consultant, David Jacobs, should have cautioned Brian as to the unbalanced percentage James and his company would receive. Years later, John complained, "Well, look what happened. With Northern Songs, we

> **COLD HARD FACT**
>
> In 1995, Sony Signatures was appointed by Neil Aspinall, chief of Apple Corp., as worldwide licensing and merchandising agent for the Beatles with a plan to expand the group's merchandising program to include products in new categories, such as limited edition collectibles, upscale apparel and accessories, house wares, gifts and novelties, paper products, toys, and games. Apple Corp. and the Beatles split these profits equally with Sony Signatures.

ended up selling half our copyrights forever. We lost 'em all and Sir Lew Grade's [chief executive of ATV Entertainment Group, who later purchased Northern Songs from James] got 'em. It was bad management. We have no company. That's where Brian Epstein f***ed up. Who got the benefit? Not us. I mean, since you ask, in retrospect he made mistakes."

Epstein also missed the mark to some extent when securing the merchandising rights and income early in the group's career as he concentrated more on their musical productions. He signed a modest 25 percent deal for himself *and* the group on any Beatle boots, guitar-shaped cakes, and mop-top wigs. These were some of the first items to be marketed in the U.K. in 1963, with the huge merchandising and commercial boon to commence once the Beatles reached American soil and eager audiences.

Making a Fortune

On the other hand, Epstein did many things right. His biggest marketing coup occurred in his negotiations with Capitol Records just prior to the Beatles' 1964 arrival in the U.S. Capitol Records, a wholly owned subsidiary of EMI, was given independence on the acquisitions it made, and its executives did not believe the Beatles would appeal to American youth at that time. Epstein was able to convince Capitol to put between $40,000 and $50,000 into promoting the group. This included a million copies of a four-page insert about the Beatles, free copies of their singles to American disc jockeys, and 5 million posters stating that "The Beatles Are Coming."

Good timing was essential to the Beatles' success throughout their career, and the group made their debut in America just when

Television host Ed Sullivan stands with the Beatles (left to right, Ringo Starr, George Harrison, John Lennon, and Paul McCartney), between rehearsals at CBS television studios in Manhattan, February 8, 1964. © Bettmann/ CORBIS

the U.S. record industry was in a period of stagnation. From 1955 through 1959, record sales had increased by as much as 36 percent each year. In 1960, however, sales were actually down 0.5 percent from the year before, and in 1963 sales were up less than 2 percent from the prior year. The problem was the music itself, as the teen idols (Frankie Avalon, Fabian, Bobby Rydell, Ricky Nelson, and Paul Anka) were quickly aging, "girl groups" were out of vogue, and the excitement early Rock 'n' Roll and R&B artists had enjoyed was subsiding in the midst of more conservative musical directions within the industry. Epstein and Capitol Records pushed open the doors for the Beatles and subsequent British Invasion groups with the U.S. release of "I Want to Hold Your Hand," which became the fastest selling single in Capitol's history. By the spring of 1964, Beatles records were flying off the shelves on both sides of the Atlantic, with an estimate of over 6 million pounds sterling (over $10 million in 2006 dollars) worth of records sold in the U.K. alone that year, boosting EMI's profits by 80 percent. By 1965, even Decca would assist in pressing Beatle records as the demand escalated.

The second and most lucrative phase of the Beatles' career began in February 1964, when they landed on U.S. soil. (During their airport interview, a reporter asked them why so many people were buying Beatles albums in record numbers, to which John replied, "If we knew that, we'd all become managers.") Epstein booked the Beatles on *The Ed Sullivan Show* in 1964 for three shows. The group earned $3,500 for the two live shows and $3,000 for the performance taped on February 23. At the time, Sullivan was paying $7,500 for single appearances to featured top acts. But Epstein astutely realized that the publicity and sales potential from these shows would be worth much more than any exorbitant performance fees he might demand.

As their careers and sales skyrocketed, Epstein booked the Beatles for larger fees, which varied from show to show. For example, the group earned $90,000 in thirty-five minutes for their August 1965 Minneapolis show; $160,000 for their August 15 Shea Stadium show and $189,000 for their second performance there; $85,000 on August 19 for the Sam Houston Coliseum Show; $155,000 for the White Sox Park show in Chicago on August 20; $47,600 for their San Francisco performance; and over $85,000 for two shows in Indiana on September 3, 1965.

Prior to 1967, the Beatles had several other sources of revenue on which to rely. Their most important collective investment was Subafilms, the NEMS-run film company that controlled the group's share of any film projects in which the group was involved.

COLD HARD FACT

Charles (Chuck) Finley, owner of the Kansas City Athletics baseball team, initially offered Epstein and the Beatles $50,000 to perform on their night off (September 17, 1964), but Brian refused this meager amount. Finley finally coughed up a record $150,000 for a night at Municipal Stadium (with the Beatles earning $4,838 per minute for their performance!). Finley lost money, however, when only 20,000 or so fans showed, filling up only half of the arena. Fans were enthusiastic, though, as the show had to be stopped briefly when fans rushed the stage.

Subafilms also produced the Beatles' promotional films (before videos were so prevalent) for television. United Artists was eager to release a Beatles soundtrack album specifically for the film *A Hard Day's Night,* and offered the group 25 percent. Epstein spoke too soon at their first meeting, suggesting that he wouldn't consider less than 7.5 percent. Luckily, Jacobs was able to finalize a deal in which they eventually received 25 percent, but of the gross, not the net. In 2010, EMI Group Ltd. had plans to sell Abbey Road due to cash flow problems, but instead is seeking an investor to help save the famous London recording studio frequented by the Beatles. Paul said he hoped Abbey Road could be preserved, and the National Trust heritage group said it was considering buying the property. But EMI expressed interest in retaining ownership and is talking to "interested and appropriate third parties" about a revitalization project.

Merchandising the Beatles

The Beatles, like Elvis, were ripe for product marketing and merchandising once the demand was there, and Epstein formed the U.S. company "Seltaeb" ("Beatles" spelled backwards) as their official merchandising company, selling over 150 different items. NEMS received 10 percent of all sales until August of 1964 when its share was raised to 46 percent through a company-wide restructuring by solicitor David Jacobs (also Liberace's attorney at the time). Unfortunately for Brian and the Beatles, Jacobs had convinced Brian to accept pennies on the dollar for all Beatles merchandise, thus losing them millions of dollars in revenue.

To be fair to Epstein, very few professionals in the music business at that time could conceive of the great sums of money music merchandising could generate. He may have believed that any revenue from the sale of Beatles merchandise was simply "gravy" to supplement their lucrative recording income. It should also be remembered that Epstein was a novice and was at the mercy of some of his new business associates, such as Jacobs and Walter Hofer (a U.S. music publishing associate of Dick James), who handled the U.S. merchandising licenses.

The various products sold as Beatle merchandise ran the full gamut of items. Fans could purchase Beatle dolls, licorice sticks, buttons, sneakers, chewing gum, toys, T-shirts, and the like, with more unusual offerings such as perfume, talc powder, used bed linens, and pillow cases available to the truly devoted. One of Jacob's duties was to prosecute licensing infringements and issue merchandising licenses at his discretion. But Jacobs got busy with other legal commitments, and so handed over this job to chief clerk Edward Marke who knew little about marketing and merchandising. Jacobs then quickly handed Marke's new duties over to Nicky Byrne, whom he had met at a party. Byrne and his associates issued licenses in exchange for 10 percent of manufacturing royalties.

But NEMS was blamed for granting some licenses to others inappropriately, and several of Byrne's partners claimed that he failed to correctly distribute Beatles' royalties, or pay taxes in the U.S. There were also claims that Byrne spent over $50,000 on personal expenses including hotel bills, two Cadillac's with a twenty-four-hour chauffeur, and on paying off a girlfriend's charge account debt.

After Epstein

When Brian Epstein died from an overdose of sleeping pills combined with alcohol on August 20, 1967, his estate was valued at over 12 million pounds sterling, but came to only a bit over 800,000 after the exorbitant British estate tax was collected. His immediate family members, who were already wealthy, were the beneficiaries.

The Beatles were rudderless, not only financially but musically as well, with the loss of Epstein, who had acted as a referee between John and Paul and always tried to keep everyone happy and everything on an even keel. Critics considered the Beatles' first self-managed project, the *Magical Mystery Tour* film (with album tie-in) an artistic failure, as it showed a lack of direction musically and a haphazard approach. (Nonetheless, the film is now considered a cult classic.) John was reportedly stoned and uninterested during the sessions, and Paul felt the need to take charge of the group at that juncture (which John also disliked). The album was seen as little more than a rehashing of the "concept album" idea so brilliantly established with *Sgt. Pepper,* offering few fresh musical ideas. Some critics said the songs seemed forced.

But a Beatles album was still a Beatles album, and *Magical Mystery Tour* sold extremely well, despite harsh criticism. After its release, the music world anxiously awaited what the group would do next.

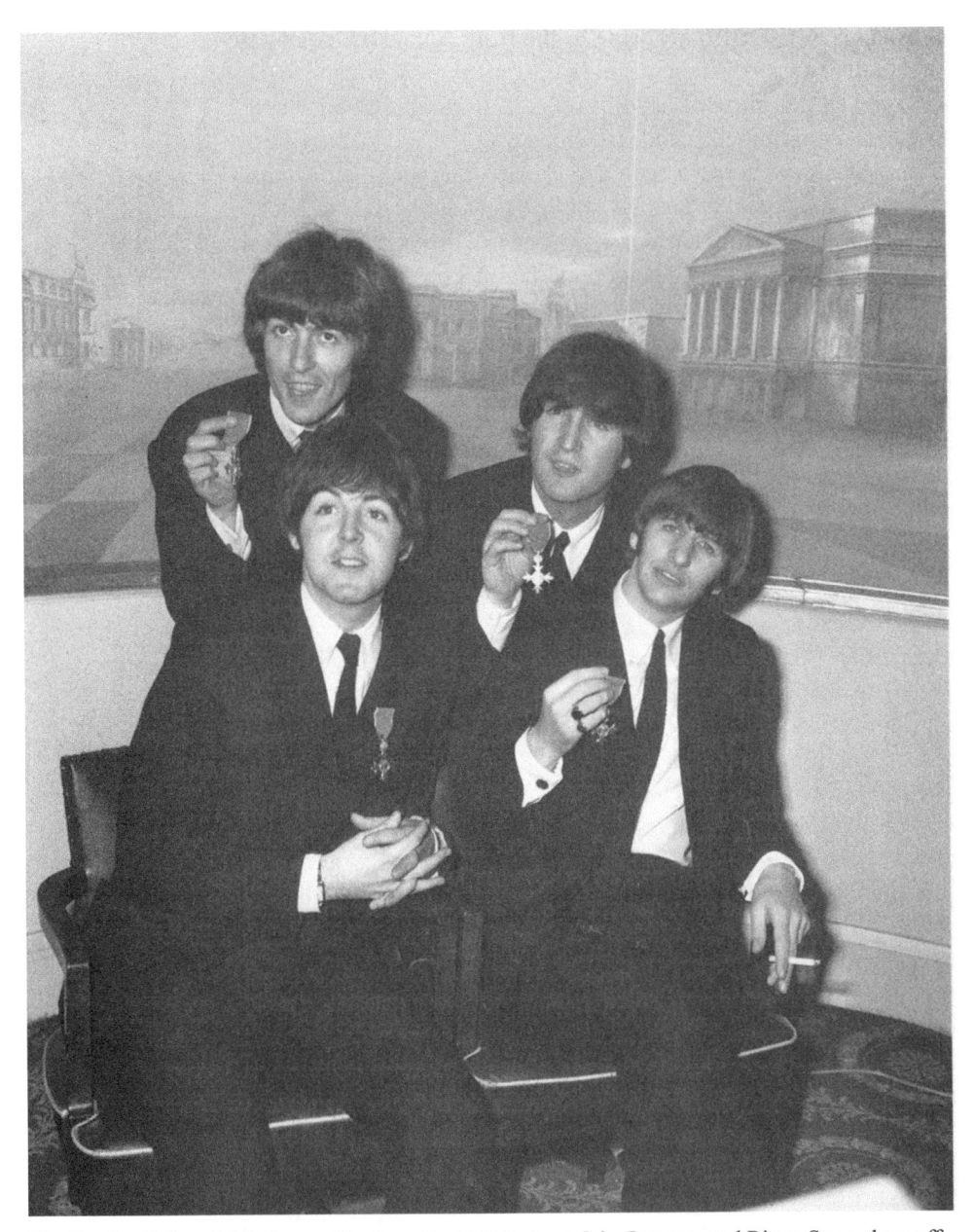

The Beatles (left to right) George Harrison, Paul McCartney, John Lennon, and Ringo Starr, show off their MBE (Member of the Order of the British Empire) awards at a press reception at the Saville Theatre in London's Shaftsbury Avenue, October 26, 1965. *(Photo by Keystone/Getty Images)*

On May 15, 1968, John and Paul appeared on *The Tonight Show,* guest-hosted by Joe Garagiola (sitting in for Johnny Carson), and announced the establishment of Apple, Corp., their own independent music and merchandise venture. Paul referred to it as "Western Communism," through which any struggling artist-musician would get a chance to be produced. But music was not the sole business of the new company. Apple Tailoring and the Apple Boutique specialized in "mod" and "psychedelic" (hippie-style) garb. But by July 31, the Apple Boutique had to close down due to lack of sales, with the remaining stock of items, from shirts to shoes, given away. The Beatles should have stuck to music, as that was the one aspect of Apple that did prove fruitful (pun intended). The single "Hey Jude" backed by "Revolution" was a huge hit, and soon Apple began producing other artists such as Badfinger, Cilla Black, and young James Taylor.

Acrimony was high among band members at this time. Even the ever-affable Ringo briefly walked out on the band during August of that year, having had his fill of John and Paul's bickering—an unpublicized incident that was just another symptom of the dissension and lack of direction within the Beatles organization. Meanwhile, Cynthia Lennon was suing John for divorce on the grounds of adultery, as his affair with Yoko Ono was by then quite public. To make matters even worse, John and Yoko were arrested for obstructing police who were searching their apartment for cannabis in October. They settled in court, with John paying a small fine, but the negative publicity hurt both their sales and their image.

Allen Klein, Ruthless Man of Business

On February 3, 1969, New York lawyer and businessman Allen Klein was appointed the Beatles' business manager. John was the driving force behind this decision, as tales of what Klein had done financially for the Rolling Stones had impressed him. Paul, on the other hand, had wanted the family of his new girlfriend, Linda Eastman, several of whom were lawyers, to take on this role. Eastman & Eastman were appointed as general counsel to Apple the next day.

By September, Klein had secured an increase in song royalties for the lads, which he had also done for the Rolling Stones. Klein renegotiated the Beatles' contract with EMI to increase their royalty rate from 17.5 percent to 25 percent on U.S. sales. The Beatles were obligated by signed contract to release two albums per year as a group or individually. They would now receive $0.58 per album through 1972 when the rate would increase to $0.72. For any reissues (re-releases of prerecorded material) the Beatles would now receive the rate of $0.55 per album, also increasing to $0.72 in 1972. The first phase of the Apple negotiations, litigations, and restructuring took ten years to clear up. But Klein, who was brought in to get rid of "the hustlers and spongers" who were buying houses and charging them to Apple's account, left his own troublesome legacy of mismanagement. Klein was eventually condemned, in the High Court action McCartney instituted in 1971, for "lamentable" bookkeeping.

Paul and the other three Beatles did not agree on Klein's management style, but admitted he was successful in renegotiating their contracts, and thus rewarded him for his efforts. For example, Apple Corp. provided a London apartment for Klein and absorbed any "reasonable expenses" incurred by Klein and other ABKCO employees in the line of doing Apple and Beatles business. Klein also received 20 percent of the gross income earned by the Beatles and Apple during the time in which Klein was their manager. And, if Klein renegotiated royalty rates or fees on any existing deals on behalf of the group, he would also earn an additional 20 percent of the new gross income generated. Klein also secured a piece of the financial action for the group's own Apple Records as part of his negotiations. This new deal was quite inventive, stipulating that EMI—which still retained ownership of the Beatles' master recordings—would now grant Apple the right to manufacture and sell Beatles albums in the United States on their own label. Apple would then pay Capitol to manufacture the actual LPs.

It was quickly recognized that Klein, though a bit brusque in his people skills, was a ruthless and skilled negotiator for both the Beatles and the Rolling Stones, garnering them new contracts and back royalties.

In March of 1970, a Danish magazine reported, "Economically the future seems brighter for the Beatles. Their finances will in the future be taken care of by the Jewish businessman Allen Klein, who used to take care of the Stones' finances. On the creative side, the only one to keep Apple going is Paul McCartney, the man behind two of the biggest hits around at the time, "Come And Get It," with Badfinger, and "Temma Habour" with Mary Hopkin.

Allen Klein gets 20% of all the Beatles' income, but McCartney thinks he's worth it."

On April 9, 1970, the personal, musical, and financial rifts among the Beatles (mainly Paul against the other three) led to Paul's announcement of a solo album release and departure from the group just as they were releasing *Let It Be*. Paul later said, "Then the job folded beneath me. Suddenly I didn't have a career anymore. I wasn't earning anything and all my money was in Apple and I couldn't get it out because I'd signed it all away." This was not totally correct. All Apple assets were frozen until the partnership was formally dissolved in court, so none of the Beatles were able to draw upon these funds. The most significant problem was that as the money piled up, a huge tax bill would be attached to any withdrawals. Thus, much of the money Klein said he was bringing in was to lie untouched for years until all legal issues were resolved. With the money frozen, of course, the Beatles had no real liquid income. They had not managed their personal finances well, nor had they made wise or substantial investments. They all owned magnificent houses, cars, and Apple Corp. itself, but had put away very little, if anything, into retirement or savings plans.

According to John's *Rolling Stone* interview of 1970, "The people around us made more money than the Beatles ever did, I'll tell you that. None of the Beatles are millionaires. But there's lots of millionaires who became millionaires around the Beatles, however."

By April 1970, John, George, and Ringo had incurred 100,000 pounds sterling (over $170,000) in legal bills. George stated, "We weren't broke, we'd earned a lot of money but we didn't actually have the money that we'd earned, you know. It was floating around, because the contracts . . . The structure of everything, you know, right back—that's really the history—Since 1962 the way everything was structured was just freaky, you know. None of us knew anything about it. We just spent money when we wanted to spend money, but we didn't know where we were spending it from, or if we paid taxes on it, you know. We were really in bad shape as far as that was concerned, because none of us really could be bothered. We just felt as though we were rich, because really we were rich by what we sold and what we did. But, uhh, it wasn't really the case because it was so untogether—the business side of it. But now it's very together and we know exactly where everything is, and there's daily reports on where it is and what it is, and how much it is. And it's really good."

In the April 16, 1971 issue of *Life* magazine, Paul stated, "Listen, it's not the boys. It's not the other three. The four of us, I think, still quite like each other. I don't think there is bad blood, not from my side anyway. I spoke to the others quite recently and there didn't sound like any from theirs. So it's a business thing. It's Allen Klein. Early in '69 John took him on as business manager and wanted the rest of us to do it too. That was just the irreconcilable difference between us. Klein is incredible. He's New York. He'll say 'Waddaya want? I'll buy it for you.' I guess there's a lot I really don't want to say about this, but it will come out because we had to sort of document the stuff for this case. We had to go and fight—which I didn't want, really."

Northern Songs and ATV: The Fab Four Lose Their Rights

The main issue regarding the Beatles' future fortunes lay with ongoing problems regarding Northern Songs Limited and NEMS. The Beatles tried to buy Northern Songs when Allen Klein came on board, as Dick James, their music publisher and owner of Northern Songs, Ltd., owned the largest share of the company at the time. But, months earlier, Sir Lew Grade, then owner of ATV music and EMI, had contacted James about acquiring Northern Songs to establish a business connection between James, Northern Songs, and his own ATV company even before the Beatles' offer. In March 1969, James, who feared that Northern Songs might soon become a Beatles-owned and -operated company or that they might file lawsuits against him, began negotiations with ATV and Grade with the idea of a sale in mind. ATV financial director Jack Gill reportedly said the deal to buy Northern Songs was quick and to the point.

In an attempt to block this sale, the Beatles contacted Henry Ansbacher and Company, a group of successful London merchant bankers. A gentleman named Ormrod, who worked for this company, tried to arrange a settlement by finding a group of investment partners for the Beatles among the various London corporate establishments. Unfortunately, during this time, John Lennon stated, "I'm not going to be f***ed around by men in suits sitting on their fat a**es in the City." This comment, among other things, kept the aforementioned businesses from showing any interest in joining with the Beatles for this financial endeavor.

The problem was that the Beatles did not have enough liquid assets (cash on hand) to make a counteroffer against ATV's bid to purchase Northern Songs, Ltd. Though the Beatles owned 29.7 percent, ATV owned 35 percent after buying over 1.5 million shares from James and his associates. On top of that, ATV had already bought 137,000 shares directly from the stock market. At this time, Paul owned 751,000 shares, Lennon 604,750, and Ringo 40,000 shares. In 1968, George had sold all of his shares when his contract with Northern Songs expired, but Pattie Boyd (Harrison Clapton) held 1,000 shares herself. NEMS (Epstein's company) was purchased by Triumph Investment, which then held 237,000 shares (4.7 percent). Three London brokerage firms had purchased 5 percent of Northern Songs from the holdings of others in Epstein's family. So, both the Beatles and ATV made public announcements that they would offer any interested shareholders a deal for their shares of Northern Song. The brokerage firms mentioned earlier combined in force to hold out for the best price possible for their shares. The Beatles soon changed positions, and, on April 18, they announced that they would now bid only for majority control instead of a complete buyout of Northern Songs, Ltd.

Finally, the brokerage consortium of interests, which had been put off by John's comments and attitude, decided to make a deal with ATV for their shares of Northern Songs, now insuring ATV's controlling interest of the company. The Beatles, wanting nothing more to do with Northern Songs, quickly converted their shares into ATV stock, which legally forced ATV to purchase them at the premium price offered during their takeover bid. So, in the short run, the Beatles had profited from ATV's takeover of Northern Songs, but lost forever any chance of ever regaining ownership of their original songs. One interesting aspect was that both Ringo and George, having not renewed their contracts as songwriters with Northern Songs in 1968, became Apple Publishing songwriters instead, so the Beatles still owned all of their musical works.

Enter Jacko

In 1985, singer-songwriter Michael Jackson purchased ATV for $47.5 million, outbidding Paul in the process. Ironically, it was Paul who advised the young Jackson years earlier to invest in song catalogs, as he himself owned music by Buddy Holly and several

> ### COLD HARD FACT
>
> Sir (later Lord) Lew Grade's lasting fame is linked to his pulling off a financial coup when he acquired Northern Songs Ltd. and a controlling interest in the Beatles song catalog. At the time, Grade's production company, ITC Entertainment, was responsible for two iconic 1960s British TV series, *The Saint* and *The Prisoner,* and produced the popular children's marionette adventure series *Thunderbirds* among others. AP Films also produced three feature films and the live-action sci-fi series *Space: 1999.* As a movie producer, Grade helped finance the 1979 big-screen incarnation of *The Muppet Show,* leading Jim Henson to immortalize him by making a Muppet in his image: Dr. Bunsen Honeydew. Henson also used Grade for the character of movie mogul Lew Lord (played by Orson Welles) in *The Muppet Movie.*
>
> Grade was the force behind the private British TV broadcasting network ATV, which dominated British TV from the 1950s into the 1970s. He received the Queen's Award to Industry in 1967—the first such award to Britain's entertainment business—and in 1969 was knighted for significantly increasing U.K. exports and bringing revenue into the realm. He lost control of ATV upon reaching the directors' age limit of seventy, but subsequently became the largest filmmaker in the world as he built up Associated Communications Corporation.
>
> Grade was seen by most as a ruthless businessman who spent his life acquiring power in the industry, and was an anathema to John Lennon. Grade died in 1998 at age ninety-one.

others, now reportedly worth over $600 million. Most believe Paul was not suggesting that Jackson buy live artists' catalogues out from under them simply because the money was there, but to acquire music portfolios of those who had passed and left legacies.

One of the things Jackson got for his many dollars was the publishing rights to between 150 and 250 original Beatles songs, including sheet music printing and distributing, public performance royalties, and fees for use (for original recordings and cover versions). So, as mentioned earlier, when Paul wanted to print the lyrics to "Eleanor Rigby" and other Beatles songs in his 1989 World Tour programs, he found that he had to pay a fee to Jackson.

COLD HARD FACT

No discussion of the Beatles or Elvis merchandise would be complete without mentioning the vast underground "bootleg" industry, which generates millions of dollars per year for unlicensed music providers. Bootleg recordings are unauthorized outtakes of sessions or performances that range in quality from good to abysmal. In his 1988 book *Do You Want to Know a Secret?* L.R.E. King writes of the reasons why fans desire such recordings: "Trying to understand the Beatles' music only through their authorized releases is like trying to understand an automobile by admiring its paint job. They are only the surface, the end product, and they say little on applying craftsmanship to basic creative genius. The final product gives great pleasure, but we have the responsibility to find out how things work and only by studying the processes of creativity can we demystify it and derive useful knowledge. Beyond that, study of their abandoned projects and failures helps keep them in perspective. We can see that they weren't godlings, but merely four human beings whose talent, skills, and chemistry, combined with hard work, and the luck of being in the right place at the right time gave them unprecedented artistic and commercial success. Today's art historians X-ray important paintings to see the rough sketches beneath. Studying the Beatles' unreleased recordings is our way of doing the same thing."

For Paul's *Give My Regards to Broad Street* album, he had to pay fees to use his own song "For No One." But in 1987, when Jackson tried to license the use of "Revolution" to Nike for a shoe commercial, he had to persuade Capitol Records, which owned the North American recording rights, to allow use of the actual recording.

Jackson did not really control the use or cover availability of Beatle songs as much as reap the profits from their earnings, outside of authorship fees paid to Lennon and McCartney of about 50 percent. But one can imagine that Paul, having lost control of his beloved Beatles songs, was not pleased. Finally, to add insult to injury, Jackson would not discuss giving Paul any increases in composer's royalties for the ever-earning Beatles catalogue. The sudden death of Jackson in June of 2009 has led to rumors of his leaving his share of the Beatles publishing rights to Paul, but this has yet to be substantiated as of the writing of this text.

Both George and John left large estates, valued at over $100 million, to their families. And of the two surviving Beatles, Paul continued to earn extremely well on both his tours and his recordings. The year 2004 was particularly lucrative for Paul, who tripled his income thanks in part to his highly successful Back to the World tour. Both Paul and Ringo continue to tour and record, with 2008 and 2009 banner years for Paul, with the release of a live New York City concert DVD and CD, and his continued work with his latest project, the Firemen.

Comparison

Ultimately, both Elvis and the Beatles had more money than most people ever dream of, yet were caught up in the web of personal and business entanglements such income can bring. John in particular tended to be cynical regarding the attention of strangers and their financial motivations. Colonel Parker made millions for Elvis but made even more for himself, choosing easy earning venues, such as concert tours and Las Vegas, over those that might have been more interesting or challenging to his boy Elvis, such as great films and international tours. Both Elvis and his dad, Vernon, allowed the Colonel to call the shots because they believed that any confrontation might anger him and cause him to drop Elvis as a client, which they feared would bring about the end of Elvis's career.

The Beatles trusted Brian Epstein to manage their band's finances, and themselves or close acquaintances to manage their personal financial affairs. Paul proved to be adept at handling his personal funds, and is now considered one of the richest men in the U.K. thanks to his well-received post-Beatles albums and continued touring. After the Beatles' demise, both George and Ringo became highly successful solo recording and touring artists, and Ringo's film and television appearances generated substantial income over the decades. John's estate earns $22 million annually (Yoko made wise investments in the 1970s in such diverse areas as prize dairy cows to substantially increase their personal fortunes.) Lastly, compilations, re-releases, and repackaging of Elvis and Beatles songs continues to generate millions of dollars in income to these artists, their estates, and all those involved.

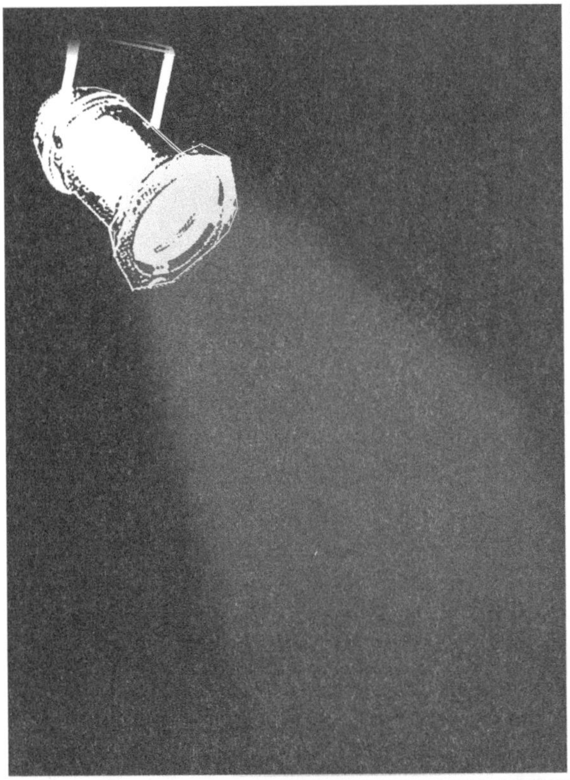

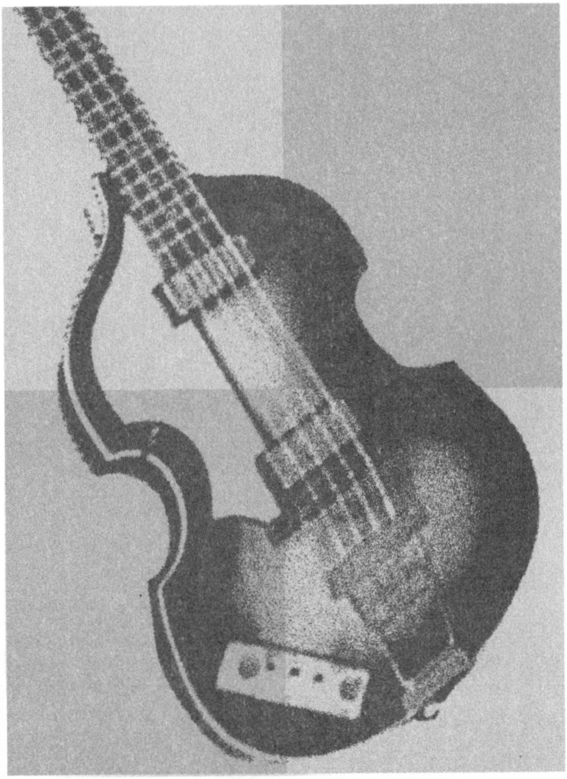

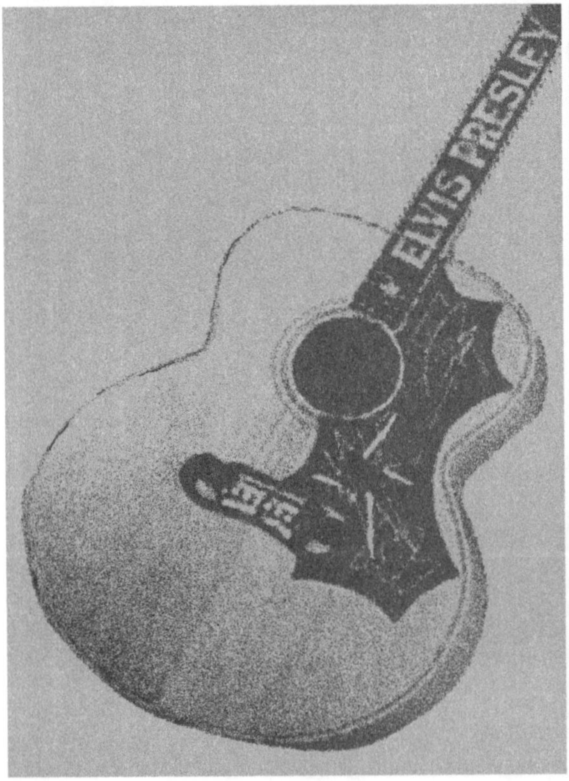
ELVIS PRESLEY

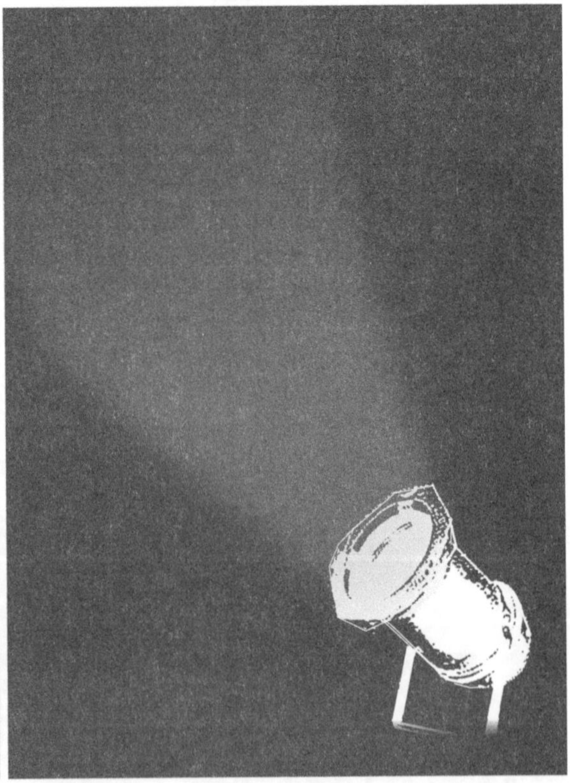

CHAPTER 7

The Manias That Wouldn't Die

"Elvismania" and its offspring, "Beatlemania," were born out of timing, talent, necessity, and luck, and forever changed our world. Musicians became larger than life, with their songs and words quoted, analyzed, and debated. George once commented that people first used Elvis, and then the Beatles, as an excuse to go crazy. Of course, the pain of losing their personal identities was somewhat assuaged by the unprecedented volume of record sales and subsequent enormous incomes they enjoyed.

New generations of fans continued to purchase Elvis and Beatles materials by the millions, and decades later these "manias" showed no signs of slowing. On March 1st of 2010, for example, there were over 30,000 Elvis-related items and 30,000 Beatles-related items for sale at the online auction house, eBay. Add to this the thousands of merchandise-related sites for each, and products and sales continue to number in the millions. In 2005, on the online auction house eBay, there were over 4 million Elvis-related items and 5 million Beatles-related items for sale, including recordings, instruments, photos, and autographs.

Another aspect of these "manias" has been the preponderance of impersonators. If imitation is the most sincere form of flattery, then even as late as the first decade of the twenty-first century there were a lot of sincere fans in the world. Beatles lookalikes and cover bands and Elvis impersonators by the dozens inhabited the stages of casinos and lounges across the globe. The Internet abounds with hundreds of websites that are "meeting" places for Elvis and Beatles impersonators, fans, critics, and collectors.

Elvis

While Elvis was alive, there were only a few aspiring rockers impersonating him, but after his death that number skyrocketed and became a mini-industry in itself. They covered the spectrum from acceptable simulation to the absolute dregs of imitation, from copycat recordings to a musical stage play entitled *Elvis,* which ran at the Astoria Theatre in London for two years in the seventies.

Two of the most famous Elvis-impersonators were Donny Edwards, who titled his show "Elvis Tribute" and showcased Presley's early look, and Rick Marino, who highlighted Elvis's later years in Vegas. There have even been Chinese Elvises, and in China, Japan, and Hong Kong, Elvis became a karaoke-bar obsession starting around the turn of the century.

Meanwhile, helping to keep Elvis alive in the public mind were the many biographical plays and films of "the King" that emerged in the years after his death, beginning with the well-crafted 1979 film *Elvis* (produced by Dick Clark), featuring remarkable performances by Shelley Winters as Gladys Presley and Kurt Russell as Elvis. In 1981, a television movie entitled *Elvis and Me,* based on Priscilla's book of the same name, aired on ABC-TV, and that same year producer David Wolper and Warner Bros. released a semi-documentary entitled *This Is Elvis,* using original footage combined with reenactments.

In 1990, ABC-TV briefly aired a series entitled *Elvis,* which focused on the years 1954 and 1955, and *Elvis–The Great Performances* (narrated by Priscilla from Graceland) aired on CBS-TV in 1992. A live pay-per-view broadcast entitled *Elvis Aaron Presley: The Tribute* was staged in Memphis on October 8, 1994, featuring Scotty Moore and the Jordanaires, and was rebroadcast on CBS-TV that December 15. In 1987, the video documentary *Elvis '56* was re-released, and in 1996, the aforementioned musical stage play *Elvis* reopened at a London theater to a successful run of several years.

The year 2001 saw the release of *3000 Miles to Graceland,* a fictional romp featuring Kevin Costner as an Elvis impersonator

Elvis Presley performs in Tupelo, Mississippi for his hometown crowd, September, 1956.
© *Bettmann/CORBIS*

> **COLD HARD FACT**
>
> In 1993, the U.S. Postal Service held a contest in which fans voted on their favorite depiction of Elvis, either as a young performer or from his Las Vegas period, with the winning picture used on a first-class postage stamp. The picture of Presley from the 1950s won by a better than 3 to 1 margin, with thousands of people voting.

and a slew of other stars including Kurt Russell, Courtney Cox, Christian Slater, and David Arquette. *The Definitive Elvis: 25th Anniversary* video, released in 2002, featured interviews with more than two hundred of Elvis's friends and acquaintances, and in 2005, CBS-TV, in cooperation with Elvis Presley Enterprises, aired a biopic produced by Red-Eye Flight Productions titled *Elvis by the Presleys: Intimate Stories from Priscilla Presley, Lisa Marie Presley and Other Family Members,* which sold extremely well in CD and DVD formats. Warner and Paramount joined forces in 2007 to release twenty-four of Elvis' films on DVD, with re-releases of his many TV appearances on two additional DVDs through 2008.

In his lifetime, Elvis's only concerts outside the United States were five shows in three Canadian cities in 1957. A world tour was an unrealized dream for Elvis and for his international fans, but more than twenty years after the superstar's death, the dream finally came true. In 1998, Elvis the Concert Tour hit the road, featuring former Elvis musicians performing songs in synch with a large-screen video presentation of Elvis singing in earlier live settings. Many former band members and Elvis's musicians participated, including: Joe Guercio (musical director/conductor), The Sweet Inspirations (female backing vocals), former members of J.D. Sumner & the Stamps Quartet (male backing vocals), former members of the Imperials (male backing vocals), former members of Voice (male backing vocals), Millie Kirkham (soprano) and the TCB Band: James Burton (lead guitar), Glen D. Hardin (piano), Jerry Scheff (bass guitar), and Ronnie Tutt (drums). Tour cities included Cleveland, New York, Las Vegas, Louisville, and a European leg that covered London, Brussels, Berlin, and Copenhagen. Attendance for the shows has been in the hundreds of thousands. Fans gathered at Graceland to celebrate what would have been Elvis' 75th birthday on January 8th, 2010, and both the Los Angeles and Washington, DC branches of the Smithsonian presented Elvis-themed exhibits. In February of 2010, Cirque du Soleil opened the extravagant "Viva Elvis" production at Las Vegas' Aria Hotel's new Elvis Theater. Highlights of the over-the-top event include a pink Cadillac and a huge blue suede shoe! Production advisor Priscilla Presley said of the show, "this tribute will help to tell a new generation about Elvis. The younger kids will get to know Elvis."

Is Elvis Alive?

Another aspect of Elvis mania has been the continuing belief among many of the King's fans that he still walks the earth, despite his death and subsequent autopsy. Some fans believe he is in hiding somewhere.

The first so-called "facts" that arose to support the "Elvis is alive" theory occurred when a number of the people who passed by Elvis's opened coffin during the viewing of his body made comments about how "unlike Elvis" the bloated, discolored body seemed to appear, and that it simply did not look like the Elvis seen by so many so often during his life. Soon after, notice was made of the "misspelling" of Elvis's middle name *Aron* on his grave marker as *Aaron*. In fact, *Aaron* was the correct spelling. Many refused to believe that Elvis had had it legally changed in 1963 to the biblically correct *Aaron* to rectify his mother's error many years earlier. (Upset by the death of Elvis's twin brother Jesse Garon at birth, Gladys Presley had accidentally misspelled Elvis's middle name on his birth certificate.)

As the myth gathered steam, fans began to speculate that Elvis might have become disillusioned with fame and fortune and faked his own death to make a clean getaway and live somewhere disguised and under an assumed name. Elvis had the connections and finances to easily accomplish this. One report, which many people took seriously, claimed that hours after Elvis's death was announced, a man by the name of Jon Burrows (Elvis's traveling alias) purchased a one-way ticket with cash to Buenos Aires. They reasoned that since Colonel Parker had faked his own identity when entering America illegally decades earlier, he could have assisted Elvis with this conspiracy. And Parker profited handsomely from the huge increase in record sales after Elvis's demise. Other fans speculated that Elvis was working in his new post as a Drug Enforcement Agency agent (see chapter 5) on a secretive case for the government—a sting

> **COLD HARD FACT**
>
> To further propagate the "Elvis is alive" myth, in 1979 C&W singer Waylon Jennings recorded a song with lyrics stating, "Elvis, may still be alive," though Jennings later denied that he believed this.

operation against an international drug ring—and had to disappear for his safety and anonymity.

In his novel *Jesse: The Post-Death Adventures of Elvis Presley,* Brian DeVall speculated that Elvis had faked his own death to escape the harsh reality of his fading glory and personal health and drug problems. According to the story, after faking his death, Elvis took on the identity of his dead twin brother, Jesse, and started a new life as the twin who had never had a chance to live. DeVall portrayed him as "the dark side of Elvis, his shadow, the yin to Elvis's yang."

As one can imagine, countless other authors quickly jumped on the "Elvis is alive" bandwagon, hoping to cash in on the phenomenon, with over a dozen books detailing this theory, many of which were discredited. The most successful, however, was Gail Brewer Giorgio, author of the controversial *Is Elvis Alive?* The book was a top-ten bestseller in the United States and sold more than 1 million copies, making it one of the biggest-selling Elvis books in history. The book package also included a cassette tape the author insisted was recorded by the King *after* his supposed demise that answers the many questions surrounding the "discrepancies" accompanying his death. In 1990, Star Video released *The Elvis Files,* a "documentary" based on Giorgio's book, featuring interviews and news footage, and Bill Bixby hosted a live show from Las Vegas of the same name that next year.

In 1992, the Presley Commission was formed to undertake a serious examination of the death of Elvis Presley and, based on inconsistencies surrounding reports of his death, to consider the theory that perhaps Elvis didn't die on August 16, 1977. Phil Aitcheson of the Presley Commission Liaison Office in Moneta, Virginia, and head of the Elvis Is Alive Museum in Wright City, Missouri, claimed in 2003 that a laboratory in North Carolina studied two tissue samples, one taken from a liver-tissue biopsy done on a living Elvis Presley in 1975, and another taken from an autopsy of the body, said to be that of Presley in August 1977. Supposedly, the laboratory's report concluded positively that these two specimens were from two different people. In other words, whoever is buried at Graceland is not Elvis Presley. This test is chronicled in Bill Beeny's 2005 book *Elvis' DNA Proves He's Alive*.

Meanwhile, Elvis "sightings" became fairly commonplace occurrences throughout the last quarter of the twentieth century and continued unabated into the twenty-first. People claimed to see Elvis in all kinds of places. In August 2002, a Dutchman claimed that a plaster bust of Elvis wept "miracle" tears.

Elvis sightings are usually lumped in with UFOs, Bigfoot, and other urban legends. The deep-seated need to explain the tragic end of an icon is perhaps the real reason for the serious tone adopted by these types of Elvis fans. In their view, the fact that Elvis died in 1977 from a drug overdose is unfathomable, therefore they adamantly refuse to give credence to it. True or not, these rumors and "sightings" appear to fill a void in some people's lives that only a living Elvis could satisfy. Since it seems a harmless fantasy, it is probably best to let them continue to dream that the King lives on and is working at a fast-food restaurant somewhere in America or relaxing on a beach in Hawaii.

The Beatles

Imitators of the Beatles began while the group was still in their heyday. Although initially created to honor the original band, many tribute bands attracted their own fan base. Tribute bands typically chose names that were related in some way to the original band—such as 1964, the Beatnix, and Classical Mystery Tour—or were derived from a famous track or record album released by the original band, such as Rain, Rubber Soul, and Strawberry Fields.

Whereas Elvis impersonators could range from the sublime to the ridiculous and get away with it, performers trying to put together a decent Beatles tribute band had a more difficult job. There had to be four guys who matched up to look and sound like the four Beatles, and they had to be willing to study films and photos until they could satisfy a demanding fan base. They needed instruments that looked like the ones the Beatles used—and the ability to play them. They needed wigs and costumes and the ability to shake

> **COLD HARD FACT**
>
> In May 2005, another musician joined the hordes that had cashed in on the Beatles' name and music, but this time there was a twist: He really *had* played with the Beatles. When John, Paul, George, and Stu Sutcliffe were making their initial forays into Hamburg, they had a drummer named Pete Best. When the Beatles signed with EMI, Pete was ousted from the group in favor of Ringo. Pete drifted about in the music industry for years. He did make a cameo appearance on *To Tell the Truth,* an American TV quiz show popular in the 1960s, but other than this glimmer of fame, he sank into obscurity until he started fronting the Pete Best Band, a group of six musicians playing mostly classic Rock from the 1950s and 1960s. Pete began touring American college campuses in 2005 with his band, touting his former relationship with his legendary ex-bandmates.

their heads and even tap their toes just like the originals. While there was plenty of demand for Beatle tribute bands, the fans could be unforgiving in their observations, pointing out every little flaw: one too many head shakes, Ringo wearing the wrong rings, Paul keeping time with the wrong foot.

One of the best-known Beatles tribute bands in the world was the Bootleg Beatles, who first performed at a small student gathering in Tiverton, Devon, England in 1980. Following tours in the Soviet Union, the Far East, the Middle East and India, they were invited to perform in the United States in 1984 to commemorate the Beatles' initial U.S. tour twenty years earlier. In 1990, the group booked ten shows in cities in which the Beatles had performed in their final U.K. tour in 1965. Audiences were small but enthusiastic, and another tour was booked for the following year. This one proved more popular, and as each year went by the crowds grew, the tours expanded, and the venues got larger. Finally, a gig in Southampton caught the attention of the band Oasis, leading to the Bootleg Beatles warming up for the Britpop band at Earls Court. This appearance helped endear the band to a contemporary audience and increased their credibility, launching them onto the premier European festival circuit. In 1999, the band performed on the rooftop of the Apple Corp. building to commemorate the Fab

Fours' farewell gig thirty years earlier. In 2006, the Bootleg Beatles toured throughout the U.K., France and Portugal, garnering high praise, increasing their fan base, and generating a level of enthusiasm reminiscent of Beatlemania.

The Impossible Dream: Reunion

After the Fab Four's breakup in 1970, Beatles fans never gave up hope for a Beatles reunion. Various promoters offered millions of dollars to get the Beatles to reunite, but none was successful.

Perhaps the closest that the Beatles ever came to a reunion while all were still alive was when they all appeared on Ringo's self-titled album released in November 1973—although not on the same track. Ringo, John, and George performed on "I'm the Greatest" (penned by Lennon), and Paul and Ringo performed on "Six o'Clock" (penned by McCartney).

In January 1976, promoter Bill Sargent offered the group $30 million to reunite (they refused), and in September, Sid Bernstein, who had been the Beatles' U.S. promoter from 1964 to 1966, took out a full-page ad begging the men to reunite for a charity event, but with no success.

In the same year, Lorne Michaels, producer of the late-night comedy program *Saturday Night Live,* made what would become a running gag with his offer of $3,000 to the Beatles to appear on his show. The camera zoomed in on an actual check made out for $3,000 from NBC and payable to the Beatles. One month later, Michaels upped the offer to $3,200 (an extra $50 each). Paul said later in interviews that he and John were watching the *SNL* broadcast from Lennon's apartment in New York City on the night Michaels made the first offer. He said the two briefly toyed with the idea of going down to the NBC studio and taking Michaels up on it.

But the Beatles did reunite, to some extent, in 1995 with the collaboration of Paul, George, and Ringo on remakes of previously unreleased demo recordings John had made prior to his death. "Free As a Bird" and "Real Love" (a single John had released earlier on his *Imagine* album) featured newly recorded vocal and instrumental tracks by Paul, George, and Ringo. These were overdubbed on tracks John had done at home, meticulously remixed by producer Jeff Lynne, and released to the accolades of eager fans.

Not even John's death quelled fans' clamors for a Beatles reunion. Paul said some had suggested to him that Julian Lennon take his famous father's role! Finally, the wild hopes of many Beatles fans for a reunion were permanently dashed with the death of George Harrison in 2001. Paul and Ringo did reunite in April of 2004, performing songs such as "With a Little Help From My Friends" for the David Lynch Foundation's benefit concert—a cause that the late George Harrison had supported.

And the Mania Went On

A huge variety of Beatles books and Beatles-oriented cartoon shows, TV specials, documentaries and related projects emerged after the group's demise. Most notable of these were the 1978 Robert Stigwood film *Sgt. Pepper's Lonely Hearts Club Band*—featuring the Bee Gees, Peter Frampton, and Earth, Wind and Fire—and the British film parody *All You Need Is Cash* by the Rutles (featuring several of the Monty Python troupe) that same year.

Meanwhile, Beatles song compilations, sheet-music collections, interview tapes, videos and DVDs, and other items continued to be marketed and sold in great quantity, and Liverpool, like Graceland, became a kind of city-wide shrine to devoted fans. Nearly 20,000 Beatles offerings appeared on the online auctioneer eBay as of September 2005, from one-cent Beatles books to a $15,000 mint condition "Butcher Block" cover. (This is the infamous "Dead Babies" cover that the Beatles did initially as a joke. It depicts the Fab Four wearing white butcher aprons and draped in raw meat and baby doll arms, legs and heads. Capitol Records refused to release the album as it was, so the boys had some plain studio shots done instead. These were then glued over the several thousand printed original album covers, but removing the substitute cover in such a way as to preserve the "Butcher" cover beneath it intact results in the high price.)

The four Beatles' authenticated autographs, together on the same item and dated prior to 1967, was the most collectable set of signatures in entertainment history, often fetching multiples of thousands of dollars. Original sets of handwritten Beatle lyrics sheets and rare or bootleg recordings were also highly sought after by fans and collectors. After the deaths of John and George, major auction houses sold a number of their personal and musical items to the highest bidders for great sums of money. For example,

John's scrawled lyrics for "All You Need Is Love" fetched $1 million at a Christie's auction, and a guitar George had owned went for $550,000.

Summary

The music of Elvis, and then the Beatles, was wild and energetic—based in the exciting melodies and rhythms of R&B music. But even as youths embraced this sound as their own, many in the established music fields saw Rock 'n' Roll as the downfall of the music business for professional musicians. With Rock 'n' Roll, it seemed anyone with a guitar and the knowledge of three chords could make an impact, and jazz and classical musicians looked down their noses at the emerging style and its uneducated performers. Critics, including some clergy, denounced Elvis as vulgar and incompetent, and feared his corruptive influence on American youth.

But no amount of verbal degradation could stop the sheer momentum of social and cultural change symbolized by first Elvis, and then the Beatles. These artists presented fresh musical alternatives and countercultural lifestyles to teens (and many adults) who were attempting to break away from the staid norms of their parents. They were viewed as dangerous symbols of rebellion by some and worshiped as gods on earth by others, but the truth lies somewhere in between.

Elvis, and then the Beatles, kicked open the doors to musical and social change by being unique as individuals and performers and by paving the way for other musicians to build upon their success (from Rockabilly-artists-turned–Rock 'n' Rollers to the continued wave of British Invasion music). Their ultimate confidence, dedication, and understanding of the musical art forms in which they were leaders seemed to have pushed many criticisms aside with the passage of time. The introduction of college music courses at many schools covering Elvis and the Beatles also elevates their stature as "legitimate" musicians, placing them among the greatest performers and composers of the millennium.

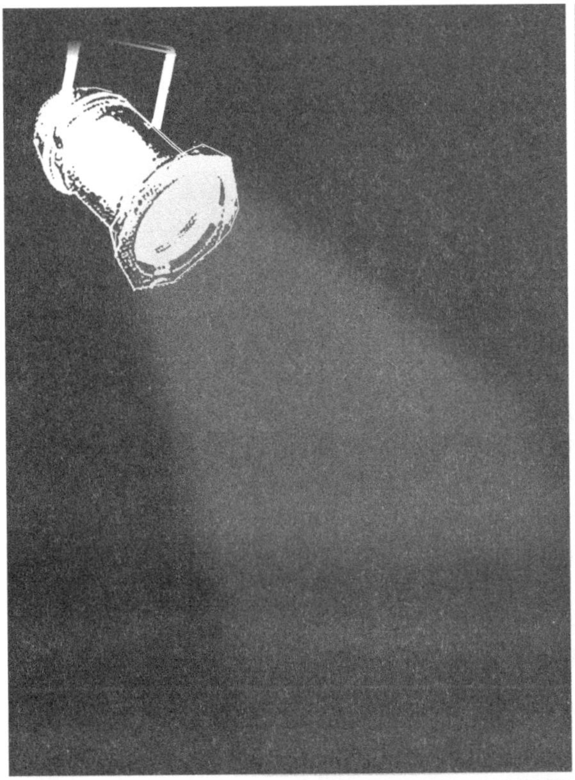

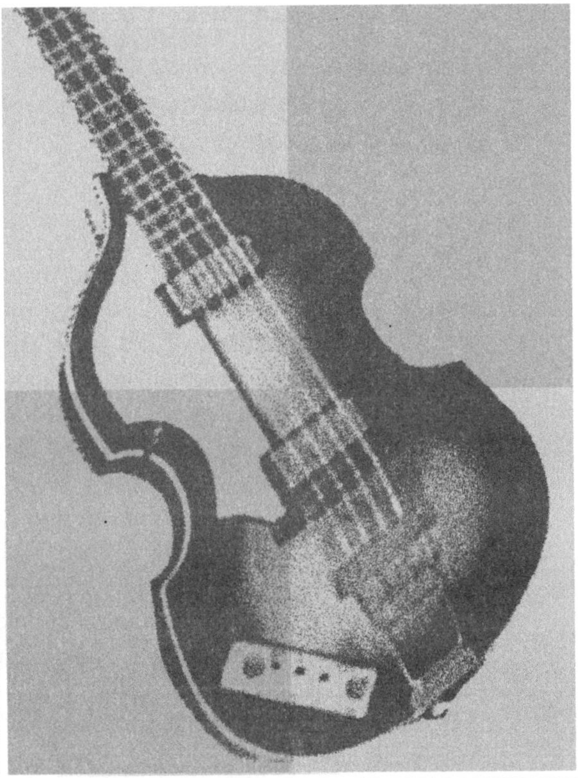

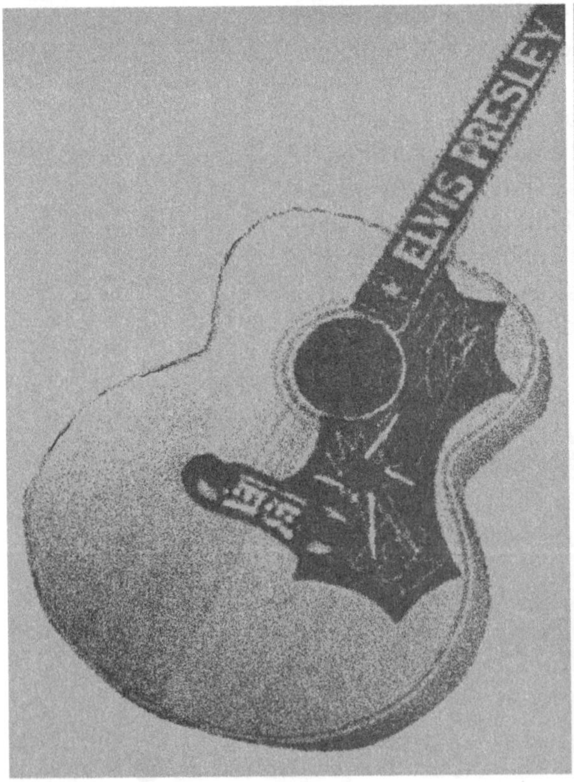
ELVIS PRESLEY

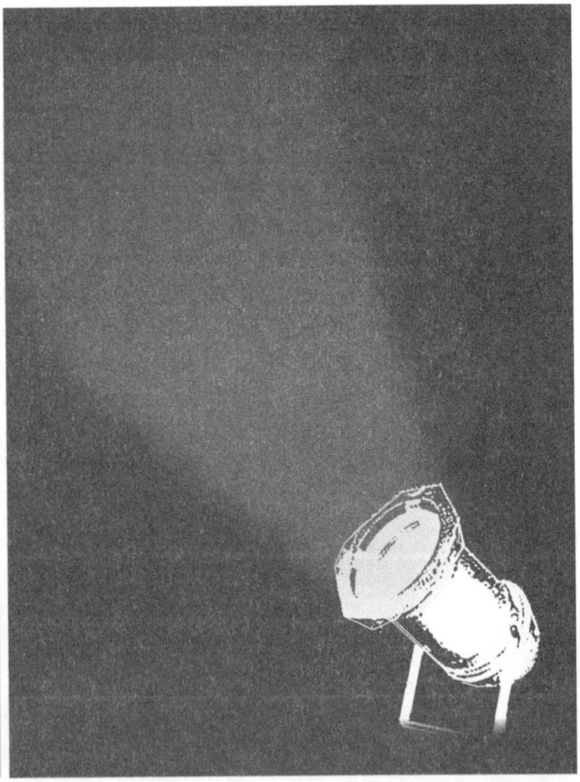

CHAPTER 8

Charts and Sales by the Numbers

Both the Beatles and Elvis were musical pioneers, each pushing the musical envelope and exploring genres in a new way. Elvis simply created a new sound intuitively—utilizing Blues, Gospel, and Country & Western to create new music. The Beatles, by their own admission, built off of the foundation laid by Elvis and others.

The recording industry has a complex way of tracking a record's success. In addition to the overall style of music, such as Rock, Pop, Country, Blues or Jazz, there are sub-categories and even sub-sub-categories within these major musical modes, all of which are tracked and charted by compilation organizations such as Cash Box, Record World, and Billboard. There are many categories of music used to chart an individual's or group's success, and things can get a little complicated! The whole racket can seem like a numbers maze that loops back on itself, causing confusion and arguments. But the essential thing to appreciate is that, in terms of numbers and charts, Elvis and the Beatles were as huge as Pop stars could get, and both set records that remained unbroken even decades after their careers were over.

SINGLES

Rock 'n' Roll was disseminated via radio to be certain, but its main impact most certainly came from the sale of two-sided

TABLE 8.1 Top 40 Singles

NUMBER OF	ELVIS	BEATLES
Top 40 singles	114	52
Gold singles (500,000 copies sold)	24	18
Platinum singles (1 million copies sold)	20	2
Double-platinum singles	5	3
Triple-platinum singles	1	0
Quadruple-platinum singles	1	1
No. 1 singles	18	20
No. 2 singles	6	3
Total singles in Top 10	40	34
Total singles in Top 20	68	40
Singles also No. 1 Adult Contemp.	7	1
Singles also No. 1 R&B	6	0
Singles also No. 1 C&W	10	0

45 rpm singles. The A side was usually the more popular of the two songs and charted higher than the B side, which sometimes went unnoticed. This was not the case, though, with the Beatles or Elvis, as their B sides were often also outstanding compositions and performances.

Elvis had more hit singles than the Beatles, with almost twice as many in the American Top 40 as the Beatles.

The Beatles had only one No. 1 hit in the category known as "adult contemporary," with "Let It Be," and no Country & Western or R&B No. 1 singles, despite the influence both of these styles had on their early music. Most of Elvis's hits in these two categories came early in his career, with his adult contemporary hits occurring after the 1960s. Elvis leads in every chart designation except No. 1 singles; the Beatles have two more No. 1 hits than Elvis. The Beatles hold the record for the most Cash Box U.S. No. 1 singles (22) and the most Record World U.S. No. 1 singles (23), which chart market success numbers.

The Beatles also hold the following U.S. singles-chart records:

- Highest jump to No. 1: No. 27 to No. 1 "Can't Buy Me Love"
- Most simultaneous songs in the Top 100: 14
- Most simultaneous songs in the Top 40: 7
- Most simultaneous songs in the Top 20: 6
- Most simultaneous songs in the Top 10: 5

A teenage Elvis fan lounges on her bed, surrounded by photos of Elvis, and listening to his records. ©
Bettmann/CORBIS

London police struggling against Beatlemania, 1965 ... Policemen struggle to restrain young Beatles fans outside Buckingham Palace as the Beatles receive their MBEs (Member of the British Empire) in 1965. John Lennon later returned his MBE in September 1969, in protest against British politics. © *Hulton-Deutsch Collection/CORBIS*

- Only act that replaced itself twice at No. 1
- Most entries in the charts within a calendar year: 30 (1964)
- Most No. 1s within a calendar year: 6 (1964)

All of these records occurred between January and April 1964, covering the Beatles' arrival and first tour of America, a time period of less than three months (February through April), comparable to Elvis's astounding rise to fame in 1956.

In addition, the Beatles' U.S. singles records include:

- Most consecutive No. 1 hits by a group: 6
- Most weeks spent on the charts by a group: 629

- Top-selling single of the '60s: "I Want to Hold Your Hand," with "Hey Jude" second
- Largest one-week sales: 940,225 ("Can't Buy Me Love")
- Largest advanced order: 1,700,000 ("Can't Buy Me Love")
- Most Top 10 hits by a group: 34

Internationally, 2,100,000 advanced orders were sold for "Can't Buy Me Love."

Worldwide, the Beatles had the most No. 1 singles in the following countries: Germany, 12; Australia, 23; Sweden, 18; Canada, 22; Holland, 23; and U.K., 5. Beatles producer George Martin is the most successful producer in the U.S. singles charts with twenty-one No. 1 hit singles.

Paul McCartney wrote the most U.S. No. 1 singles (thirty-two) and John Lennon wrote the second most (twenty-six) to combine as the top songwriting team in Pop history. The most covered song in history (done by artists other than the Beatles) as of 2005, was Paul's "Yesterday," with over 2,500 versions, including one by Elvis. The Beatles were also the only group whose individual members all had No. 1 solo singles in the U.S. Paul had nine No. 1s, with "Say Say Say" going platinum (over 1 million in sales) in 1983. John had three No. 1 singles, including the gold record "Just Like Starting Over" in 1980. George came in with three No. 1 singles, with "My Sweet Lord" going Gold in 1970. And Ringo earned two No. 1 single spots, with Harrison's composition "Photograph" a huge hit for Ringo in 1973. As for million-selling singles, both Elvis and the Beatles had twenty-nine.

COLD HARD FACT

Who had the most No. 1 hits, Elvis or the Beatles?

Elvis had a career span from 1956 (the year of his first No. 1 with "Heartbreak Hotel") to 1977, or twenty-one years. The Beatles charted from 1963 (with "She Loves You"/"I'll Get You" in the U.S. and "Please Please Me"/"Ask Me Why" in the U.K.) to 1970, or seven years. So longevity should count for something. But total No. 1 hits are the questions of the moment, and in the end the Beatles lose to Elvis: Liverpool 22, Memphis 29.

The biggest selling Beatles single was "Hey Jude" with "Revolution" on the B side. Entering the Billboard Top 40 charts on September 14, 1968, it was the first Beatles release on their new Apple Label (Apple 2276) and was the most commercially successful single of their career, reaching No. 1 in twelve countries. The Beatles performed "Hey Jude" and "Revolution" on *The David Frost Show* in 1968, their first performance since touring ended in 1966. Paul composed "Hey Jude" for John's son, Julian (although John always felt it was a song to him), while Paul was driving out to visit John and his family during the final days of John's marriage to his first wife, Cynthia. Paul said he originally sang "Hey Jules" but decided "Hey Jude" sounded stronger and more Country & Western. "Hey Jude" is the Beatles' longest song, at seven minutes and eleven seconds. (Although the musical montage "Revolution 9" from *The White Album* comes in at over eight minutes, it is not really considered a "song.")

"Hey Jude" was the first lengthy song to get radio airplay, as radio stations still preferred short songs that lasted no more than three minutes or so. When "Hey Jude" became a hit, radio programmers realized that listeners would stay tuned if they enjoyed the songs regardless of their length, paving the way for such extended anthems as "Layla" by Derek and the Dominos (Eric Clapton), and Don McLean's "American Pie," and much of the Progressive and Art Rock music of the 1970s. "Hey Jude" was the thirty-eighth Top 40 single for the group. It was No. 1 on the charts for nine weeks and in the Top 40 for nineteen weeks, and it sold over 4 million copies. (The great Memphis Soul singer Wilson Pickett recorded a cover version later that year that reached No. 23 on the U.S. charts.)

The biggest selling Elvis single was "Don't Be Cruel," backed by "Hound Dog," which entered the charts on August 4, 1956. Elvis's fourth single for RCA (RCA Victor 47-6604) is often referred to as "double A sided," as both songs reached No. 1 on the charts and remained there for eleven weeks. "Don't Be Cruel" was on the Top 40 charts for twenty-three weeks and sold over 4 million copies. It is the only single in history to have had both the A and B sides reach No. 1 in the United States.

"Don't Be Cruel" was an Otis "Bumps" Blackwell–style composition (also co-credited to Elvis). Elvis did twenty-eight takes of this song before finding the right sound. He went on to record many Blackwell-penned songs, including "All Shook Up,"

> ### COLD HARD FACT
>
> **Who wrote the most No. 1 hits, Elvis or the Beatles?**
>
> Numbers are funny things—they don't show authorship, for one thing. While Elvis is co-credited with some of his biggest hits, it was standard practice at the time for songwriters to submit songs to him to perform by agreeing to relinquish half the publishing rights to Hill & Range/Gladys Music, Elvis's song publishing companies. This allowed Elvis to have his name on "Heartbreak Hotel," "Don't Be Cruel," "Hound Dog," and many others in his catalog, while his actual writing contributions to these songs were dubious at best. The Beatles, on the other hand, were the authors of *all* of their No. 1 singles, and all except Harrison's "Something" in 1969 were penned by Lennon and/or McCartney. So when it came to *writing* songs as well as performing them, the Fabs won this one.

"Return to Sender," "One Broken Heart for Sale," and "Fever," which was made famous by Peggy Lee. "Don't Be Cruel" also reached No. 1 on Juke Box charts, Top 100 charts, Jockey (Disc Jockey charts), and the R&B and Country & Western charts but was not released on an album until Elvis's *Golden Records* in March 1958. The song proved durable throughout the years, as Elvis's bass player, Bill Black, released a No. 11 instrumental cover version in 1960, and Cheap Trick had a No. 4 hit in 1988 with their rendition. "Don't Be Cruel" was inducted into the Rock 'n' Roll Hall of Fame in 2002.

"Hound Dog," the B side to "Don't Be Cruel," was a Jerry Leiber–Mike Stoller R&B-style composition first made popular by Willie Mae "Big Mama" Thornton in 1953. Leiber and Stoller wrote several other songs for Elvis, including the soundtrack for the *Jailhouse Rock* film. During Elvis's first (unsuccessful) Las Vegas gig in 1956, he heard Freddie Bell and the Bellboys performing a comedy version of "Hound Dog" when they appeared as his opening act. Working largely as his own producer, Elvis recorded "Hound Dog" during the same session as "Don't Be Cruel," recording thirty-one takes. This song was also a No. 1 hit

No. 10 - "Don't Be Cruel / "Hound Dog" - Elvis
Peak year: 1956
18 weeks on the charts
24 weeks in the Top 40
21 weeks in the Top 10
11 weeks at No. 1

No. 19 - "All Shook Up" - Elvis
Peak year: 1957
30 weeks on the charts
22 weeks in the Top 40
15 weeks in the Top 10
9 weeks at No. 1

No. 21 - "Hey Jude" - Beatles
Peak year: 1968
19 weeks on the charts
19 weeks in the Top 40
14 weeks in the Top 10
9 weeks at No. 1

No. 28 - "Heartbreak Hotel" - Elvis
Peak year: 1956
27 weeks on the charts
22 weeks in the Top 40
15 weeks in the Top 10
8 weeks at No. 1

No. 40 - "Jailhouse Rock" - Elvis
Peak year: 1957
27 weeks on the charts
19 weeks in the Top 40
15 weeks in the Top 10
7 weeks at No. 1

No. 42 - "(Let Me Be) Your Teddy Bear" - Elvis
Peak year: 1957
25 weeks on the charts
18 weeks in the Top 40
14 weeks in the Top 10
7 weeks at No. 1

No. 49 - "I Want to Hold Your Hand" - Beatles
Peak year: 1964
15 weeks on the charts
14 weeks in the Top 40
12 weeks in the Top 10
7 weeks at No. 1

No. 80 - "Are You Lonesome Tonight?" - Elvis
Peak year: 1960
16 weeks on the charts
14 weeks in the Top 40
11 weeks in the Top 10
6 weeks at No. 1

No. 92 - "Love Me Tender" - Elvis
Peak year: 1956
23 weeks on the charts
19 weeks in the Top 40
15 weeks in the Top 10
5 weeks at No. 1

Chart 8-1 Top 100 Singles 1955–1999 (from Whitburn's *Billboard Book of Top 40 Singles*)

on the Juke Box charts, Top 100 charts (No. 2), Jockey, and the R&B and Country & Western charts. During his first appearance on *The Milton Berle Show* on June 5, 1956, Elvis's hip-swiveling leg-shaking performance ignited the first real controversy of his career. Though the audience fans squealed with delight, television critics across the nation called the performance "vulgar" and "animalistic" and observed an "appalling lack of musicality." In July of that year, Elvis appeared on *The Steve Allen Show,* where Allen, not an Elvis or Rock 'n' Roll fan, insisted that the "new and improved" Elvis wear formal white-tie-and tails while singing this song to a basset hound. Elvis did it good-naturedly, and laughed all the way to the bank.

Elvis had more Top 40 singles than did the Beatles and frequently crossed over to the Country, R&B and easy listening charts with great success. His versatility with singles in different musical sales arenas is unmatched in music history.

ALBUMS

LPs, or long-playing records, quickly became the industry standard for releasing multiple songs and/or singles by one group or artist in a concise package. Elvis dominated in most categories (see Table 8.2).

Comparing soundtrack and live albums is significant to the comparison between Elvis and the Beatles, because the King had so many more soundtrack albums—seventeen—compared to the Beatles' mere four. Elvis's soundtrack albums were drawn from his large film catalog of thirty-one feature films, plus two film documentaries. The Beatles made only five feature films (*A Hard Day's Night, Help!, Magical Mystery Tour, Yellow Submarine,* and *Let it Be*). Furthermore, the Beatles released only one major live album

TABLE 8.2 Top 40 Albums

NUMBER OF	ELVIS	BEATLES
Top 40 albums	50	34
Gold albums (500,000 copies sold)	25	10
Platinum albums (1 million copies sold)	14	5
Double-platinum albums	8	2
Triple-platinum albums	2	2
Quadruple-platinum albums	0	3
Quintuple-platinum albums	1	4
6 million or more sold	1	4
No. 1 albums	10	19
No. 2 albums	2	6
Total albums in Top 10	26	29
Total albums in Top 20	39	32

(*Live at the Hollywood Bowl*) before the advent of *The Beatles Anthology* in 1995, while Elvis's movie work spawned both soundtrack and live albums over most of his career. As for live or concert recordings, Elvis had eight albums culled mainly from performances, while the Beatles had only one–*Live at the Hollywood Bowl*–though *Let It Be* does have live songs from the Abbey Road studio's rooftop performance in London in January 1969. Elvis dominates in this category, as the Beatles only toured internationally from 1964 through 1966, with very few commercial concert recordings made.

Twenty-one of Elvis's most successful albums were collections, including the more recent *Elvis: 30 No. 1 Hits,* a No. 1 Pop and Country & Western multi-platinum success. Released September 24, 2002, it became the first album ever released by Elvis to debut at the top of the U.S. charts and was No. 1 in seventeen countries and territories. Elvis had three Gospel albums in the Top 40, and won three Grammys in that field of music. He also had five Christmas albums in the Top 40. *The Elvis Christmas Album,* first released in 1957, had sold 9 million copies as of 2002.

Twenty-first-century observers sometimes find it hard to understand why albums were so meaningful in the 1950s and 1960s. This was a pre-video, pre-MTV, pre-Internet radio culture; mass media consisted of the three television networks (none of which broadcast programming twenty-four hours a day), radio airplay for music, and the occasional live performance. Albums provided the one constant link between a performer and his or her audience, and failure to issue records on a timely basis could make or break an act.

The Beatles did release Christmas albums, but these were fan club records that did not chart (but became quite collectible). Parlaphone, the Beatles U.K. label under EMI Company, released only twelve "official" Beatles albums in Britain, but Capitol released twenty-three Top 40 Beatles albums on its label, including several collections and reissues, plus the three platinum anthologies. The most successful Beatles albums included the multi-platinum *Sgt. Pepper's Lonely Hearts Club Band, The Beatles (The White Album), Abbey Road,* and *The Beatles 1,* which, as of 2006, was still the fastest-selling album in history, with 20 million copies sold in nine weeks.

In albums, the Beatles held the following U.S. records, as of 2006:

- Most No. 1 albums: 19
- Cash Box No. 1 albums: 15

- Most Record World No. 1 albums: 17
- Most weeks spent on the album charts by a group: 1,985
- Most weeks at No. 1: 132
- Most consecutive No. 1 hit albums: 8
- Most No. 1 albums within a calendar year: 3 (1964–66)
- Most Recording Industry Association of America (RIAA) diamond awards for sales exceeding 10 million: 5
- Highest RIAA certified album sales: 163.5 million
- RIAA-certified album sales equal to 328 gold albums
- RIAA-certified album sales equal to 161 platinum albums
- Top-selling album of the 1960s: *Sgt. Pepper's Lonely Hearts Club Band,* (*A Hard Day's Night* album holds second place)

In 1964, the Beatles sold approximately 35 million singles and albums in the U.S. and nearly 75 million worldwide. The Beatles dominated the U.S. singles and album charts in 1964, with the top five singles, and the No. 1 and No. 2 albums on the charts. They also held the No. 1 and No. 2 positions for nine consecutive weeks on two occasions in 1964, and completely dominated both the U.S. and U.K. charts. In 1997, New York radio station WNEW-FM (102.7) conducted a listener's survey, and the Beatles came away with three albums in the Top 10: *Sgt. Pepper's Lonely Hearts Club Band, Abbey Road,* and *The Beatles* (*The White Album*). *Sgt. Pepper's* was also elected Album of the Century and Album of the Millennium in 2000 by the writers at *Rolling Stone* magazine.

Elvis had a lifetime career span nearly double that of the Beatles, yet simple extrapolation of their respective numbers shows that the boys from Liverpool accomplished almost as much as the King in a shorter period of time.

Posthumous Sales

Chart sales following a group's breakup or the demise of its members is a relatively new phenomenon, at least in terms of the degree of success achieved by Elvis and the Beatles. This can largely be attributed to their continuing popularity: In both cases, their respective musical catalogs sold for the same price per unit as did current musical acts, and in some cases even more.

Even after the breakup of the Beatles in 1970 and the release of *Let It Be,* the group had five Top 40 singles and fourteen Top 40 albums, as of 2005. These singles included "Free As a Bird" and "Real Love," both created in the mid 1990s by combining late 1970s home

> **Points are awarded this way:**
> No. 1 = 100 points for its first week at No. 1, plus 10 points for each additional week
> No. 2 = 90 points for its first week at No. 2, plus 5 points for each additional week
> No. 3 = 80 points for its first week at No. 3, plus 3 points for each additional week
> Nos. 4-5 = 70 points
> Nos. 6-10 = 60 points
> Nos. 11-20 = 50 points
> Nos. 21-30 = 45 points
> Nos. 31-40 = 40 points
>
> **TOP 100 ARTISTS 1955-1999**
> No. 1 - Elvis Presley - 8,067 points
> No. 2 - Beatles - 4,703 points
>
> **TOP ARTISTS BY DECADE**
> 1950s ('55-'59)
> No. 1 - Elvis Presley - 3,324 points
>
> **1960s ('60-'69)**
> No. 1 - Beatles - 4,142 points
> No. 2 - Elvis - 3,455
>
> **1970s ('70-'79)**
> No. 2 - Paul McCartney - 2,020 points
> No. 11 - Elvis - 1,238
>
> **1980s ('80-'89)**
> No. 21 - Paul McCartney - 963 points

Chart 8-2 Top 40 points earned by Elvis and the Beatles

recordings by John with vocals and instruments added by the remaining three Beatles. Very few groups continue to be as successful as the Beatles after disbanding. Post-breakup albums included the Beatles 1962–66 and 1967–70 compilations, the *Live at the BBC* collection of early radio performances, the three *Anthology* albums made up of rarities and outtakes, and *The Beatles 1* album, which had sold over 8 million copies as of 2005. In the first five days after the 9/9/09 release of the Beatles re-mastered albums on CD, over two million copies were sold worldwide. In the same year, an apple-shaped USB drive was released containing all fourteen re-mastered Beatles albums with artwork, photos, and new and expanded descriptive materials.

At least two dozen albums of Elvis material were released after his death, including one live album, fourteen collections, four

Most charted singles
No. 1 - Elvis - 114
No. 3 - Beatles - 52
No. 13 - Paul McCartney - 37

Most Top 10 singles
No. 1 - Elvis - 38
No. 2 - Beatles - 34
No. 9 - Paul McCartney - 22

Most No. 1 singles
No. 1 - Beatles - 20
No. 2 - Elvis - 18
No. 11 - Paul McCartney - 9

Most weeks in No. 1 position
No. 1 - Elvis - 80
No. 3 - Beatles - 59
No. 8 - Paul McCartney - 30

Chart 8-3 Top 40 Artist Achievements

Christmas albums, and one Gospel LP. In December 1977, four months after his death, Elvis's version of "My Way" (from his earlier CBS television special *Elvis in Concert*) reached the Top 40. In 1981, guitarist Jerry Reed's remix of the 1968 Elvis recording of "Guitar Man" also entered the Top 40, reaching No. 28. Recent contemporary dance-style remixes of Elvis songs, including "A Little Less Conversation," have also done well on the charts. The *Elvis: 30 No. 1 Hits* continued to sell into the twenty-first century.

As of 2005, Elvis Presley had sold more than a billion records worldwide, more than anyone in music history. Both Elvis and the Beatles had sold more than 100 million records domestically. RIAA recognized the Beatles for the highest combined singles and album sales (192.5 million records sold) and in 1999 named the Beatles the Most Successful Recording Act of the Twentieth Century in America. In October of 2009, Elvis' 17-year-old grandson Benjamin Presley signed a five-album, $5 million recording deal with Universal.

AWARDS AND HONORS

Both Elvis and the Beatles received various awards and honors outside the field of music for their humanitarian and charitable

TABLE 8.3 Elvis's Grammy Awards

YEAR	CATEGORY	SONG/ALBUM
1967	Best Sacred Performance	"How Great Thou Art"
1971	Lifetime Achievement Award	
1972	Best Inspirational Performance	"He Touched Me"
1974	Best Inspirational Performance	"How Great Thou Art"
1978	Music City News Country Album of the Year	
1986	Special American Music Award	
1988	Hall of Fame Awards	
1995	Hall of Fame Awards	
1998	Hall of Fame Awards	

contributions. In 1965, the Beatles were honored with MBE awards (Members of the British Empire). Elvis was named "One of the Ten Most Outstanding Young Men of the Nation" by the U.S. Junior Chamber of Commerce in 1971, and the "Young Elvis" commemorative stamp, when issued in 1993, became the most successful in the history of the U.S. Postal Service.

The Beatles won thirty-one Grammy Awards from 1964 to 2004; Elvis won nine (see tables 8.3 and 8.4). The Beatles as a group and its individual members also received thirty-two non-winning Grammy nominations as of 2005. In November of 2009, Paul McCartney was honored with the Library of Congress Gershwin Prize for Popular Song, with an all-star tribute concert planned for Spring of 2010. Paul is the third artist to receive this award, following Paul Simon and Stevie Wonder. Ringo Starr was given a

> **COLD HARD FACT**
>
> The Grammy Awards, the recording industry's most prestigious honor, are presented annually by the Recording Academy. A Grammy (so named because it uses a gramophone as its symbol) is awarded by the Academy's voting membership to honor excellence in the recording arts and sciences. There are various categories within the award process, including Lifetime Achievement Awards, Trustees Awards, Technical Awards and Hall of Fame Awards, to name a few.

TABLE 8.4 The Beatles' Grammy Awards

YEAR	CATEGORY	SONG/ALBUM
1964	Best New Artist	
1964	Best Performance by a Vocal Group	"A Hard Day's Night"
1966	Best Contemp. Pop Vocal Perf., Male	Paul, "Eleanor Rigby"
1966	Song of the Year	"Michelle"
1967	Album of the Year	*Sgt. Pepper's*
1967	Best Contemp. R&R Recording	*Sgt. Pepper's*
1967	Best Album Cover	*Sgt. Pepper's*
1967	Best Engineered Recording	*Sgt. Pepper's*
1969	Best Engineered Recording	*Abbey Road*
1970	Best Motion Picture Original Score	*Let It Be*
1975	Hall of Fame	
1990	Lifetime Achievement Award	Paul McCartney
1991	Lifetime Achievement Award	John Lennon
1993	Hall of Fame	*Sgt. Pepper's*
1995	Lifetime Achievement Award	George Martin
1995	Hall of Fame	*Abbey Road*
1996	Best Pop Perf. By a Duo or Group w/ Vocal	"Free As A Bird"
1996	Best Music Video, Short Form	"Free As A Bird"
1996	Best Music Video, Long Form	*The Beatles Anthology*
1997	Hall of Fame	"Yesterday"
1998	Hall of Fame	"I Want to Hold Your Hand"
1999	Hall of Fame	*Revolver*
1999	Hall of Fame	"Strawberry Fields"
1999	Hall of Fame	"Imagine", John
2000	Hall of Fame	*Rubber Soul*
2000	Hall of Fame	*White Album*
2000	Hall of Fame	*A Hard Day's Night*
2001	Hall of Fame	"Hey Jude"
2001	Hall of Fame	*Meet the Beatles*
2002	Hall of Fame	"Eleanor Rigby"
2004	Hall of Fame	"Let It Be"

star on the Hollywood Walk of Fame in February of 2009, with the Beatles having received one as a group in 1998.

The National Academy of Recording Arts and Sciences (NARAS) gave Trustee awards to the Beatles in 1972 and to George Martin in 1996. Four other groups or artists won Grammys for covers of Beatles songs. In 2004, the Beatles won the NARAS President's Award, a special Grammy award to mark the group's inspirational achievement and to celebrate the band's anniversary of their arrival in the US.

Rock 'n' Roll Hall of Fame

Induction into the Rock 'n' Roll Hall of Fame in Cleveland, Ohio, is a tremendous honor for any artist or group, since it means recognition from musical peers as well as from the record industry itself. It is the best indication of the significance of a musician or group to the industry in general and the world as a whole. An artist or band that achieves placement in the Rock 'n' Roll Hall of Fame is akin to any sports figure honored in comparable halls of fame regarding power of recognition and longevity. Only the cream of the crop in the Pop music world are considered for induction. Elvis was inducted in 1986, and the Beatles as a group in 1988. (See Table 8.5 for the induction dates for the individual members of the Beatles.) Elvis was also inducted into the Country Music Hall of Fame, in 1998.

When Elvis and the Beatles were in their recording heyday, charting singles and albums were used as both a public relations device and a way to increase an artist's revenue base by demanding higher performance and recording fees. No one could have predicted that, decades later, these same statistics would provide a means to codify popularity and start arguments among fans the world over. In the final analysis, they can only determine historical fact. They are a window into the past, but one that only shows static images—merely the indicators, not the individuals.

"What is essential is invisible to the eye," said Antoine de Saint-Exupéry, and this has never been truer than in the case of the Beatles and Elvis Presley. Numbers cannot convey their respective power to elevate, inspire, and delight audiences the world over, from one generation to the next. They are truly immortal.

TABLE 8.5 Year of Induction Into the Rock 'n' Roll Hall of Fame

YEAR	ARTIST
1986	Elvis
1988	Beatles
1994	John Lennon
1999	Paul McCartney
1999	George Martin
2004	George Harrison

Appendix A
Elvis's Musicians

Elvis's musicians (in recording / performance order):

YEAR	PERFORMER	INSTRUMENT
1954	Scotty Moore	guitar
	Bill Black	bass
	Jimmy Day	steel guitar
	Floyd Cramer	piano
1955	Scotty Moore	guitar
	Bill Black	bass
	Jimmie Lott	drums
	Johnny Bernero	drums
1956	Scotty Moore	guitar
	Bill Black	bass
	Chet Atkins	guitar
	D.J. Fontana	drums
	Floyd Cramer	piano
	Gordon Stoker	piano
	Shorty Long	piano
	Marvin Hughes	piano
	Vito Mumolo	guitar
	Mike "Myer" Rubin	bass
	Richard Cornell	drums
	Luther Roundtree	banjo
	Dom Frontieri	accordion
	Carl Fortina	accordion
1957	Scotty Moore	guitar
	Bill Black	bass
	D.J. Fontana	drums
	Gordon Stocker	piano
	Hoyt Hawkins	piano / organ
	Tiny Timbrell	guitar
	Dudley Brooks	piano
	George Fields	harmonica
	Mike Stoller	piano
1958	Scotty Moore	guitar
	Bill Black	bass

continued

	D.J. Fontana	drums / bongos
	Ray Siegel	bass / tuba
	Gordon Stocker	bongos
	Hoyt Hawkins	cymbals
	Bernie Mattinson	drums
	Dudley Brooks	piano
	Mahlon Clark	clarinet
	John Ed Buckner	trumpet
	Justin Gordon	saxophone
	Elmer Schneider	trombone
	Warren D. Smith	trombone
	Hank Garland	guitar
	Buddy Harman	drums
1960	Scotty Moore	guitar
	Bob Moore	bass
	Hank Garland	guitar / electric bass
	Buddy Harman	drums
	Floyd Cramer	piano
	Boots Randolph	saxophone
1961	Scotty Moore	guitar
	Bob Moore	bass
	Hank Garland	guitar
	Buddy Harman	drums
	D.J. Fontana	drums
	Floyd Cramer	piano / organ
	Boots Randolph	saxophone / claves
	Neal Matthews	guitar
	Gordon Stoker	piano / accordion
	Jerry Kennedy	guitar
1962	Scotty Moore	guitar
	Harold Bradley	guitar
	Grady Martin	guitar / vibes
	Bob Moore	bass
	Buddy Harman	drums
	D.J. Fontana	drums
	Floyd Cramer	piano
	Boots Randolph	saxophone
1963	Scotty Moore	guitar
	Grady Martin	guitar
	Jerry Kennedy	guitar
	Harold Bradley	guitar
	Bob Moore	bass
	Buddy Harman	drums
	D. J. Fontana	drums

	Floyd Cramer	piano
	Boots Randolph	saxophone / vibes / shakers
1964	Scotty Moore	guitar
	Grady Martin	guitar
	Harold Bradley	guitar
	Bob Moore	bass
	Buddy Harman	drums
	D.J. Fontana	drums
	Floyd Cramer	piano / organ
	Boots Randolph	saxophone / vibes
1966	Scotty Moore	guitar
	Chip Young	guitar
	Bob Moore	bass
	Henry Strzelecki	bass
	Charlie McCoy	bass / harmonica
	Buddy Harman	drums / tympani
	D.J. Fontana	drums
	Floyd Cramer	piano
	David Briggs	piano / organ
	Henry Slaughter	piano / organ
	Peter Drake	steel guitar
	Rufus Long	baritone saxophone
	Boots Randolph	tenor saxophone
	Ray Stevens	trumpet
1967	Scotty Moore	guitar
	Chip Young	guitar
	Grady Martin	guitar
	Bob Moore	bass
	Buddy Harman	drums
	D.J. Fontana	drums
	David Briggs	piano
	Peter Drake	steel guitar
	Charlie McCoy	harmonica / organ / guitar
	Jerry Reed	guitar
	Harold Bradley	guitar
	Boots Randolph	saxophone
1968	Scotty Moore	guitar
	Chip Young	guitar
	Jerry Reed	guitar
	Bob Moore	bass
	Buddy Harman	drums
	D.J. Fontana	drums
	Floyd Cramer	piano
	Peter Drake	steel guitar
	Charlie McCoy	harmonica

continued

	Tommy Tedesco	guitar
	Mike Deasy	guitar
	Al Casey	guitar / bass
	Charles Berghofer	bass
	Larry Knechtal	keyboards
	Don Randi	keyboards
	Hal Blaine	drums
	John Cyr	percussion
	Frank DeVito	percussion
	Tommy Morgan	harmonica
	Billy Goldenberg Orchestra	
1969	Reggie Young	guitar
	Tommy Cogbill	bass
	Mike Leech	bass
	Gene Chrisman	drums
	Bobby Wood	piano
	Ronnie Milsap	piano
	Bobby Emmons	organ
	John Hughey	steel guitar
	Ed Kollis	harmonica
	The Memphis Horns:	
	Andrew Love	tenor sax
	Wayne Jackson	trumpet
1970	James Burton	guitar
	John Wilkinson	guitar
	Charlie Hodge	guitar
	Jerry Scheff	bass
	Bob Lanning	drums
	Glen Hardin	piano
	Chip Young	guitar
	Norbert Putnam	bass
	Jerry Carrigan	drums
	David Briggs	piano / organ
	Charlie McCoy	organ / harmonica
	Farrell Morris	percussion / vibes
	Weldon Myrick	steel guitar
	Bobby Thomas	banjo
	Buddy Spicher	fuddle
	Ronnie Tutt	drums
	Eddie Hinton	guitar
	Harold Bradley	guitar
	Bobby Morris and his Orchestra	
	Joe Guercio and his Orchestra	
1971	James Burton	guitar
	Chip Young	guitar
	Charlie Hodge	guitar

	Norbert Putnam	bass
	Jerry Carrigan	drums / percussion
	David Briggs	piano
	Charlie McCoy	harmonica / organ / percussion
	Kenneth Buttrey	drums
	Joe Moscheo	piano
	Glen Spreen	piano
	Ronnie Tutt	drums
	Glen Hardin	piano
	Joe Guercio and his Orchestra	
1972	James Burton	guitar
	John Wilkinson	guitar
	Charlie Hodge	guitar
	Jerry Scheff	bass
	Ronnie Tutt	drums
	Glen Hardin	piano
	Emory Gordy	bass
	Dennis Linde	guitar
	Jerry Carrigan	drums / percussion
	Joe Guercio and his Orchestra	
1973	James Burton	guitar
	John Wilkinson	guitar
	Charlie Hodge	guitar
	Jerry Scheff	bass
	Ronnie Tutt	drums
	Glen Hardin	piano
	Reggie Young	guitar
	Tommy Cogbill	bass
	Bobby Manual	guitar
	Johnny Christopher	guitar
	Donald Dunn	bass
	Al Jackson	drums
	Jerry Carrigan	drums
	Bobby Wood	piano
	Bobby Emmons	organ
	Dennis Linde	guitar
	Thomas Hensley	bass
	Don Sumner	piano
	Norbert Putnam	bass
	David Briggs	piano / organ
	Per-Erik "Pete" Hamlin	piano / organ
	Alan Rush	guitar
	Rob Galbraith	percussion
	Bob Ogdin	piano
	Randy Cullers	organ
	Joe Guercio and his Orchestra	

continued

1974	James Burton	guitar
	John Wilkinson	guitar
	Charlie Hodge	guitar
	Duke Bardwell	bass
	Ronnie Tutt	drums
	Glen Hardin	piano
	Joe Guercio and his Orchestra	
1975	James Burton	guitar
	John Wilkinson	guitar
	Charlie Hodge	guitar
	Duke Bardwell	bass
	Ronnie Tutt	drums
	Glen Hardin	piano
	Tony Brown	piano
	David Briggs	clavinet
	Greg Gordon	clavinet
	Johnny Christopher	guitar
	Chip Young	guitar
	Norbert Putnam	bass
	Mike Leech	bass
	Buddy Spicher	fiddle
	Weldon Myrick	steel guitar
	Richard F. Morris	bells / percussion
1976	James Burton	guitar
	Jerry Scheff	bass
	Glen Hardin	piano
	David Briggs	piano / electric piano
	Bill Sanford	guitar
	Norbert Putnam	bass
	John Wilkinson	guitar
	Charlie Hodge	guitar
	Ronnie Tutt	drums
	Dennis Linde	bass
	Chip Young	guitar
	Farrell Morris	congas / tympani
	Shane Keister	Moog synthesizer
	Tony Brown	piano
	David Briggs	electric piano
	Randy Cullers	percussion
	Weldon Myrick	steel guitar
1977	James Burton	guitar
	John Wilkinson	guitar
	Jerry Scheff	bass
	Ronnie Tutt	drums
	Tony Brown	piano / organ

Bobby Ogdin	piano / electric piano
Norbert Putnam	bass
Alan Rush	guitar
Dennis Linde	guitar
Randy Cullers	drums / percussion
Richard F. Morris	bells / percussion
Tony Brown	organ
Charlie Hodge	guitar
Chip Young	guitar
Mike Leech	bass
Ralph Gallant	drums
Joe Guercio and his Orchestra	

Elvis's Back-Up Singers: Groups

YEARS	GROUP: MEMBERS	EVENTS

1956–1970	The Jordanaires:
	  Gordon Stoker (first tenor)
	  Neal Matthews (second tenor)
	  Hoyt Hawkins (baritone)
	  Hugh Jarrett (bass) (up to 6/58)
	  Ray Walker (bass) (6/58 on)
		That's The Way It Is
		Elvis Country
		Love Letters
		Loving You
		G.I. Blues
		all major singles
		all major concerts

1956	The Ken Darby Trio:
	  Chuck Prescott
	  John Dodson
	  Rad Robinson
		Love Me Tender

1962–1963	The Amigos:
	  Jose Vadiz
	  Miguel Alcaide
	  Felix Melendes
	  Pedro Berrios
	  German Vega
		Girls! Girls! Girls!
		Fun in Acapulco

1962–1965	The Mello Men:
	  Thurl Ravenscroft (bass)
	  Max Smith (tenor thru '66)
	  Gene Merlino (tenor–'66-'72)
	  Bill Lee (baritone)
	  Bob Hamlin (lead tenor thru '55)
	  Bob Stevens (lead tenor- '55-'61)
	  Bill Cole (lead tenor–'62-'72)
		It Happened at the World's Fair
		Roustaboout
		Paradise Hawaiian Style

continued

1963–1964	The Carole Lombard Quartet / Trio	*Viva Las Vegas* *Girl Happy*
1963–1965	The Jubilee Four	*Viva Las Vegas* *Girl Happy*

1966–1971	The Imperials:
	    Jake Hess
	    Jim Murray
	    Gary McSpadde
	    Armand Morales
	    Sherrill Nielsen
		How Great Thou Art
		He Touched Me
		Elvis: That's the Way It Is
		studio recordings
		live concerts

1968 & 1970	The Blossoms:
	    Darlene Love
	    Jean King
	    Fanita James
		Comeback Special
		Change of Habit

1969–1977	The Sweet Inspirations:
	    Emily (Cissy) Houston
	    Myrna Smith
	    Estelle Brown
	    Sylvia Shemwell
		Elvis: That's The Way It Is
		Elvis On Tour
		Las Vegas performances
		tours and concerts

1970–1971	The Nashville Edition:
	    Dolores Edgin
	    Hurshel Wiginton
	    Joe Babcock
	    June Page
		recording sessions

1971–1977	J.D. Sumner & The Stamps Quartet:
	    Ed Enoch (lead)
	    Ed Hill (baritone)
	    Larry Strickland
	    Donnie Sumner (lead)
	    Bill Baize
	    Buck Buckles
	    Richard Sterban (bass)
	    J.D. Sumner (bass)
	    Pat Brown (first tenor)
	    Dave Roland (baritone)
		Elvis On Tour
		major concert performances
		major studio recordings

1973–1975	The Voice:
	    Donnie Sumner
	    Per-Erik (Pete) Hallin
	    Tim Baty
	    Sherrill Nielsen	

Elvis's Back-Up Singers: Individuals

YEARS	NAME	EVENTS
1956	Gordon Stoker Ben Speer Brock Speer	recordings
1957	Millie Kirkham	recordings
1958	Kitty White	*King Creole*
1960	Charlie Hodge	recordings
1961	Millie Kirkham	recordings
1962	Millie Kirkham	recordings
1963	Joe Babcock Millie Kirkham	recordings
1964	Millie Kirkham	recordings
1966	Millie Kirkham June Page Dolores Edgin Sandy Posey	recordings
1967	Millie Kirkham	recordings
1968	Charlie Hodge	*Comeback Special*
1969	Charlie Hodge Mary Green Mary Holladay Donna Thatcher Susan Pilkington Sandy Posey Millie Kirkham Sonja Montgomery Joe Babcock Hurshel Wiginton	recordings
1970	Mary Holladay Ginger Holladay Mary Green Sandy Posey Millie Kirkham James Glaser Temple Riser	Las Vegas

Year	Singers	Notes
1971	Mary Holladay Ginger Holladay Sonja Montgomery June Page Millie Kirkham Temple Riser	recordings
1972	Kathy Westmoreland	Las Vegas concerts and tours
1973	Kathy Westmoreland Mary Holladay Ginger Holladay Mary Cain	*Aloha from Hawaii* recordings
1974	Kathy Westmoreland	concerts and tours
1975	Mary Holladay Ginger Holladay Millie Kirkham Lea J. Beranati	recordings
1976	Kathy Westmoreland Myrna Smith Wendellyn Suits Dolores Edgin Hurshel Wiginton Sherrill Nielsen	Graceland recordings

APPENDIX B
THE BEATLES' USE OF OUTSIDE INSTRUMENTS

Beatles' Outside Instrumentation

YEAR	STRINGS	BRASS	WINDS	ORCHESTRA	EAST INDIAN	CHOIR
1965	Yesterday		You've Got to Hide Your Love Away			
	Eleanor Rigby					
1966		For No One Got to Get You Into My Life Penny Lane Yellow Submarine		Strawberry Fields Forever	Love You Too	Yellow Submarine
1967	She's Leaving Within You Without You Hello Goodbye Blue Jay Way	Good Morning Good Morning Magical Mystery Tour Sgt. Pepper's Lonely Hearts Club Band I Am the Walrus	When I'm 64	A Day in the Life All You Need Is Love	Within You Without You	All You Need Is Love
	I Am the Walrus					I Am the Walrus
1968		Revolution Only a Northern Song It's All Too Much Ob-La-Di, Ob-La-Da Martha My Dear Wild Honey Pie Mother Nature's Son	Lady Madonna Ob-La-Di Ob-La-Da Savoy Truffle	Hey Jude Glass Onion	The Inner Light	Bungalow Bill Birthday
	Martha My My Dear Piggies Don't Pass Me By			Good Night		Good Night

YEAR	STRINGS	BRASS	WINDS	ORCHESTRA	EAST INDIAN	CHOIR
1969	Across the Universe Something Here Comes the Sun Golden Slumbers Carry that Weight The End	Carry that Weight				Across the Universe
1970	The Long and Winding Road I Me Mine					The Long and Winding Road

Conclusions from the Authors—Who Is the Greatest?

Mike Shellans

When all is said and done, Elvis was really #1. As John Lennon so eloquently stated, "Before Elvis, there was nothing." Would there have been a group like The Beatles had Elvis not paved the way? Likely so, but perhaps not with the same notoriety, depth or diversity that Elvis first brought to the Popular Music scene, and The Beatles used as their musical springboard.

When all the numbers and statistics are put aside for a moment, one must consider influence and impact. Yes, The Beatles accomplished in a decade what it took Elvis three decades to do, and they wrote virtually all of their own hits, while Elvis composed very little. But Elvis kicked the doors of Popular Music wide open by legitimizing the musical commingling of black and white styles, which The Beatles later drew upon when covering early Soul and Motown songs. Elvis personified Rock and Roll, bringing a living, breathing physical presence to this new music. He mesmerized the teenage Beatles and compelled them to sing his songs, imitate his style (the early, leather clad Elvis, not the rhinestone-covered jumpsuit Elvis!) and eventually, to compete with him. Elvis was the musical source, and The Beatles the greatest exponents and innovators springing from his musical well.

Bill Slater

The Beatles are #1, without a doubt!

While it is true that Elvis started it all, The Beatles took the simple form of Rock and Roll Presley originated and synthesized it into an entirely new art form. As great artists do, they took raw ingredients and shaped them into wholly new varieties of expression that still amaze and delight us, transforming the raw three-chord sound of Rock and Roll into a kaleidoscope of cultural explosions.

The lists of "firsts" by The Beatles is very long, from the initial concept of music videos, new technical achievements in recording, use of new instruments, a tapestry of lyrics with phrases that shine to this day, ground breaking visual art and a host of others.

Pioneers do what they do, and deserve credit for being first. But visionaries create new ways of seeing our world, and in the final analysis, ought to be seen as greater than those who went before . . .

And that's exactly what The Beatles did.

BIBLIOGRAPHY

Babiuk, Andy. *Beatles Gear.* San Francisco: Backbeat Books, 2001.

Badman, Keith. *The Beatles Diary, Volume 2: After the Breakup.* New York: Omnibus Press, 2001.

Badman, Keith. *The Beatles: The Dream Is Over: Off the Record 2.* New York: Omnibus Press, 2002.

Baird, Julia, with Geoffrey Giuliano. *John Lennon, My Brother.* New York: Henry Holt, 1988.

Berkenstadt, Jim and Belmo. *Black Market Beatles: The Story Behind the Lost Recordings.* Ontario: Collector's Guide Publishing, 1995.

Best, Pete, and Patrick Doncaster. *Beatle! The Pete Best Story.* New York: Dell Publishing, 1985.

Blake, John. *All You Needed Was Love.* New York: G.P. Putnam's Sons, 1981.

Brewer-Giorgro, Gail. *Is Elvis Alive?* New York: Tudor Publishing Co., 1988.

Brown, Peter, and Steven Gaines. *The Love You Make.* New York: McGraw-Hill Book Co., 1983.

Carr, Roy. *Beatles at the Movies.* New York: HarperCollins, 1999.

Carr, Roy, and Tony Tyler. *The Beatles: An Illustrated Record.* New York: Harmony Books, 1981.

Castleman, Harry, and Walter Podrazik. *All Together Now.* New York: Ballantine Books, 1975.

Choron, Sandra, and Bob Oskam. *Elvis! The Last Word.* New York: Carol Publishing Group, 1991.

Clayton, Marie. *Elvis Presley: Unseen Archives.* New York: Barnes & Noble Books, 2004.

Clayton, Marie, and Tim Hill. *The Beatles Unseen Archives.* London: Parragon, 2002.

Coleman, Ray. *Lennon.* New York: McGraw-Hill Book Co., 1984.

Coleman, Ray. *The Man Who Made the Beatles: An Intimate Biography of Brian Epstein.* New York: McGraw-Hill Book Co., 1989.

Cott, Jonathan, and Christine Doudna, eds. *The Ballad of John and Yoko.* New York: Doubleday, 1982

Davies, Hunter. *The Beatles.* New York: McGraw-Hill Book Co., 1998.

Delano, Julia. *The Beatles Album.* New York: Smithmark Publishers, 1991.

DiLello, Richard. *The Longest Cocktail Party.* Chicago: Playboy Press, 1972.

Dowlding, William J. *Beatlesongs.* New York: Simon & Schuster, 1989.

Escott, Colin, with Martin Hawkins. *Good Rockin' Tonight: Sun Records and the Birth of Rock 'n' Roll.* New York: St. Martin's Press, 1991.

Evans, Mike. *The Art of the Beatles.* New York: Beech Tree Books, 1984.

Evans, Mike, ed. *Elvis: The King on the Road.* New York: St. Martin's Press, 1996.

Everett, Walter. *The Beatles as Musicians: Revolver through the Anthology.* New York: Oxford University Press, 1999.

Fawcett, Anthony. *John Lennon: One Day at a Time.* New York: Grove Press, 1981.

Friede, Goldie, Robin Titone, and Sue Weiner. *The Beatles A to Z.* New York: Kingsport Press, 1980.

Fulpen, H.V. *The Beatles: An Illustrated Diary.* New York: Putnam Publishing Group, 1982.

Goldman, Albert. *Elvis.* New York: McGraw-Hill Book Co., 1981.

Goldman, Albert. *The Lives of John Lennon.* New York: William Morrow, 1988.

Golson, Barry, ed. *The Playboy Interviews with John Lennon and Yoko Ono.* New York: Playboy Press, 1981.

Goodgold, Edwin, and Dan Carlinsky. *The Complete Beatles Quiz Book.* New York: Bell Publishing, 1975.

Gottfridsson, Hans Olof. *The Beatles with Tony Sheridan: Beatles Bop- Hamburg Days.* Hamburg: Bear Family Records, 2004.

Green, John. *Dakota Days.* New York: St. Martin's Press, 1983.

Greenwald, Ted. *The Beatles Companion.* New York: Smithmark Publishers, 1992.

Grove, Martin A. *Beatle Madness.* New York: Manor Books, 1978.

Guiliano, Geoffrey. *George Harrison.* Secaucus: Chartwell Books, 1993.

Guiliano, Geoffrey. *The Beatles: A Celebration.* Toronto: Methuen Publications, 1986.

Guiliano, Geoffrey. *The Beatles Album.* New York: Penguin Books, 1991.

Guralnick, Peter. *Careless Love: The Unmaking of Elvis Presley.* New York: Little Brown, 1999.

Guralnick, Peter. *Last Train to Memphis: The Rise of Elvis Presley.* New York: Little Brown, 1994.

Guralnick, Peter. *Lost Highway: Journeys and Arrivals of American Musicians.* New York: Random House, 1979.

Harbison, W.A. *The Illustrated Elvis.* New York: Grosset & Dunlap, 1975.

Hayward, Mark. *The Beatles Unseen.* New York: Barnes & Noble Books, 2005.

Hertsgaard, Mark. *A Day in the Life: The Music and Artistry of the Beatles.* New York: Delacorte Press, 1995.

Hunt, Chris, ed. *MOJO Beatles* (magazine). London: EMAP Metro, 1997.

Hutchins, Chris, and Peter Thompson. *Elvis Meets the Beatles.* London: Smith Gryphon, 1994.

Kane, Larry. *Ticket to Ride.* Philadelphia: Running Press Book Publishers, 2003.

Kozinn, Allan. *The Beatles.* London: Phaidon Press Limited, 1995.

Leen, Jason. *Peace at Last: The After-death Experiences of John Lennon.* Bellingham: Illumination Arts Publishing, 1989.

Lennon, Cynthia. *A Twist of Lennon.* New York: W. H. Allen Publishers, 1980.

Lewisohn, Mark. *The Complete Beatles Chronicle.* New York: Harmony Books, 1992.

Lewisohn, Mark. *The Complete Beatles Recording Sessions.* London: Hamlyn Publishing, 2004.

Lichter, Paul. *Elvis in Hollywood.* New York: Simon & Schuster, 1975.

MacDonald, Ian. *Revolution in the Head: The Beatles' Records and the Sixties.* New York: Henry Holt, 1994.

Mackenzie, Maxwell. *The Beatles Every Little Thing.* New York: Avon Books, 1998.

Marcus, Greil. *Mystery Train: Images of American Rock 'n' Roll Music.* Third revised ed. New York: Plume Books, 1900.

Marsh, Dave, and Ken Stein. *The Book of Rock Lists.* New York: Dell Publishing, 1981.

Martin, George. *All You Need Is Ears.* New York: St. Martin's Press, 1979.

McCabe, Peter, and Robert D. Schonfeld. *John Lennon: For the Record.* New York: Bantam Books, 1984.

McCartney, Michael. *Remember: Reflections and Photographs of the Beatles.* New York: Henry Holt, 1992.

Mellers, Wilfrid. *The Music of the Beatles: Twilight of the Gods.* New York: Macmillan Publishing, 1973.

Miles, Barry, ed. *Beatles in Their Own Words.* New York: Omnibus Press, 1978.

Miles, Barry. *Paul McCartney: Many Years From Now.* New York: Henry Holt, 1997.

Naha, Ed, ed. *John Lennon and the Beatles Forever.* New York: Tower Publications, 1978.

Nash, Alanna. *The Colonel: The Extraordinary Story of Colonel Tom Parker and Elvis Presley.* New York: Simon & Schuster, 2003.

Norman, Philip. *Shout: The Beatles in Their Generation.* New York: Simon & Schuster, 1981.

O'Neal, Sean. *Elvis, Inc. The Rise and Fall of the Presley Empire.* Rocklin, Calif.: Prima Publishing, 1996.

Pang, May, and Henry Edwards. *Loving John: The Untold Story.* New York: Warner Books, 1983.

Pascall, Jeremy, ed. *The Beatles.* London: Octopus Books, 1973.

Patterson, R. Gary. *The Walrus Was Paul: The Great Beatle Death Clues.* New York: Simon & Schuster, 1998.

Pawlowski, Gareth L. *How They Became the Beatles.* New York: E.P. Dutton, 1989.

Presley, Priscilla Beaulieu, with Sandra Harmon. *Elvis and Me.* New York: G. P. Putnam's Sons, 1985.

Rayl, A.J.S. *Beatles '64: A Hard Day's Night in America.* New York: Bantam Doubleday Dell Publishing Group, 199.

Riley, Tim. *Tell Me Why.* New York: Random House, 1988.

Robertson, John. *The Art and Music of John Lennon.* New York: Omnibus Press, 1990.

Robertson, John. *The Complete Guide to the Music of the Beatles.* New York: Omnibus Press, 1994.

Rovin, Jeff. *The World According to Elvis*: Quotes from the King. New York: HarperCollins Publishers, 1992.

Saimaru, Nishi F. *The John Lennon Family Album.* San Francisco: Chronicle Books, 1982.

Saltzman, Paul. *The Beatles in Rishikesh.* New York: Penguin Putnam, 2000.

Schaefer, G.W. Sandy, Donald S. Smith, and Michael J, Shellans. *Here to Stay/Rock and Roll Through the '70s, Second* ed. Scottsdale, Ariz.: Gila Publishing Co., 2001.

Schaffner, Nicholas. *The Beatles Forever.* New York: McGraw-Hill Book Co., 1977.

Schaumberg, Ron. *Growing up with the Beatles.* New York: G. Putnam's Sons, 1976.

Seaman, Fredric. *The Last Days of John Lennon.* New York: Dell Publishing, 1991.

Shotton, Pete, and Nicholas Schaffner. *The Beatles, Lennon and Me.* New York: Stein & Day, 1983.

Solt, Andrew, and Sam Egan. *Imagine: John Lennon.* New York: MacMillan Publishing Co., 1988.

Somach, Denny, and Ken Sharp. *Meet the Beatles . . . Again!* Havertown: Musicom International Publishing, 1996.

Southall, Brian. *Abbey Road.* Wellingborough: Thorsons Publishing Group, 1982.

Spence, Helen. *The Beatles Forever.* New York: Crescent Books, 1981.

Spignesi, Stephen J. *The Beatles Book of Lists.* Secaucus, N.J.: Carol Publishing Group, 1998.

Stanley, David E., with Frank Coffey. *The Elvis Encyclopedia.* Santa Monica, Calif.: General Publishing Group, 1997.

Stark, Steven D. *Meet the Beatles.* New York: HarperCollins Publishers, 2005.

Swenson, John. *The Beatles: Yesterday and Today.* New York: Kensington Publishing, 1977.

Swenson, John. *The John Lennon Story.* New York: Nordon Publications, 1981.

Taylor, Derek. *It Was Twenty Years Ago Today.* New York: Simon & Schuster, 1987.

Taylor, Derek, ed, et al. *The Beatles Anthology.* San Francisco: Chronicle Books, 2000.

Tobler, John. *The Beatles.* New York: Exeter Books, 1984.

Toropov, Brandon. *Who Was Eleanor Rigby...and 908 More Questions and Answers about the Beatles.* New York: HarperCollins Publishers, 1996.

Turner, Steven. *A Hard Day's Write: The Stories Behind Every Beatles Song.* New York: Carlton Books, 1994.

Vellenga, Dirk, with Mick Farren. *Elvis and the Colonel.* New York: Delacorte Press, 1988.

Wallgren, Mark. *The Beatles on Record.* New York: Simon & Schuster, 1982.

Wenner, Jann. *Lennon Remembers: The Rolling Stone Interviews.* New York: Popular Library, 1971.

West, Red and Sonny, with Dave Hebler. *Elvis: What Happened?* New York: Ballantine Books, 1977.

Whitburn, Joel. *The Billboard Book of Top 40 Hits.* New York: Billboard Books, 2004.

Wiener, Jon. *Come Together: John Lennon in His Time.* New York: Random House, 1984.

Williams, Allan, and William Marshall. *The Man Who Gave the Beatles Away.* New York: Ballantine Books, 1975.

Wootton, Richard. *John Lennon.* New York: Random House, Inc., 1985.

Zmuesky, Steven and Boris. *The Films and Career of Elvis Presley.* New York: Citadel Press, 1991.

INDEX

A

Abbey Road Studios, 17
Aberbach, Jean, 71
Aberbach, Julie, 71
Aerosmith, 54
African-American music, 16, 24, 27
    influence on Elvis, 28, 33, 37
    sexuality in performances, 28
All You Need Is Cash (film), 172
Apple Boutique, 153
Apple Corp., Ltd., 17, 86, 153
Apple Records, 17
Arias, Olivia Trinidad, 22
Armstrong, Louis, 123
Aronowitz, Al, 129–130
Aspinall, Neil, 42, 72
Associated Independent Recording (AIR), 80
Atkins, Chet, 64
ATV Music, 89, 156–160

B

Bach, Barbara, 23
Beach Boys, the, 39, 70
Beale Street, 5
Beatle hair cut, 75
Beatlemania, 17, 113, 119, 163
Beatles, the. *See also* Beatles albums;
        Beatles films; Beatles songs;
        Harrison, George; Lennon, John;
        McCartney, Paul; Starr, Ringo
    album rankings, 183
    awards and honors, 187–189
    band name changes, 16
    booking fees, 149
    breakup of, 18
    collaborators, 43
    collector's items, 172
    cover/tribute artists, 54, 85
    discography, 87
    drug experimentation, 52, 81, 128–135
    early recordings, 17
    final live performance, 18
    Elvis comparisons, 53–54, 90–91, 121, 134–135, 160
    and EMI (Capitol) Records, 85–86
    the fifth Beatle, 43, 77–78
    financial affairs of, 144–150, 151–160
    formation of band, 15–16
    Grammy Awards of, 189
    growth and evolution of, 51–53
    hairstyles, 75
    Indian influence on, 41, 83
    instrumentation and orchestration, 39–45
    and manager Allen Klein, 153–156
    and manager Brian Epstein, 72–77
    members, early lives of, 10–15
    and merchandising, 150–151
    musical influences, 38–39
    no. 1 hits, 179
    and Northern Songs, Ltd., 88–90, 156–157
    and outside instrumentation, 201–203
    performance techniques, 47
    Philippines concert, 48
    posthumous sales, 185–187
    and producer George Martin, 77–85
    singles, 175–183
    song credit feud, 21

song rights, loss of, 156–160
rehearsal techniques, 45, 46
reunion, 170–171
Rock 'n' Roll Hall of Fame, 190
top-40 points earned, 186
tribute bands, 169–170
versus Elvis, summarily, 205–206
vocal styles and techniques, 45
Beatles albums, 183–185
Abbey Road, 18, 20, 53, 84
Anthology, 18, 52, 76, 85
complete discography, 87
Let It Be, 39, 40, 43, 44, 53
Let It Be Naked, 44–45
Magical Mystery Tour, 40, 83, 151
Please Please Me, 17, 40, 80, 144
Revolver, 129
Rubber Soul, 40, 81, 129
Sgt. Pepper's Lonely Hearts Club Band, 39, 40, 52, 82, 83, 131, 133, 151
The White Album, 51, 53, 84, 180
Beatles films
A Hard Day's Night, 50, 81, 99, 112, 113–114, 150
Help!, 50, 81, 99, 112, 114–116
Jungle Book, the (not filmed), 119
Let It Be, 18, 44, 84, 112, 117–118
Lord of the Rings (not filmed), 119
Magical Mystery Tour, 50, 112, 116–117
Shades of Personality (not filmed), 120
Talent for Loving, A (not filmed), 119
Three Musketeers, The (not filmed), 120
Up Against It (not filmed), 120–121
Yellow Submarine, 81, 112, 117
Yellow Teddybears, the (not filmed), 118–119
Beatles songs, 17, 175–183
"Baby, You're a Rich Man," 39
"Being for the Benefit of Mr. Kite," 82
"Bungalow Bill," 133

"Can't Buy Me Love," 179
"Come Together," 53, 133
"Day in the Life, A," 133
"Eleanor Rigby," 81
"Fixing a Hole," 133
"Get Back," 43
"Got to Get You into My Life," 41, 54
"Hey Jude," 50, 52, 54, 86, 180
   recording of, 50–51
"I Am the Walrus," 49
"I Want to Hold Your Hand," 17, 45, 86, 148
"I Want You (She's So Heavy)", 53, 133
"I'm a Loser," 39
"The Inner Light," 39
"Lady Madonna," 54
"Let It Be," 43, 176
"Love Me Do," 17, 41, 76, 79, 81, 89
"Lucy in the Sky with Diamonds," 82, 131
"Money," 41
"Norwegian Wood," 41, 130
"Not Guilty," 52
"Not a Second Time," 41
"Octopus's Garden," 45
"Oh, Darling," 53
"Only a Northern Song," 88
"Penny Lane," 82
"Please Please Me," 17, 89
"Revolution," 86
"She Loves You," 45, 80
"She's Leaving Home," 82
"Something," 22, 54
"Strawberry Fields Forever," 52, 81–82
"Taxman," 22
"Tomorrow Never Knows," 81
"Twist and Shout," 49
"When I'm Sixty-Four," 39, 82
"While My Guitar Gently Weeps," 22, 43
"With a Little Help from My Friends," 45, 133

"Within You Without You," 39, 83
"Yer Blues," 133
"Yesterday," 41, 54, 80, 179
"Your Mother Should Know," 39
"You've Got to Hide Your Love Away," 39, 41
Beatles tribute bands, 169–171
Beatlesongs (Dowlding), 78, 81, 82
Beaulieu, Priscilla, 9
Beeny, Bill, 169
Belew, Bill, 35
"Besame Mucho," 15
Best, Mona, 16
Best, Pete, 16, 17, 76, 170
Binder, Steve, 106–107, 109
Black, Bill, 5, 30
Book of the Dead, 81
Bootleg Beatles, the, 170–171
Bootleg music industry, 159
Boyd, Patti, 22
Brando, Marlon, 24, 47
Brewer Giorgio, Gail, 168
British Invasion, 9, 25, 31, 148
Brooks, Dudley, 31
Byrds, the, 132

C

Capitol Records, 147. *See also* EMI (Capitol) label
Cellar Full of Noise, A (Epstein), 72, 73
Chapman, Mark David, 20
Churchill, Winston, 10
Clapton, Eric, 22, 43
Cobain, Kurt, 123
Cocker, Joe, 54
Coltrane, John, 132
Columbia Records, 61
Complete Beatles Recording Sessions, The (Lewisohn), 80
Concert for Bangladesh, 22

Costello, Elvis, 21
Counterculture, 123
Country & Western (C&W), 5, 28
Cox, Maureen, 22
Cramer, Floyd, 31
Creedence Clearwater Revival, 29
Crosby, David, 132
Crudup, Arthur ("Big Boy"), 5
Curtis, Tony, 10

D

Davis, Miles, 123
Dean, James, 24
Decca Records, 75, 85
DeVall, Brian, 168
DiLello, Richard, 86
Do You Want to Know a Secret? (King), 159
Donegan, Lonnie, 39
"Don't Knock Elvis" (Jarvis), 63
"Don't You Rock Me Daddy-O" (Sherrell), 15
Dorsey Brothers TV show, 27, 103
Dowlding, William, 78, 81, 82
Drug use
    by Beatles, 128–135
    by Elvis, 9, 24, 124–128
    in music industry, 123
Ducktail hairstyle, 10, 12
Dykins, John "Bobby," 11
Dylan, Bob, 22, 29
    influence on Beatles, 39, 129

E

Eastman, Linda, 20
Ed Sullivan Show
    Beatles appearance, 17, 77, 86, 149
    Elvis appearance, 103
Eddie Clayton Skiffle Group, 15
Edwardian-style clothing, 12
Elvis. *See* Presley, Elvis

Elvis (film), 164
Elvis albums, 183–185
   Aloha from Hawaii, 9
   Elvis Is Back, 9
   Way Down, 10
Elvis' DNA Proves He's Alive (Beeny), 169
Elvis Files, The (film), 168
Elvis films, 8–9
   from 1956 to 1964, 93–99
   from 1965 to 1969, 99–103, 104–105
   Blue Hawaii, 9, 96–97, 99
   Change of Habit, 102
   Charro!, 102
   Clambake, 102
   Double Trouble, 99–100
   Easy Come, Easy Go, 99
   Flaming Star, 9, 96
   first 15 films, 97
   Follow That Dream, 97
   Frankie and Johnny, 99
   Fun in Acapulco, 98
   G.I. Blues, 96, 99
   Girl Happy, 99
   Girls! Girls! Girls!, 38
   It Happened at the World's Fair, 97
   Harum Scarum, 99
   Jailhouse Rock, 9, 64, 94, 95
   Kid Galahad, 97
   King Creole, 9, 94, 95
   Kissin' Cousins, 98
   Live a Little, Love a Little, 102
   Love Me Tender, 8, 93–94, 95
   Loving You, 39, 94, 95
   Paradise, Hawaiian Style, 99
   Roustabout, 98
   Speedway, 102
   Spinout, 99
   Stay Away Joe, 102
   Tickle Me, 99
   top-selling songs from, 101
   Trouble with Girls, The, 102

   Viva Las Vegas, 9, 98
   Wild in the Country, 96
Elvis impersonators, 164–166
Elvis, Inc. (O'Neal), 72
Elvis Is Alive Museum, 168
Elvis Presley Enterprises, Inc. (EPE), 139–140
Elvis sightings (after his death), 168–169
Elvis songs, 175–183
   "All Shook Up," 180–181
   "Are You Lonesome Tonight?" 32
   "Baby Let's Play House," 38, 52
   "Blue Moon of Kentucky," 5
   "Blue Suede Shoes," 96
   "Burning Love," 9
   "Can't Help Falling in Love," 38, 97
   "Don't Be Cruel," 70, 180, 181
   "Fever," 181
   "Heartbreak Hotel," 7, 27
   "Hound Dog," 70, 180, 181
   "How Great Thou Art," 29
   "If I Can Dream," 35
   "In the Ghetto," 29
   "It's Now or Never," 29
   "Love Me Tender," 53, 95
   "My Happiness," 5, 30
   "One Broken Heart for Sale," 181
   "Return to Sender," 38, 97, 181
   "Teddy Bear," 94
   "That's All Right (Mama)," 5
   "That's When Your Heartache Begins," 5, 30, 32
   "Suspicious Minds," 9
      recording of, 35–37
   "U.S. Male," 32
Elvis stamp, 166
Elvis TV performances, 29, 31, 33, 34, 69–70, 103, 110–111
   Aloha from Hawaii, 107–109
   song lineup for, 112
   Dorsey Brothers show, 103

Ed Sullivan Show, 103
Frank Sinatra–Timex Show, 103
Milton Berle Show, 182
Singer Special/Comeback Special, 106–107
    credits for, 108
Steve Allen Show, 181–182
Elvismania, 163
EMI (Capitol) label, 17, 80
    and the Beatles, 85–86
Epstein, Brian, 16–17, 48, 72
    as Beatles manager, 73–77
    death of, 17, 77
    and drug use, 77
    and homosexuality, 74
    and Northern Songs, Ltd., 88
Evans, Mal, 42, 48, 72
Eymond, Wally, 17

F

Flack, Roberta, 29
Foley, Red, 4
Folk music, 38
    influence on Beatles, 39
Fontana, D. J., 30
Franklin, Aretha, 54
Freed, Alan, 16, 27

G

Giliham, Cherri, 130
Gleason, Jackie, 27
Goodman, Benny, 28
Gospel music, 5, 24, 37
Graceland, 139, 140
Graceland Plaza, 140
Grade, Lew, 158
Grammy Awards, 188
Grand Ole Opry, 5
Grateful Dead, the, 70

Graves, Harry, 15
Guthrie, Woody, 32

H

Haley, Bill, 28
Hank Snow Attractions, 5, 7
Harrison, Dhani, 22
Harrison, George. *See also* Harrison solo songs
    early life of, 14
    first marriage of, 22
    Indian influence, 22
    second marriage of, 22
    stabbing of, 22
Harrison, Harold, 14
Harrison, Louise, 14
Harrison solo songs
    "All Those Years Ago," 22
    "Give Me Love," 22
    "Got My Mind Set on You," 22
    "My Sweet Lord," 22, 179
Hendrix, Jimi, 70, 123
Hill and Range Music, 33, 38
    and Elvis's career, 71–72
Hinduism, 22
Hippies, 123
Hitler, 10
Hodge, Charlie, 31, 32
Holiday, Billie, 123
Holly, Buddy, 16, 28
How I Won the War (film), 81, 82
Howlin' Wolf, 5
Hullabaloo TV series, 65
Humes High School, 4–5
Hurricanes band, 17

I

Indian music, 22
Is Elvis Alive? (Brewer Giorgio), 168

J

Jackson, Michael, 21
    relationship with Paul, 89
    rights to Beatles songs, 89–90, 157–160
Jagger, Mick, 83
James, Dick, 88
Jarvis, Felton, 63
    as Elvis's producer, 64–65
Jazz music, 123
Jennings, Waylon, 168
Jesse: The Post-Death Adventures of Elvis Presley (DeVall), 167
Jim Mack Jazz Band, 14
Joplin, Janis, 123
Jordan, Lewis, 33
Jordanairres, 30–31, 32, 33

K

Kaempfert, Bert, 16
Kennedy, Aaron, 4
King, B. B., 5
King, L. R. E., 159
Kircherr, Astrid, 75
Kirkham, Millie, 32
Kirkland, Kenny, 123
Klein, Allen, 153–156

L

Leek, Ed, 142
Leitch, Donovan, 83
Lennon, Alfred, 10–11
Lennon, John. *See also* Lennon solo albums; Lennon solo songs
    adult life, 18–20
    birth, 10
    death of, 20
    drug use of, 24
    early life, 10–12
    Elvis parallels, 23–25
    first marriage, 18
    mother's death, 12, 14
    recordings with Yoko, 18
    second marriage, 18
    solo albums, 18
    spirituality of, 24
Lennon, Julia, 10–12
Lennon, Julian, 18
Lennon, Sean, 20
Lennon solo albums
    Double Fantasy, 20
    Imagine, 20
    John Lennon/Plastic Ono Band, 20
    Live Peace in Toronto 1969, 18
    Milk and Honey, 20
    Mind Games, 20
    Rock 'n' Roll Album, 20
    Walls and Bridges, 20
Lennon solo songs
    "Cold Turkey," 20
    "Give Peace a Chance," 20
    "Instant Karma," 20
    "Just Like Starting Over," 179
Lewis, Jerry Lee, 28
Lewisohn, Mark, 80
Live and Let Die, 21
Liverpool College of Art, 11
Longest Cocktail Party, The (DiLello), 86
Lowe, John, 16
Lymon, Frankie, 123
Lynne, Jeff, 22
LSD, 24, 123, 132
    and "Lucy in the Sky with Diamonds," 131

M

Manila, Philippines, Beatles concert, 48
Marcos, Imelda, 48
Margret, Ann, 9
Marijuana, 123
    and the Beatles, 129–131

Martin, George, 17, 40–41, 42, 43–44
    as Beatles' producer, 77–85
    and drug use in the music industry, 133
Max, Peter, 117
McCartney, Mary, 14
McCartney, Jim, 14
McCartney, Paul. *See also* McCartney solo albums; McCartney solo songs
    adult life of, 20–22
    early life of, 14
    feud with Yoko, 21
    first marriage of, 20
    second marriage of, 21
McCartney solo albums
    Band on the Run, 21
    Give My Regards to Broad Street, 158–159
    McCartney, 20
    Ram, 20
McCartney solo songs
    "Coming Up," 21
    "Ebony and Ivory," 21
    "For No One," 159
    "The Girl Is Mine" (with Michael Jackson), 21
    "Live and Let Die," 81
    "Maybe I'm Amazed," 20
    "Say, Say, Say" (with Michael Jackson), 89, 179
    "Veronica" (Elvis Costello), 21
McGuinn, Roger, 132
    Mellers, Wilfred, 53, 76
Memphis Mafia, 3, 24, 98, 125, 139
Memphis Recording Service, 5, 30
Miles, Eddie, 15
Miller, Mitch, 61
Mills, Heather, 21
"Moondog" radio show, 16
Moore, Scotty, 5, 30
Moore, Tommy, 16
Mowtown, 28, 45

N

Nesmith, Mike, 83
New Clubmoor Hall Conservative Club, 15
Nilsson, Harry, 23
Nixon, Richard, 125
Norman, Phillip, 70
Northern Songs, Ltd., and the Beatles, 88–90

O

Oasis (band), 170
"Old Shep" (Foley), 4
O'Neal, Sean, 72
Ono, Yoko, 18–20, 24
    feud with Paul, 21
Orbison, Roy, 22

P

Pang, May, 18
Paramount Records, 64
Parchman Penitentiary, 3
Parker, Charlie, 123
Parker, Colonel Tom, 7, 33, 57–63
    estate settlement after Elvis' death, 63, 140
Parlophone Records, 85–86
Perkins, Carl, 28
Petty, Tom, 22
Phillips, Sam, 5, 30
Phish, 54
Plastic Ono Band, 18
Polydor Records, 16
Powell, Cynthia, 18
Preludin ("Prellies"), 129
Presley, Elvis. *See also* Elvis albums; Elvis films; Elvis songs; Elvis TV performances
    album rankings, 183

alive myth/mania, 167–169
army service, 7–8
awards and honors, 187–189
back-up singers, 197–200
Beatles comparison, 53–54, 90–91, 121, 134–135, 160
birth of, 3
costumes, 35
as DEA assistant, 125, 167
documentary/biographic films about, 103, 126, 164, 166
divorce of, 9
and drug use, 9, 24, 124–128
early employment, 4–5
early life, 3–5
early recordings, 5, 7
estate of, 139–141
extramarital affairs of, 9
final live performance of, 10
financial affairs of, 137–139
Grammy awards, 38
growth and evolution of, 37–38
guitar lessons, 4
guitarist collaborators, 31
health of, 126–128
and Hill and Range publishing, 71–72
instrumentation and orchestration, 30–32
Lennon parallels, 23–25
management, career, 57–64
marriage of, 9
and merchandising, 141–144
middle name debate, 4, 167
as movie star, top ten, 101
musical influences on, 28–29
musicians, collaborative, 191–197
no. 1 hits, 179
performance techniques, 33–34
posthumous sales, 185–187
and producer Jarvis Felton, 64–65
and producer Steve Binder, 65, 66
and RCA Records, 7
and RCA Victor, 67–71
rehearsal techniques, 32–33
Rock 'n' Roll Hall of Fame, 190
sexuality in performances, 29
singles, 175–183
singles versus album promotion, 30
spirituality of, 24
and Steve Sholes, 67–71
top-40 points earned, 186
versus Beatles, summarily, 205–206
vocal style and technique, 32
weight struggle, 126–128
Presley, Gladys, 3, 94
    illness of, 7–8
Presley, Jesse Garon, 3
Presley, Lisa Marie, 9, 139
Presley, Minnie Mae, 139
Presley, Priscilla, 9, 139
Presley, Vernon, 3, 4, 94, 137, 139
Presley Commission, 168
Preston, Billy, 43
Psychedelic music, 39, 82

Q

Quarry Bank High School, 11
Quarry Men band, 12, 15, 40, 52

R

Raving Texans band, 15
RCA Records, 7, 64
Rhythm & Blues (R&B), 5, 27–28, 38
    influence on Elvis, 28
Ringo Star and His All-Starr Band, 23
Rock 'n' Roll, 9, 16, 25, 27, 28
"Rock Island Line" (Donegan), 39
Rockabilly, 28, 39, 45, 52

Rodgers & Hammerstein Organization, 140–141
Rolling Stones, the, 54, 125

S

Seeger, Pete, 32
Seltaeb company, 150
SFX Entertainment, 141
Shankar, Ravi, 132
Sheridan, Tony, 16
Shotton, Pete, 12
Shout (Norman), 79
Sillerman, Robert F. X., 141
Sinatra, Frank, 54
Sinatra, Nancy, 9
Skiffle music, 12, 14, 15, 38, 39
Smith, Frank, 4
Smith, Johnny, 4
Snow, Hank, 7
Spector, Phil, 44
St. Peter's Parish Church Garden Fete, 15
Starkey, Richard. *See also* Starr, Ringo
    early life of, 15
    renaming of, 15
Starr, Ringo, 17. *See also* Starr solo albums; Starr solo songs
    adult life of, 23
    film roles of, 23
    first marriage of, 23
    second marriage of, 23
Starr solo albums
    Ringo, 23
Starr solo songs
    "Photograph," 23
    "You're Sixteen," 23
Steppenwolf, 70
Storm, Rory, 15, 17
Sun Records, 142
Sun Studios, 5
Sutcliffe, Stu, 16, 47, 72
Sweet Inspirations band, 31–32

T

Talking blues music style, 32
T.A.M.I. (film), 65
Taylor, James, 29
Teddy boy style, 11, 12, 24, 47
"That'll Be the Day" (Holly), 16
"That's All Right (Mama)" (Crudup), 5
Tonight Show, the, Beatles appearance, 86
Townsend, Ken, 133
Transcendental meditation, 25
Traveling Wilburys *band,* 22
Twilight of the Gods (Mellers), 53, 76
Tyler, Steven, 54
Tyme Records, 15

V

Vaughn, Ivan, 15
Voice band, 32

W

Walker, T-Bone, 33
West, Red, 24
Westmoreland, Kathy, 32
WHBQ radio station, 5
Williamson, Sonny Boy, 5
Wings, 21

Z

Zappa, Frank, 23
    influence on Beatles, 39